Digging Deeper

A Memoir of the Seventies

epicpress

Digging Deeper

A Memoir of the Seventies

Peter Weissman

Digging Deeper

An Epic Press book

Copyright © 2010 Peter Weissman

ISBN 978-1-906557-05-8

Thanks to Gene Greathouse, who went over the manuscript with sharp eyes and a keen mind ... to Tom Braden and Jess Harpur for feedback on certain chapters, Brent Higgins for his steadfast encouragement; and, belatedly, to Stuart Braman, for his work on *I Think, Therefore Who Am I?*

Thanks also to Rich Conti for the cover and Beth Lonergan for the design; Atif Farooq Qureshi of Epic Press, for his patience during the editing process; to my daughter Raphaela, a writer herself, whose reactions suggested solutions, and my wife, Rita, for recognizing the bubble around me while I write, and not bursting it.

Rehabilitation

In the morning, when the alarm went off, I'd pad into the bathroom, splash cold water on my face, brush my teeth; a creature of long ingrained habit. Back in the studio room, I'd put on a T-shirt, then the white shirt, or maybe the pale blue one, and then the dark blue suit hanging in the otherwise empty closet, the limited wardrobe once again reminding me of my estrangement from my own circumstance.

The super who had shown me the one-room apartment weeks before opened the venetian blinds to reveal the courtyard entrance to the building, leading to the most ordinary of streets. I'd stood there looking out longer than necessary, perhaps searching for something more than concrete and brick, until I sensed her impatience and tore myself from the soporific view. She then led me toward the closet, where I averted my eyes from the mirrored doors, to avoid ego confusion, and then *she* was the one to linger, considering the mirrored doors a selling point, expecting me to say something. What could I say? That I'd seen myself before? That it wasn't something I wanted to see every moment of the day?

I finessed the medicine cabinet mirror in the bathroom by scrutinizing the shiny faucets and the tile floor, eliciting her impatience again. Again I could see my behavior was inappropriate. Who cares about faucets? But she had a short attention span; not attenuated like mine by psychedelic drugs, but by a notion of propriety that moved her from here and there according to her own internal directives. They ushered her out of the bathroom, across the parquet floor to the front door, then up the second floor hallway, and I followed, stopping when she opened another door, to showcase the garbage disposal.

"It's a good apartment," she said when we were back in the studio apartment, the door closing with a *thunk* more impressive than anything else she'd shown me. "No riffraff," she remarked, and when I looked at her with tilted head, she added, "In the building, you know."

I was clean-shaven, my hair cut and combed. I looked presentable. But at the mention of riffraff, in association with the solid *thunk* that threw me back to the flimsy wooden doors of the East Village tenements, I wondered if she'd recognized me as an impostor, had seen through my clean-cut look to the person who dealt nickels and dimes of this and that just a few months ago.

No, I'd told myself. *Calm down. You're paranoid.* I could see from the pleasure that washed over her when I said I'd take the place that she was just waiting on me.

Now, in the morning, as I regarded my smooth-walled domain before heading to work, from that solid door to the mattress on the floor in the far corner, beneath the faux Arabian canopy tacked to the ceiling, I knew I'd put something over on her. What would she think to see me in the evening, when I didn't turn the light on but instead struck a match to the candle and sat cross-legged in my hippie corner, staring at the mandala I'd tacked to the wall, breathing methodically, the beat of my heart pounding in my ears? She was Italian, and Catholic. Had she witnessed my nighttime behavior in a monastery, she would have considered it admirable. But here, I had to be careful. One person's monk is another's nut job.

As usual, I idled at the tie rack within the closet, trying to choose between the three silky specimens, staring at them as if to divine the elements of the day in the patterns and colors …

Catching myself amidst this magical thinking, I grabbed the red and gold one, looped it over my neck, then quickly put on my raincoat; I couldn't afford a winter overcoat and liked to believe the zip-in lining sufficed. It didn't. Leaving, taking the stairs instead of the elevator, I thrust my hands into the flimsy coat after stepping out of the building, hunching my shoulders in primitive reflex to combat the freezing chill.

The morning world was already in motion, stepping along the sidewalks on both sides of the street, its denizens all heading in the same direction, toward the hole in the ground a few blocks away. Perhaps because I knew I was different, not truly of this world, it was comforting to join the herd movement, to ostensibly belong to it. I watched it swell with foot traffic flowing from side streets onto the long incline that led to Main Street, past a church on one side and a synagogue on the other, past a library and a plate-glass wall of stores on the ground floor of apartment buildings like my own. Farther down, beyond the railroad overpass, buses pulled to the curb, exhaust smoke steaming in the cold air as disgorged passengers joined the ever thickening flow. The crowd, hemmed in now by buildings and traffic, bubbled to a froth at the subway entrance, where only two or three at a time could head downstairs, to mill on the platform there and then file into the waiting subway cars that would take us to Manhattan.

An hour or so later we'd fairly explode out of deceptive placidity, pour from the confining tubes of glass and steel, erupt up other steps to flow in all directions like lava. And then my circumstantial solidarity with this mass would fragment, at my surprise over the faces reflecting hurry and strain to get to work on time. In contrast, instead of rushing off I'd breathe deeply, exulting in freedom from confinement. A high point to the day, a blessing I would not have experienced if not for rush hour. In the evening, heading back the other way, emerging from the outlying station on Main Street, I'd merely be relieved, too enervated to fully appreciate that second liberation.

On a typical morning, I now confronted a more personal ordeal than mass transit, as the smaller gathering that entered my particular office building waited for the elevator, and when the doors opened, squeezed in. The same neutral look that deadened faces on the train would mask these faces too. Inside the box enclosure, they all stared straight ahead, at the doors that sealed us in, and though by then I'd adopted the same neutrality, I couldn't lose myself in it, not with the whirring sound of pulleys and wheels as we ascended, the numbers advancing as the elevator moved up, my heart beating loud enough to hear.

How could they not realize there was an empty shaft below us and only a cable holding us aloft? Was it frayed? Would it snap? It happened in the movies. Why not now? A moving room, taken for granted, becoming in an instant a death chamber.

It didn't matter that we always averted disaster, that every morning I'd step out on the fourteenth floor as the doors gently slid shut behind me; it was still an immense relief to finally got there safely … a sense of relief I of course kept to myself.

In the past year or so my parameters had been altered by certain synthetic laboratory drugs, and now I couldn't help but reflect upon fundamentals I'd never paid much attention to before. In high school, eager and earnest at my first job, I'd had a surfeit of false courage. Death never occurred to me while working alongside grown-ups.

And later, as a college graduate, I insouciantly rode elevators all over the place, to make a few bucks to pay the rent and cover the cost of meals. It never occurred to me I would someday, inevitably, die. And now I couldn't escape that fact of life: I would not live forever. In the guise of my office worker identity I might look as oblivious as everyone else, but the persistent presence of death's inevitability made me different.

After the close-quarter subway ride and the elevator ordeal, my empty office cubicle was a godsend. I'd hang up my raincoat, lean back in the swivel chair and breathe in and out, in and out, as I did in the evening beneath my corner canopy in the studio apartment. Only here I'd stare at a plaster indentation on the wall instead of the midpoint of a mandala.

Unseen others were also easing into the day while I practiced my particular morning routine. I assumed at first that this daily respite before work began had been designed with meditative intent, rather than haphazardly come about through custom. I liked to think that together, in our separate cubicles, we were in silent communion with a greater meaning, whether the ten or fifteen minutes of morning quietude involved drinking coffee, reading newspapers, or doing crossword puzzles.

And then, one morning before the clacking typewriters sent a signal up and down the hallway that the workday had officially begun, my office neighbor peered around the pebbled glass partition and saw me staring at the wall.

"Oh, I'm sorry," she said, flustered. "I didn't mean to interrupt … I assumed … It was so quiet, I didn't realize anyone was here …"

How naive of me, to believe that drinking coffee and reading the paper were modes of meditation. They were well-worn rituals. In comparison, sitting and staring at a wall … well, there was a word for people who stared at walls.

It seemed I was caught, found out—or would have been if not for an aspect of office culture that ensured my coworker's silence. She'd peeked into my space, after all, which breached an unspoken rule. And, too, we worked for an enlightened company—an outfit that did research and development into educational methods and materials—one that hewed to a social attitude of tolerance, which included people who stared at walls, if such crazy behavior were ever to come up. Which is to say I had nothing to fear from my office neighbor; she would keep my oddness to herself.

But it reminded me that I had to be vigilant. Odd behavior alarms most people, however much they might deny it. It was what kept me in line; that and the restraint imposed by the obligatory suit and tie I wore. In time I would discover that when I merged into the tribal office community, in behavior and appearance, I would have the option of becoming an iconoclast; let hair grow on my face if I kept it neat and trim, arrive fifteen minutes late or leave fifteen minutes early. But meanwhile, uncertain about the ins and outs of tribal custom, I shaved every day, got to work on time and left at five. And in truth I would never make use of iconoclastic exception.

Yes, my office neighbor would keep my secret. Still, the day after being accidentally peeked in upon, I bought a *New York Times* on the way to work, unfolded its massive pages in my cubicle, and stared into it instead of at the wall. I found a lowercase letter *i* in a subhead and used the dot as a meditative focal point. If anyone had peeked in on me, there would have been nothing to remark upon. Reading the *Times*, or appearing to, was the definition of normalcy.

Did I fool anyone? Or was this a game played between myself and the unimpressed observer who looked over my shoulder? Perhaps the people I feared would discover the real me were more acceptant than my paranoia led me to believe.

But I wasn't taking any chances.

Occasionally, in committee meetings, at lunch in the company cafeteria, and in the lounge during the afternoon coffee break, someone would eye me with the hint of a smile. I didn't know what it meant, but sensed that it wasn't hostile. There might have been a secret knowledge in that surreptitious perusal. An awareness that I wasn't who or what I purported to be, and a certain pleasure in that assumption.

Another day, I saw an assessing look that was easier to recognize, because it bespoke rejection.

Our team of five was in one of the tedious weekly meetings when I caught the slant-eyed glance, a look not unlike that of some drug dealers and undercover cops I'd come across not long ago. It was followed by a frown, and then aversion, as if my inspector was too disgusted to look at me any longer … though I hardly said a word in those meetings. Dick, the guy's name was. My suit and tie and smooth-shaven face apparently meant nothing to him. Clearly, he wanted nothing to do with me.

It was a jolt, to be discovered, and I reacted without thinking, with panic, seizing upon obsequious friendliness; an on-the-fly ploy to disarm him. I asked this Dick about a committee report the team was working on, listened with fascination to his grudging answer, then thanked him profusely. But I knew I hadn't won him over, nor did similar fake questions I posed the following week. In fact, I could see he now despised me even more. And now, having prostrated myself before him, I didn't much like myself either.

So, in the face of his continued disdain, I came up with a different attitude—stoic indifference. I regarded him, or avoided even looking at him, with a detachment that erected a wall against his evident hostility. And to my surprise—since I hadn't adopted this attitude to persuade, but rather, to protect myself—Dick began to talk. He even began to seek me out, approaching me in the hallway after committee meetings and in the employee lounge, to ask about projects, to solicit my opinion.

It should have pleased me, for I am an essentially friendly person, but out of continued wariness, I hewed to purposeful indifference ... and then the poor guy came apart at the seams, nearly begged for a response of some kind, anything. It unnerved me, realizing that I'd brought his sorry state about. Stirred up his insecurities and manipulated him by pretending he didn't matter. That was my own great fear! Not to matter. His own well of loneliness had brought him down. How could I celebrate that?

But I get ahead of myself, since I could hardly string more than a few words together then. A cipher when I arrived, I was barely capable of speech, the drugs I'd taken short-circuiting the commonplace verbal transitions that enable conversation. In the silence between phrases uttered by others, I'd remain mute, inexpressive—not out of rudeness, but because of my inability to concentrate, to link disparate phrases into sentences and sentences into paragraphs, as I recalled Henri Bergson describing the difference between being and becoming when I read him on acid. It seemed the cumulative effect of those acid trips had rendered my senses predominant, presaging thoughts or overlapping them. When an opening in a line of discourse called upon me to contribute, I didn't have the time, or space, to gather up information and craft an answer. And so, when I managed to respond, it was in monosyllables.

That no one remarked on this didn't mean they hadn't noticed, only that they were being polite.

But despite appearances, I was not an idiot. I was capable of learning, and in rehabilitation. Observing the impression I made, I taught myself to react appropriately, to learn the social graces, as they're called, to relearn the basic skills of communication: returning a greeting when greeted, nodding in order to indicate that I'd heard and grasped what had been said, and offering affirmative words or sounds to put a speaker at ease. And later, when I got better at the basics, I hastened to speak when an idea occurred to me in association with something that had been said, knowing, with my short attention span, that I would lose it altogether if I waited. As a result, following long moments of silence, I spoke in staccato outbursts, which made me no less odd, but more acceptable.

Realizing that people don't need much to be put at ease put me at ease as well, made me less guarded. And when I was more relaxed, they more easily accepted me, and more: a few even began to seek my company, since my still notable silences made me the ideal listener.

One woman in particular, a retired schoolteacher, latched onto me. She sat down across the table in the cafeteria, took a chair next to me in committee meetings, then took to popping in on one pretext or another.

Somewhat like me, she'd blurt out random bits of information at the weekly meetings, about school rooms and schoolteachers. As befit the tribal adherence to tolerance, people were constrained to hear her out without interruption, though I could see that the old lady's ramblings drove them to distraction. Outside the committee room, however, they avoided her, and so she came to me, the young man who always wore the same suit, the listener; and given my passivity, the perfect sounding board.

She'd pop in for a chat, as she prefaced it, and tell me about her years in the public school system, her former pupils, her fellow teachers … She missed that life so much, it left me tongue-tied. What could I say to alleviate her longing for the past? At some point, as I nodded and made listening sounds, she'd become even more animated and lose control, sentences running into each other in a stream of consciousness, the pauses between phrases disappearing, and then, anticipating interruption at my simple "Uh-huh"—since everyone else eventually interrupted her and found an excuse to leave—she'd speak even faster, overrunning anything I might say.

She began to wear on me. I'd nod and make agreeable sounds, but no longer hearing details, tuned into the underlying meaning within the rapid flow of words. And then one day I heard myself break in and say the words she dreaded: "Listen, Ruth, there's something I have to do…"

A startling breakthrough. Posing with the *New York Times* and learning to nod and grunt had rendered me a member of the tribe. But at that moment, I'd gone beyond the perfunctory, was not just in it, but of it.

It struck me, as she apologetically excused herself and left my office cubicle, that I'd lost something important.

Not long ago, I'd lived in the moment. A drug had thrust that momentary state upon me, the wonderment of a yawning, spacious reality in which boredom and impatience were impossible. And now, having adjusted to a different, less immediate world, I'd lost a certain innocence that accompanied that Edenic state. I felt comfort and discomfort, acted as jury and judge, concluded that I didn't have to listen to people, could tune them out if I wanted to.

In the evening of that day, returning to my apartment, I took off the uniform suit, as usual, put on jeans and the splashy cowboy shirt I'd found in a garbage can in Haight-Ashbury, slipped into a pair of moccasins. Then, as usual, I turned off the electric light and lit a candle and a cone of incense, sat cross-legged beneath the canopy and stared at the midpoint of the mandala tacked to the wall. But it felt different; a custom of mine, not a preparation to enter a transcendent state. Breathing in and out, in and out, self-meditating, my pristine alienation from the world-at-large did not reappear. It was gone, the sharp edges of my former clarity blurred by a new, less salutary consciousness.

The Letter that Changed My Life

One evening, returning to the red brick apartment building after another day of rehabilitation, I was surprised to find an actual letter in my mailbox, instead of an advertisement or the occasional bill. I stood in the fluorescent lobby staring at my name written in childlike script that covered most of the square white envelope.

It was postmarked Philadelphia. Who did I know there?

But despite my curiosity, I didn't rip it open on the spot. Instead I brought it upstairs and tossed it on the bulky dining room table, as if I received such letters every day. It sat there while I stripped off my suit and took off the shoes, put on jeans, the fraying cowboy shirt, and slipped into the moccasins. Then, in the relaxed manner of a man home from work, I shuffled across the parquet floor to the envelope, feeling childishly mature, having played a waiting game in which enough time had passed to prove I was capable of self-discipline.

The thick white card stock inside was marked by black ink splotches; in the style of Hans Hoffmann, I would eventually learn. I opened it to more splotches and two lines done by the same hand as the address on the envelope.

It said: *Sagittarius-Aquarius.*

And farther down, screaming from the corner: *Help! I need you desperately!*

Astonishment threw me back in time to a morning when I'd stared at another, similarly frantic message and wondered if I'd written it myself the night before, when the walls, ceiling, and floor had begun whispering to me.

I knew I was Sagittarius. But who was Aquarius?

As on that memorable morning, after the most chaotic night of my life, I idly turned the greeting type card over and was startled to see more writing and a name scrawled on the back.

Noreen.

And like the other name, months ago, on a scrap of grocery bag, it took a moment before I recalled who it was.

Noreen …

She was sitting in a jalopy convertible spattered with paint in what was considered the psychedelic style as I drifted down Avenue A, stoned and heading nowhere in particular. When she called out to me, I looked up, took in pale skin, flaxen hair falling over the shoulders of a tattered hippie blouse, and veered over. She said something to me, but I was too transfixed by her blue-gray eyes to respond, and then the sound of my name, again, followed by a smile, snapped me out of my trance. How did she know my name? I finally said something, perhaps asking how she knew me, and then backed away, waving goodbye in embarrassed retreat. When she called to me a few days later in the park, I was still stoned, perhaps on something else, and having forgotten her name, stumbled over a greeting. My awkwardness didn't put her off, amused her in fact as she regarded me with the same transfixed stare, as if she couldn't take her eyes off me. This time I sat down beside her on a patch of worn grass and we spoke for a while, or maybe, disconcerted by her rapt attention, I talked and she listened; about what, I couldn't recall.

And just like that, there was something going on between us.

But I was surprised when Michael, who was living in my pad at the time, ushered into the apartment one afternoon. "I met her in the park," he told me. "She recognized me, and said she was looking for you."

And then he left, which was not unusual for Michael, who left stray people at my pad as if they were lost kittens.

She was in distress, kneading her hands together, pupils tick-tocking in alarm. I sat her down on the couch and asked what was wrong. She explained that she'd taken acid with a half-dozen people she thought she knew, but when the drug hit, was freaked out by their suddenly unfamiliar faces, which was when she went to the park, looking for me.

Sitting on the couch, she hugged herself to quell her trembling. I put an arm around her shoulder and comforted her with platitudes, but the solicitous sound of my voice calmed her down. I brought her a blanket, lit a candle as dusk came on, made her tea. And as she sipped, cupping her hands around it for warmth, I told her what I knew about fear: that if you don't think about it, it goes away; a hippie nostrum. But like the platitudes, I uttered this with concern, which was what mattered. Eventually she pulled herself together and was all right.

And now she'd written me a greeting card letter, asking me to help her, again.

It's a powerful thing, to know someone needs you. Sitting at the table I'd scavenged from an immigrant's leavings in the Bronx, it seemed Noreen had thrown *me* a lifeline. None of the furniture felt like mine, no more than the skin I inhabited. In my dissociated state, and its plenitude of isolation, the words she'd written and the feelings they conjured could not have been more significant.

I need you desperately.

I was leading the most ordinary life imaginable. I put one foot in front of another to get from here to there, and imagined more of the same forever. The job, and the routine that went with it, were my prescription reconstituting my scattered self, versions of which congealed around this or that association. At times it seemed this regimen was working, when I forgot myself in moments brimming with perception … in a busy coffee shop in the city, windows fogged with the moisture of cooking and close-packed customers … when orange-tinted sunlight poured into my office window in late afternoon, or I

looked down at the tidy people fourteen floors below, in Bryant Park …
emerging from the subway in the evening and heading back to the red
brick building past a splash of color, a whiff of sweet odor, from the
flower stall beneath the railroad overpass on Main Street. I even had
objective proof that of one such carefree moment, in a Polaroid
snapshot a fellow worker had taken, capturing me in my blue suit and
crimson tie, smiling at the camera.

But in the solitary cell block of my studio apartment, the evanescent
sensations that momentarily brightened life lost their sparkle, attached
themselves to meaning: the impermanence of all things. In some ways
my sense of isolation had grown more pointed as I recovered my drug-
addled wits and functioned with less uncertainty.

I could talk now, engage in conversation—if it didn't go on too
long, and overtax my still limited attention span. I could read a book
without the words bouncing on the page. I could look at a mirror, if I
moved close, and took in the details rather than the wider configuration
that constituted me.

But I had never felt so alone.

And now this letter, from someone I somewhat remembered, who
needed me.

That night, too hyped to sit cross-legged beneath the canopy and
breathe myself into a soothing state, I could do nothing but think about
Noreen, recalling things we'd done together. We'd hitchhiked to
western Massachusetts and taken acid in a meadow, angering the
uptight, politically oriented people—friends of a friend of mine—who'd
put us up. We went to Boston, hung out in Cambridge, slept in a local
commune. Then we hitched down the coast and stayed with the family
of a friend of hers, moneyed people. The father, who wore a knitted
shirt and white tennis shoes, took me sailing, and with real class, which
money can't buy, pretended not to notice that I looked like a
ragamuffin. In contrast, his daughter, Noreen's friend, didn't try to hide
her disgust. And then I said goodbye and hitchhiked back to Manhattan,

while Noreen flew to Michigan to get ready for school in the fall.

I hadn't thought about her since.

That night, I couldn't sleep, got up and wrote my own letter, responding to hers.

A few days later I heard from her again, thirty or so words filling two pages, her handwriting enormous. She was in art school, she wrote, and hated it. Would I come down to Philadelphia and visit that weekend?

I wrote back, telling her I couldn't, that I had a job.

The mail wasn't fast enough for her. The following week she called instead. If I couldn't come to her, she said—what a mellifluous voice!—then she would come to me.

If I had a philosophy of life, it was the fatalistic belief that things merely happened, and the way to deal with inevitable change was to go with it, whatever it was. To resist or fight only made life more difficult, which might not have been a philosophy at all, merely an attitude of resignation. But then, I was what you might call an old hippie, a psychedelic survivor. And I knew people with even less structure than a guiding attitude who hadn't made it.

Sure she could come, I told her, looking forward to being with another person, though not without trepidation; we grow used to our own misery.

After work on Friday, I went to meet her at Grand Central. I spotted her in the cavernous main hall, walking toward me with a loping stride, flaxen hair sawing on either side of her long face. It came back to me then: who she was. And when she got closer and smiled, it was like the late afternoon filling the office window; a perfect moment.

I still hadn't gotten around to buying a winter overcoat, wore the flimsy slicker with its zip-in lining, and that seemed to be who I was—a misfit in a grown-up world—when she stopped a few feet away, blue-gray eyes riveted to mine, struck dumb, it seemed, as was I …

And then I was babbling, filling the space between us with words, to fill a vacuum that would otherwise have swallowed me. I couldn't shut up, as Noreen kept pace beside me through the labyrinth tunnels that led to the subway station on the lower level. On and on I babbled, about I don't know what, and kept it up as we stood on the crowded rush hour platform, waiting for the train to arrive, and then in the subway car, where I had to shout to be heard over the clattering wheels as we barreled underground and then up to the elevated tracks in Queens.

The car was jammed, and we stood all the way, but despite the crush of people and the nighttime scenery outside, we were encapsulated in my logorrheic bubble. If only she would have stopped staring with such unnerving adoration! It was unbearable. To deflect her, I continued to blather, all but disembodied as we rolled along above the peripheral dreamscape of freight yards, factories, and warehouses; ramshackle row house neighborhoods; old and new apartment buildings; streets and stores and traffic lights, then highways and a glimpse of open nighttime sky before we tunneled underground again, plunging into pitch-darkness before the final stop.

In the illuminated Main Street station, the interior train lights went off and I finally fell silent as we waited for the doors to open. Then we filed out and upstairs and I was at it again, launching into a personal travelogue of the aboveground streets.

The curb where I'd waited for the bus every morning to take me to college, because my parents couldn't afford to send me away— consigning me to live there, with them, though I would have preferred not to, which was probably why we hadn't gotten along since then … And there, on the corner, the bar where my friends and I sometimes went after school, for a hot dog and a beer. And over there, the Long Island Railroad (which meant nothing to me; I'd never been on it), and beneath that overpass, the flower stall where Jimmy Avena, who was on my Little League baseball team, worked for his father now …

Which brought me down a side street where I hadn't been in years and into a particular restaurant, as if I trafficked that route every day, though I was only following a stream of consciousness from a more distant past, when my parents took us—my brother and I—to one of the first places we ever ate out, because we could finally afford to do it.

"Amazing, that it's still here, and serving the same bread sticks and green minestrone soup!"

It turned out Noreen wasn't hungry. She ordered something anyway, at my insistence, then hardly ate it, as I continued discoursing—meanwhile devouring an entire basket of bread sticks, out of nervousness—through the salad, the signature bowl of green soup, and the entree, which was maybe chicken. In fact, I wasn't hungry either. I could have been eating wood as she adored me with her lucent eyes and I fought against drowning in the all-too-real fulsomeness of her proximity.

When we left the restaurant, which was only a couple of blocks from my place, I looked around for some other distraction—my throat sore by then—and seizing upon a movie marquee, suggested we go inside and watch it, whatever was showing; I'd never heard of it.

"No," Noreen said, finally speaking up; and adamantly, at that. "Let's go to your apartment."

The door had hardly closed behind us, with its solid *thunk,* before she was pressing me to the wall, pinning me there with an open-mouthed kiss. Lip-locked, there was nothing I could say now as we stumble-waltzed across the parquet floor to the mattress beneath the canopy in the far corner. Not the meditation canopy now, as we tore off our clothes, but the tent flap of a sheik, in his apartment oasis, horny as a longtime celibate breaking his fast, foregoing foreplay, fucking with wild urgency.

When had the light been turned off and the candle lit? The flickering flame threw our humping shadows on the wall—I thought of camels—lusty inflations billowing on the swooping canopy above us …

Afterward, the air flickered with postcoital fireflies as we lay on the mattress rolling cigarettes, tobacco falling on our sweat-slick chests, clinging to our skin. Now, in the satiated calm, I felt no urge to talk, and for a change Noreen had a few things to say.

She began with her parents, and stuck with them awhile, blaming them for being insensitive. Yes, they'd agreed to send her to art school, but in Philadelphia, of all places, when what she wanted, *needed*, was to be in New York. And she hated it there. If not for amphetamines, she would have gone crazy.

The volubility I'd unsuccessfully attempted to hide behind earlier as she stared at me hungrily, now flipped the other way, into silence, as I listened, surprised by her contempt. I didn't understand it. It seemed to me her parents had been trying to accommodate her. So why was she so scornful? There was a whiff of entitlement there, of feeling sorry for herself; that she expected reality to accommodate her. Who liked their parents? No one that I knew.

But in the aftermath of our ferocious coupling, after months of abstinence, I was not about to point that out. Languid satisfaction trumped disagreement. I wanted her again. All I could manage to assuage my integrity was to keep myself from commiserating.

*   *   *

The next morning I set off for work, as usual, with hands thrust deep into the pockets of the faux winter coat, arms pressed to my torso to commune with the heat of my body. But things were different; it seemed I was noticing more. The vapor my breath produced in the cold air as I walked down the incline toward the subway, startled me: I hadn't made a casual scientific discovery in a long time.

When I returned that evening, Noreen had cleaned up the place. It inspired me to go back out and pick up Chinese food for the two of us.

In all the months I'd been there, buying a precooked meal and bringing it to the apartment had never occurred to me. I put the take-out bag on the table, and as she went about setting plates, glasses, napkins, and silverware, I took off the raincoat and suit and changed into my casual clothes, though the now ragged cowboy shirt seemed an affectation, an advertisement for the so-called Summer of Love, which in truth hadn't been so lovely; I was homeless, after all, and starving, my teeth wobbling in my gums.

In retrospect it hardly seemed my life at all. Accentuating the difference, the electric lights in the apartment were on. What a difference it made! There were no hidden spots in the room, no candle-flame shadows, and the incandescent brightness gave a new aspect to the old furniture, which now had a surprising sheen. And then, sitting down at the bulky table with its claw legs, there was someone on the other side, waiting to share the meal with me.

Noreen had a plain face, thin lips arrowing into a smile as she gazed back at me, but arresting blue-gray eyes; they sparked, as they had when we met in Grand Central, only it didn't freak me out now. Instead, I was content to bask in her attention and felt no urgent need to talk.

She spoke first, as we ate, recalling a walk she took that day. Ambling through the local streets, she'd come upon a sprawling park.

"That must be ten blocks from here," I said, surprised. "Kissena Park."

"It's beautiful," she said, "with its old art deco gaslight lamps. I'd like to see it at night, how it looks when they're lit up ... There were hills, a lake—and ducks ... and no one else there. I had the whole park to myself."

It wasn't that far away. I wondered why I'd never gone.

"We should go together!" she said. "Maybe this weekend."

A stroll. "That would be great," I replied, before realizing she'd invited herself to stay, and that I'd accepted.

Then I told her about my day, the subway, the office, the hole in the wall where I ate lunch, my life sounding so civilized, so manageable, as if I were reading it in a book situated in a different era. Not my life at all, and pleasant, viewed from a distance. So it surprised me when she jumped in to commiserate, at how dehumanizing it was to take a crowded subway and then sit in an office all day.

I wanted to say, *No, it's okay. It used to bother me, but it doesn't anymore.*

But she was so solicitous, it seemed I might hurt her feelings if I corrected her. And I could see why she'd come to the conclusions she had. So I said nothing, and she went on to talk about abstract expressionism, Franz Klein, Adolph Gottlieb, and other names I didn't know. She got up and brought a book from her knapsack back to the table to show me, a foreplay of mental excitement as she sat beside me and flipped pages. She felt it too, closing the book, taking my hand and leading me to the corner canopy. Quickly, we shed our clothes, the bright lights turned off and the candle lit, throwing our humping bodies on the canopy and wall …

Afterward as we lay on the mattress rolling cigarettes, she said, "I'm quitting school."

To live with me, it seemed, though she didn't say so; and I didn't ask.

But then, it didn't matter. I had a philosophy, or maybe an attitude, that guided me in the face of all possibilities: go with it, whatever it is.

Walking to the subway station the following morning, I thought about what Noreen had taken for granted; was sure of it now—that she would move in with me, unless I told her otherwise. It was a rare moment in which a person confronts a choice that will determine their future. There aren't as many of these as fiction would have us believe.

I could go on as I had, with no idea where it might lead; or give up my solitary existence for a life that included companionship.

Though I'd come to distrust so-called thoughtful judgment in my drug-influenced year, and still held to the notion that what you felt in the moment was all that mattered, I knew this was something I should think seriously about.

And yet, before I even reached the stairs down to the subway, I knew what I'd do.

I was twenty-three years old, but felt older; an old man, in fact, looking back wistfully, recalling a certain orderliness to his isolation; a foundation, I liked to think, for a truer life. And then one morning I agreed to accept my apparent fate, because I couldn't stand being alone anymore.

Old Demons

We fell into a comfortable pattern. Noreen dropped out of one art school and applied to another, and, in the apartment we now shared, she was the quiet girl she'd been when we were hippies. When I came home from work, she had dinner waiting, though except for salads, not anything she prepared herself, but bought on Main Street and brought back. She'd set the place settings on the scavenged table, fading flowers adorning the edges of plates, vines curling on the silverware stems, the aesthetic of an immigrant family that had prospered enough to afford the upward move from a tenement in Manhattan or Brooklyn to an elevator apartment building near the Grand Concourse in the Bronx.

The plates and silverware and furniture had been a match for my own indeterminate state of mind, and now, for some reason, the old-fashioned stuff bothered me. But Noreen was unaffected by the oddity, was less inclined to attach meaning to inanimate objects. Did that explain the difference between us that impregnated the silence when we sat down at the ancient table? To my eyes, we were two strangers—before I began to expostulate, about the subway commute, office encounters, and the restaurant where I'd eaten lunch, details that emerged in no narrative order but as a stream of recollection, as if I were recalling someone else's life.

She listened with attentive curiosity.

"I *am* Sagittarius, after all," I threw in, the first time I went on a jag, interrupting myself, apologizing for my discursive stream. "I like to talk—but you already know that."

When I finally eased off, reeled in by the food sitting on my plate—having been too busy talking to eat, then prodded by habit to pick up the knife and fork or the chopsticks—she spoke, to commiserate.

She still considered it a hardship that I had a job. And I still didn't feel that way; it's not what I'd meant while relating this or that seemingly surreal scene. In fact I hadn't actually meant anything, I was just talking. At times I was on the verge of pointing out that she'd misinterpreted me, but I always let it slide.

The adaptations we make when we share our lives with others struck me as destructive when I thought about my parents, trapped in their own till death do us part relationship. But I soon stopped conjuring that. It was good to be with someone who listened, after all, and the fact that I didn't challenge her, or myself, by airing disagreements seemed a sensible trade-off.

But it went further. Not only didn't I question Noreen, I didn't reveal important things about myself; feelings that floated in a cloud and that only announced themselves in dreams. Like my nervousness when we were together after being apart. She seemed a stranger then. Why was that? Nor did I ask questions that might have elicited what she was thinking or feeling. For all I knew, she might have felt the same way about me.

Meanwhile, surreptitiously aware of avoiding more significant stuff made me reconsider my psychedelic year. I liked to think it had been transformative. It certainly tongue-tied me afterward, rendered me an alien along ordinary people, though I'd hidden the extent of my alienation by adopting various acceptable guises. But I soon dismissed those speculations as well, because contemplating them before Noreen showed up had been unnerving. One night, in fact, I'd all but come apart at the seams, recalling a candlelit tenement pad and the hovering spirit of a dead man in the abandoned apartment across the hall. I didn't want to go through that again.

So, to finesse those visitations, I thought about other things; Noreen, for instance, whose presence made me edgy when I came home from work until I recognized her as someone I knew, whose quietism became a positive trait I wished I could emulate. She was Aquarius, with alabaster skin and a graceful, swanlike way of moving about. Not an intellectual, but ruled by perception, intuitively grasping the truth of things, while I needed a few millimeters more time before comprehending the meaning of what I sensed.

"You know," I told her one evening as we ate dinner, "at work, I usually don't say much, but at the weekly committee meeting—like the one we had today—I'm expected to contribute, so I labor to string phrases and sentences together, while keeping the larger point I want to make in mind, so I don't forget it. I keep the thrust of it in my head while moving on in increments, barely holding everything together. If I pause to take a breath, the whole thing—the edifice I had in mind to build—might turn to gibberish …

"And then I finally get there—to the point I'd been holding onto— and get it all out, and stop … and notice that everyone sitting around the table is staring at me as if I'd just said something brilliant." I shook my head at the recollection. "The thing is, they're not amazed because of what I *said,* but the *way* I said it, quilting thoughts together and delivering them in my choppy Brooklyn accent. It disarms them, that my disjointed … concoction eventually comes together into something intelligible."

When I fell silent, Noreen replied, "I like the way you string things together."

It was not the first time I marveled at her intuitive economy.

"Yes, that's it exactly. They like the way I string things together."

How much of what I said did she actually grasp? I'd wonder about that later. Not to judge her, but to figure her out. Did she glide over the details, the nuances that made the disparate parts of a story interesting, and only see the final, conclusive picture?

Unlike our feelings, we'd talk about that. She was more abstract that I was, never had a problem understanding me, so long as we trafficked in observation and I didn't jar her by delving into the meaning of things. When I did, she'd glaze over.

But then, I was Sagittarius, and she was Aquarius. Which to my mind explained everything.

And then one evening when I came home from work and we sat down to eat, she broke her usual silence and spoke first; and about details, at that.

She said, "I think we should move into the city …"

My mind went blank.

"I miss the streets there," she explained, "the things to see."

"Where in the city?" I asked, though I already knew the answer.

The numbered streets and alphabet avenues where we'd met.

She didn't want to be too far from school where she'd start classes in the fall, she explained. She'd be working in the studios, and it might get late, so it would be better for her not to be too far from where we lived.

I said, "The lower east side, you mean."

"Why not?" she asked.

Because it was the last place I wanted to be.

But it was the only neighborhood we could afford, and, as she pointed out, only twenty blocks from her new school …

"All right," I said, and in the space of ten minutes went through one of those changes we'd refer to all the time as hippies.

I was Sagittarius, after all; quick change artist.

*   *   *

After walking down the six flights to the street from the railroad flat that first time, I stood rooted to the sidewalk, looking up and down the block with uncertainty, wondering which way to go. To the right, toward the numbered avenues, or to the left, where my trepidation mainly resided. Avenue A ... Tompkins Park ... Avenue B ...

I went toward the park, hesitating when the trees came into view, then ducking my head, as I often had back then, while walking to the corner and onto the avenue. In the illusory refuge of buildings that loomed to my right, I took in the park across the street ... the cyclone fence around the concrete softball field and basketball courts ... the promenade—

I flinched, seeing it, the brush with death trilling through me.

The paths, outlined with iron railings, the trees ... the band shell at Sixth Street, resembling a trepanned skull that fateful night ...

I looked away and trod past the plate-glass window of the Polish restaurant where I'd eaten so many cheap meals, when I could afford to eat, saw two men perched on counter stools up front, the cook at his grill, the tables in back, empty, as always.

What was there about this grim place and others like it that left me feeling hopeful?

Head down again, I clanked across the storage cellar doors, walking faster now, as if toward a destination, as so often back then, though I never had any place in particular to go, or else chased an idea, an inchoate notion that would somehow make everything better.

All you need is love ...

Blasting from the sub shop on the corner.

All you need is love ...

The words had mocked me. How could that be? What sense did it make?

And now, on that same avenue, I wondered how much I'd changed since then.

My rehabilitation so far had consisted of adjusting to a new place, resetting my metabolism to a workday schedule, overcoming a short attention span. I'd sacrificed loose-limbed clothing for clothes appropriate for a midtown office, discovered the social utility of responding when spoken to, gradually began to initiate speech, with words and in sentences others would accept Ψ all of this motivated by the fear of being discovered.

But this was something else. Returning to the scene. Confronting the larger fears, whatever they were. No mere costume change or manner of presentation and speech would suffice to quell those old demons.

What happened here? How much of it was real, and how much imagined?

I would discover that just asking the questions made a difference.

*   *   *

Heading to work in the morning, I felt what I supposed an actor might feel, playing a role. I moved along, easy within my skin, clothed in my office disguise. I felt competent, ambling toward the subway stop at Astor Place. Until, reaching the first corner, waiting for the light to change, I put a hand in a pocket and realized I'd forgotten my keys. Turning back, I'd retrace my steps down the block, up the six flights, burst inside, find them, and head back out again … and then, beyond the point where I'd stopped before, discover there was no money in the other pocket and double back, in a hurry now, recognizing that my attention span still needed work.

Eventually I made it all the way to the subway, arriving at work ten or fifteen minutes late. Not that anyone cared. By then I'd been accorded the status of iconoclast, without even trying.

When not heading toward work, when I went in the other direction, the old streets still conjured their associations, but it was getting easier to brush them aside before they could take hold. And for that I had Noreen to thank, though she had no idea while going about her business that her presence had altered my life.

Within weeks after we moved into the flat, she turned it into an art gallery. The sketches I'd seen in her pad in Flushing, the black and white splotches of her abstract expressionist period, were now splotches of paint on canvases she tacked to the walls, like drapery. She'd roll them up, bring them back from school; a new one every few days, adding color, crayon strokes, polka dot cutouts the size of pizzas safety-pinned to gessoed canvas.

"Larry Poons," she said, pointing to one when I asked about it. And "Josef Albers," for the geometric stripes she'd framed and hung in the kitchen; lines of vibrant color. "Morris Louis," for a humongous canvas in the living room; a breakthrough, she told me. Names I'd read on plaques when I accompanied her to museums and galleries.

It was all there when I came home from work, evidence that life could be livelier and more interesting, that it didn't have to be bleak. Now, when I turned my back on the street and opened the door to the building, I looked forward to walking into the top floor apartment, to decompressing in the creative cocoon the flat had become.

*   *   *

On the morning of the day I was scheduled to go to the induction center, Noreen got up early to make me breakfast. At the door, before I left, she me as though I were going into battle, which indeed I was.

"Don't worry," I told her. "It'll be all right." As if I had any idea. But knowing she shared my fate, that she would be with me afterward, whatever happened, I thought she could use some cheering up.

The psychiatrist I'd gone to for a while, as part of the bargain I'd struck with my parents when they fronted me money to rent the apartment in Queens, agreed to write a letter to the authorities. He'd shown it to me afterward, to see if I approved, and then I sealed the envelope, which I now had with me.

I hadn't slept much that night but was wide-awake, taking in the scenery as if imprinting the images in my brain as I walked to Astor

Place. The tenement streets, the utilitarian station, the numbing familiarity of the fluorescent-lit subway as it rattled and shrieked its way down Manhattan and into Brooklyn ... the unfamiliar station names conjuring aboveground locales I'd never seen. At every one, I imagined getting off, climbing up to the street and finding myself somewhere exotic. Yet after today, who knew whether I'd ever see Nevins Street, or Bergen, or Prospect Avenue? Whatever they looked like. I might be a citizen of Toronto, and my life—our life—would change forever. Because if the army accepted me, we'd be splitting for Canada that evening.

A cosmic joke, then, the marshal gods grinning, when I emerged from the subway and the scene was not at all dreary. On the contrary, the streets near the induction center were surprisingly, incongruously, attractive. I'd expected some sort of gulag, not tree-lined sidewalks and the startling blue expanse of the Verrazano strait. There were ships out there, freighters, waiting to be welcomed into the New York harbor. Vessels of the wider world, from far-flung ports of call, more places I'd never been.

Past the entrance gate, into the leafy confines of the fort, I followed the arrows to a barrack, with its classrooms, blackboards, desks, chairs, prospective inductees filling out official forms. And when we were done there, we moved to another barrack, a locker room where we took off our clothes, then shuffled into line to await various tests.

It cauterized my optimism, to stand there in my underwear with the others, waiting for the next in a battery of physical examinations. The letter clutched in my hand—the simple ruse I'd concocted about not knowing what was in the sealed envelope, in order to vehemently deny its assertions—now seemed feeble, a transparent fraud. How could I, a solitary individual, prevail against the inexorable designs of a System that could so effortlessly compel us to disrobe?

In my pessimism, I thought seriously about Canada then, which had only been a notion before, and abstraction, the idea of moving to another country. It hadn't bothered me. But now that it seemed a certainty I would be going—fleeing, not voluntarily moving—it made me angry. This was my country, after all. Its leaders as callous as anywhere else, easily manipulating and being manipulated by the patriotic bombast and self-congratulation of its simpleton citizens. But it was mine, this place where I'd been born and had lived all my life. I wanted to stay, to picket draft boards and compounds such as this one, to protest, to shout out in opposition, to demonstrate against its stupidity.

And then it was my turn to give blood, and the odds of my prevailing abruptly changed.

Life has a way of dealing you opportunities when you least expect them.

As squeamish as I am, the sight of the red liquid being syringed from my arm was a blessing. If I could hold onto the woozy feeling that made me feel faint, I thought, stay on my feet and nurture that sensation, I might become the person in the sealed envelope, a trembling wreck who could hardly walk and barely speak.

A few deep breaths and I could have pulled myself together; I knew that. But instead I thought back to the bright red stuff filling the syringe, and thinking about it, almost fainted again as I moved shakily to the next station, and the one after that, preserving that squeamish head all the way to the last room, a gymnasium where the army psychologist sat at a desk behind a partitioned cubicle within the larger room.

Swaying on my feet after another recollected extraction, I collapsed onto the metal folding chair facing his desk, pitifully weak as I handed the shrink the sealed letter and recited my rehearsed line: "My doctor said I shouldn't open it."

He looked at the envelope, turned it over once, then again, then briskly sliced it open with a miniature dagger, withdrew and read the letter. He looked up for a moment, stole a glance at me, then finished reading, leaned back and said, "It says here you attempted suicide six times."

I'd read that too, of course, and that I was a suicidal, latent homosexual addicted to narcotic drugs, a paranoid schizophrenic who would be a danger to anyone in my outfit. My cooperative shrink had written everything I'd asked him to, and thrown in a few extras.

Yes, I'd read it. Only now, as my heart pounded and the army shrink asked me *how* I'd tried to kill myself those six times, I realized I hadn't given it any thought at all.

I had no idea how I tried to kill myself once, much less half a dozen times!

"Well," I said, desperately holding to my wobbliness, "the first time, I took an overdose of sleeping pills ..."

"Yes," he said when I didn't continue. "And the other times?"

Perhaps I'd made myself too woozy to think straight, for now, as I frantically tried to imagine another suicide attempt, how I'd gone about it, what method I'd employed, my mind went blank.

I couldn't think of a thing.

Panic rippled though me ...

And then another, less flustered part of me boldly stepped in and took charge. It told me that anything I said, any attempt I might make to explain myself, would sound false, and that would be that.

So I sat in my self-induced squeamish haze, watching them draw blood from my vein once again ... sat staring over the shrink's head at the partition behind him, at the bright, high-ceilinged gymnasium beyond his ersatz enclosure, and sensing him sitting there waiting on me, I did the hardest thing I'd ever done, because I've always been a social animal, unable to resist explaining myself or filling demanding silences with the sound of my own voice ...

I said nothing.

More silent seconds passed, and I continued to say nothing.

And then, abruptly, he tore a page from a pad on his desktop, made a check with his pen, tore the page off, thrust it at me and said, "You can get dressed now."

I traipsed out without looking at the notation. Nor did I look while walking through the gym to the locker room where we'd all disrobed earlier. Who knew who might be watching? And even then, sitting on the plank bench in front of my locker, I only peered at the page surreptitiously, then contained my exultation until I was outside, where I shouted it at the sky.

"Four F!"

Unfit for military service.

My Little Notebook

It was inspiring, how dedicated Noreen was to her art. On the way home from work one day, thinking about it, I bought a spiral notebook. It was only five-by-seven inches, as if an ordinary size would have been presumptuous. And then, sitting in the front room with her gargantuan canvases surrounding me, I gazed at the street below, through the iron bars on the window meant to deter thieves, and the fire escape railings beyond, and made my first entry.

> Halfway up the block, at the top of a stoop, the usual fat guy leans back in a chair propped next to the bathhouse entrance. He sits there napping. Why? I've never seen anyone go in or come out. What is he guarding?
>
> As I watch, a group of neighborhood kids come down the block and stop at the foot of the bathhouse stoop. They taunt him from the sidewalk, counting on the fact that he's too fat to chase them down the steps, knowing they can easily get away.
>
> They're right. The fat man doesn't even attempt to stand up, just throws a stick at them, shakes his fist, shouts, "Get the fuck outta here or I'll call the cops!"
>
> "Gaw head," one of the kids says scornfully, "call the cops," sure that he won't. Like they have something on him.
>
> What exactly is going on in the bathhouse?

I read the piece to Noreen that night, thinking she'd like it because it was about what I saw, rather than my usual existential musings on the human condition. A short piece, hardly more than an anecdote, but I sensed her restlessness as she listened.

Not that it mattered. I didn't need her affirmation. Writing was my thing, I'd decide later, and painting hers. That we were both doing what we wanted was enough.

Eventually I'd fill that little notebook with short pieces, a few paragraphs each, always on a single page. And when I finished, and then reworked each piece, I felt different; younger, more playful. Somewhat like the self that hovered within me when I headed to work now, lighting up the cigarette I'd prepared the night before: squeezing tobacco out of the end, inserting a small piece of hashish into the hollow, then repacking the tobacco. My morning cocktail. By the time I got to the subway stop at Astor Place, my parietal lobe was pleasantly adrift, and in the office, my morning sojourn beneath the usually annoying fluorescents was a smooth affair.

When I finished the first notebook, I bought another, this one full-sized. And now I no longer confined myself to a single page.

Why had I done that anyway? Because I was self-conscious about seriously considering myself a writer?

Up the block there's a candy store, of sorts, that sells nothing but gum, cigarettes, and a few newspapers. It's always crowded with middle-aged men smoking, drinking coffee, hanging out as if something unseen were going on.

When I bought a *Sporting News* there one day, thinking to handicap the day's races at Aqueduct, to play with prognostication for a while, the owner, who had never said a word to me before, when I bought gum or cigarettes, remarked, "They're good."

"What's good?" I asked.

"The paper," he replied. "The one you got there."

"Thanks," I said, as if in response to a compliment, though I didn't get it.

Around the corner, the Italian restaurant on First Avenue is never open, yet somehow hasn't gone out of business. Across the avenue, the People's Fruit Stand burned down last month, the entire three-story building above it gutted. But the Three Guys From Brooklyn fruit stand next door survived intact, and since then has prospered. Everyone shops there now.

And then this morning at seven o'clock a limousine pulled up to the Turkish bathhouse up the block. Two guys in expensive suits got out, lugging laundry bags. They went up the stoop and inside, and minutes later came back out without the bags.

I find it hard to believe they were delivering towels.

*   *   *

I've come to the state employment office wearing my blue, dry-cleaned suit, looking like a guy who looks for work. But the transformation is incomplete: my elbow on an armrest, I cradle my cheek in a hand and notice that my fingers smell like fried onions and green peppers—what I had for supper last night. The smell induces a moment of panic, but before I freak out, fearing I might be discovered, I realize that the brown-suited clerk across the desktop, studying the form I filled out earlier, is too far away, that he'd have to be inside my nostrils to smell my pungent fingers.

"When you were here last," he says, looking up from the file folder splayed open on the green blotter, "the job market was slow ... but it's picked up somewhat since then." He knows better, of course. I can see as much in the way he almost looks at me, managing not to meet my eyes. "Have you been actively looking for work?"

In fact, I consider my unemployment check a subsidy to the arts. It pays for my necessary idleness while walking around lower Manhattan, sitting on park benches, gazing out my apartment window, and then while describing these scenes, courtesy of the federal government. Not that I don't feel occasional twinges of guilt. My father was a cutter, after all, a manual worker, when I grew up, and my family valued hard work above almost all else.

In my imagination, I discuss it with him. I don't want to disappoint, to be misunderstood as a parasite, so I explain the situation in a way he might understand and thus empathize.

I say, "George, they've been taking money out of my paycheck since I was sixteen. You know, that job I had in the book warehouse every afternoon in high school. And then working nights in the post office while I was in college. And recently, sitting in an office, pretending to work, which is actually worse than the real thing. So it seems to me I've paid my dues, that for now, while unemployed, I'm entitled to do whatever I want …"

Hearing clacking typewriters and ringing phones, seeing the other job or supposed job seekers at other desks with their own clerks, I look back at my man and say, "Of course I've been looking."

He pulls a yellow legal pad from the corner of the desktop, slides it over the file folder and the form I filled out, asks, "Who have you spoken to?"

I take out the notebook in which I write stories, while reserving the last few pages for official things, and recite the names and addresses of two places I visited and four others I found in the phone book.

He finishes recording all this on his yellow pad, says, "Let's see," and taking his pad with him, splits; leaves the room.

While he's gone I imagine him making calls, uncovering my fictions. But he reappears as bland as before, sits down without looking at me, holds up an index card in front of his face and says, "Unfortunately, I found only one active position in our files…It pays a hundred ten dollars a week …"

I tell him, "I can't support myself on that," leaving Noreen out of it.

He writes on the yellow pad *NEEDS MONEY,* in big letters. I almost laugh. He looks up and says, "Have you considered looking for a position in a field other than marketing research?"

"Marketing research? I haven't been looking for that."

He's surprised. "You haven't?"

"No. I'm looking for work as an educational research assistant."

He rechecks my folder. "It says here, 'Marketing research.'"

"I did that part-time, years ago, when I first got out of college. I applied for unemployment then too, which is probably why you have it down there, but my last job," and I gesture at the splayed file, "was as an educational research assistant."

He looks at the file, frowns, says, "Wait here," and leaves me alone again.

The law requires a person to subject himself to this every two months, so the little book you present at the check window each week is up-to-date. This bimonthly visit is a drag. But then, to collect a government subsidy, a certain amount of red tape can't be avoided.

My counselor returns, abashed. He has bad news: "You'll have to go back to the center on Worth Street and change your job classification."

Quickly, I say, "I've been thinking"—of the tedious trip downtown—"I guess you *could* say I'm a survey research worker. I mean, I once was … as you pointed out."

The instant career shift, so suspicious that it seems I should be taken away in handcuffs, doesn't faze him at all. On the contrary, he appears relieved. The official record and my place in it are now in accord. Without further questions, he stamps and signs my little weekly book.

*   *   *

I spend the afternoon at the Board of Education on Montague Street in Brooklyn, actually, seriously, looking for work. Time is running out on my creative period. I can tell because when I walk the streets, waiting for inspiration, or sit in the apartment, enveloped by Noreen's prolific art, I berate myself as a laggard doing work he doesn't get paid for.

So now I'm seriously looking for a job as a substitute teacher. I did it for one day, two years before, took my second dose of LSD that afternoon, after school let out, and never went back. But I enjoyed what little I did, so I fill out the forms, turn them in, sit in the waiting room awhile until my name is called.

After a while they show me to the fingerprint room, roll each of my digits in ink, as though browning sausages, then let me wait some more before calling me into another room to sign a release of my draft records. This I can't do, because those records were carefully designed, by me, to get me out of the army. So I refuse to sign.

Given the circumstance that underlay my draft record—that I declined to kill anyone—when they send me to another waiting room to wait some more, I lose myself in a fantasy in which I'm both Dreyfus and Emile Zola writing about Dreyfus.

Finally I'm summoned and an official of some kind, who perhaps wears a better suit than the other people I've briefly met, informs me that since I won't release my records, I had to be evaluated by a Board of Ed psychologist the following month.

I take this as good news, since I'm not ready to give up my freedom just yet, and because the fact that I actually tried to land work will silence my inner workingclass gnome between now and then. But before that interview could take place, something else came up. And that was a good thing too: I'd had enough of evaluative shrinks.

*   *   *

After washing my hands I sit down to eat supper in the railroad flat, vaguely noticing that the radio is playing and the room is too brightly lit. Noreen is about to crumple fried bacon into the viscous yellow liquid that will become scrambled eggs.

I say, "Can you put my bacon *next* to the eggs?"

She dries her hands on a dish towel, waits for the toast to pop. "Then I would have to cook yours and mine separately," she replies.

"All right," I say. "Make them the way you like."

From the counter, she regards me questioningly, across the gaping space between us.

"Make it any way you like," I repeat. In the bright room, with its yellow walls, my glass of cider looks like urine.

Noreen says, "I can make two batches if you want your eggs plain."

"It's all right," I say, for the third time, but louder now. "Mix mine with bacon."

After a moment she says, "Tell me how you want them," looking at me from the stove, gripping the spatula with a fist, as if it's a hammer.

The music on the radio is no more than noise, but it doesn't occur to me to turn it off. Instead I light a cigarette. "It really doesn't matter," I say, smoke scattering from my mouth.

"I just wanted to make it this way for once," she says. "We always eat it the other way."

Suddenly, I'm shouting: "You've lived with me for more than a year and you don't know me at all!" Whatever that means. And then I'm bellowing: "I don't give a shit what we eat! What the fuck do I care?"

Noreen, trembling, turns back to the stove as I finish the cigarette, screwing it angrily into the ashtray.

Neither of us talks for a long time. There's a grating ad on the radio, and still I make no move to turn it off. She brings the frying pan to the table and spoons the bacon-flecked eggs into two plates, her knuckles white from her death grip on the spatula.

The air is screaming, demanding resolution, so it's almost no surprise when she shouts, "I can't stand it anymore!" and sweeps the dishes off the table with an arm like a scythe. They shatter on the floor, shards bouncing everywhere, scrambled eggs with bacon bits, cider, heeps of brown sugar—an art piece, I think irrelevantly—as she runs out of the apartment, barefoot, without a coat, in the winter.

I run after her, down six flights, up the nighttime street to Avenue A and around the corner, keeping her in sight. She dashes across the avenue without looking, her bare feet slapping the pavement, and I give chase, hoping to catch her before she runs into the park.

Abruptly, she stops, looks around as if she doesn't know where she is, and I catch up. She tries to claw me then, and I try to pin her hands together between us, pushing her against a lamppost as she flails and thrashes. She's out of control, possessed, face contorted, eyes wild. Then her pupils roll up into the sockets of her eyes and disappear, except for a crescent of color visible above the white.

She freezes then, stops struggling, as if all the life has gone out of her, and collapses to the pavement.

*   *   *

I eat lunch on a balcony overlooking white-cloaked bartenders who pace the floor between cash register and customer. The uneaten meat loaf on my plate congeals. There must be a formula for how quickly it happens: the relation of volume and density to air temperature, perhaps.

Sports photos adorn the walls, for we're near the latest incarnation of Madison Square Garden. The athletes are elbowing each other, screaming, shaking fists … but it's pleasant, biding time there between job interviews, sipping my beer, watching the meat loaf congeal.

In retrospect I'll reflect on the inauspicious details that fall in proximity to notable events; how prescient they seem, looking back, and how meaningless they were at the time.

A few minutes before the appointed interview, I enter a carpeted office where the secretary tells me to take a seat. I'm wearing the old blue superhero suit and my favorite yellow-flowered Van Gogh tie, and feeling pretty good. Then I'm summoned into another, inner, office, walk the psychological distance to the boss's desk, shake hands with him and his assistant, who hovers nearby. With the curious sense of confidence that's come over me—or maybe just resigned indifference, after failing to get a job nibble for so long—I take a chair before it's offered. Small talk immediately ricochets between the three of us: concerning sports, for which I'm now ambiently prepared, having eaten lunch beneath the giant posters of muscular men.

Eventually the boss gets down to business. "You have a very impressive résumé," he says.

Having unsuccessfully sought work for weeks, his statement startles me, which is followed by a shot of hope, and adenaline on top of it, inflating this optimism. It's one of those rare days, I realize, when for no clear reason I'm suddenly in demand; certainly it has nothing to do with my résumé; more likely it's the position of the planet Jupiter.

Impressive ...

This assessment cues my glib tongue. Without effort I spew the right words. No, more than that, I can hardly believe how eloquent I am, weaving job interview gibberish. Pausing for breath, I notice the boss and his assistant exchanging a surreptitious glance. They're communicating mutual cleverness, which all but tells me I have the job. They covet me, want me to put out the annual state housing report. And I can't acknowledge my eagerness to do it, lest it reduce their offer.

I don't resume my pitch, selling myself as a valuable object, now that I know what's what. And into the silence, the boss crisply says: "This is a contractual job. You'll have a six-month deadline to meet, if we decide to hire you."

"I thrive on deadlines," I reply, forgetting to act blasé.

"Good, good ..."

"What's the salary?" I ask, and in the ensuing overlong pause, sense a shift, the two guys appraising me cannily through close-set eyes.

The boss snaps out of it first, inclines his head over a blotter and scribbles figures on a piece of paper. He's adding, subtracting ... Who knows what he's calculating? His assistant, meanwhile, picks up the reins of pseudoconversation, trying to engage me in ... hockey, I realize. I'm not much up on the sport, but pretend to be ...

"How 'bout those Blueshirts!"

... to show that I too don't care about the ongoing salary negotiation, that I just happen to be up there on the nineteenth floor to talk about the New York Rangers.

Finally the boss looks up from his incomprehensible scribbling and says, "We can only pay you as a consultant, you understand, not a regular, full-time employee ... You'll be working on a per day basis."

It jolts me that he doesn't say *per diem*, and though I am the most regular of guys, I feel a rush of uncharacteristic disdain.

"We can offer forty dollars a day."

Forty dollars!

My disdain is blown away, replaced by incredulity. I have just pulled off the biggest bamboozlement of my life.

"Okay," I reply solemnly. "It's a deal."

Later, of course, it occurs to me I've been screwed. But since I have no true notion of what I'm actually worth, I quickly get over it.

Scenes from a Marriage

I don't recall proposing to Noreen. That we would get married just seemed to emerge out of circumstance, and had something to do with how she felt about her parents. She talked about them with a curious mixture of anger and resentment, which I assumed had something to do with being adopted. That it would be easier for her to live with me if she didn't have to explain herself to them seemed a good reason to get married, especially since I didn't care one way or the other.

I met them for the first time when they visited the city during a business trip her father made on behalf of his company. He was one of a dozen vice presidents at Dow Chemical. Noreen and I went uptown and had tea with them in their posh hotel facing Central Park. Then they took us to dinner at a French restaurant, where we sat in a plush leather booth and ate snails, foie gras, duck and chicken, imbibed an expensive bottle of wine. Afterward we went to a Broadway play. They seemed nice enough, but Noreen bristled on the way home, complained about how little they understood her.

A few months later, when we flew out to small-town Michigan to visit, she was nervous about whether they'd make an issue over us sleeping in the same room, though they already knew we were living together. I pointed this out, but her mixture of defiance toward them and a contrary need to please clouded her usual clear thinking. Clearly, being adopted had left a mark.

For me, with my parents, there was just resentment.

My father, with whom I'd had problems since I was a teenager, pretended not to care that I'd apparently gone off the deep end again, shacking up with some girl who wasn't even Jewish—which might have been acceptable if she were—then losing my job at the research company and still out of work, though I claimed to have found a dream job—one that did not include health coverage. He kept these grievances to himself when we had dinner at their apartment, but shot my mother meaningful glances, silently warning her not to say anything that might set me off.

Of course, she did anyway, her seemingly innocent questions about our living arrangements and future plans conveying a subtext of guilt I was expected to alleviate.

There's too much talk about Jewish mothers being a hoot. It's a shtick. But you don't hear as much about Jewish sons. It drove me up the wall to be cajoled by her passive aggression. And my father too, with his transparent, withdrawn silences; as if nothing were wrong, when clearly everything was. So after that visit, Noreen and I didn't see them again for a while.

In contrast, my younger brother, with whom I hadn't much contact in several years, got along better with them. While I'd been doing who knew what in the East Village and Haight-Ashbury, he was at school, getting good grades, on an ineluctable upward career path. Indeed, he was at Harvard now. And unlike me, he had a live and let live temperament that precluded arguments. I was a hothead; around them, at any rate.

That first time Noreen and I flew to Michigan, we were picked up at the little airport by my future brother-in-law, a tree trimmer who played the drums and swore he was a demo tape away from playing with John Sinclair and the MC5. And why not? It was still the sixties, albeit the waning cusp, and anything seemed possible as we drove through the pancake flat landscape, immersed in "Hey, Jude," on our way to the company town of Midland and the Ainsworths' split-level house in the managerial suburbs.

They were glad to see me again, even more so than before; now that their daughter had officially chosen a mate, they wanted him to approve of him. Midwesterners. Hospitable people. What a relief, not to contend with my parents' undercurrent of judgment.

But the Ainsworths' open-ended welcome made me nervous. Why so agreeable? They hardly knew me, after all.

Was it the Jew in me, suspicious of unconditional acceptance, who wondered about their friendliness?

My thoughts were churning, and I hadn't even taken my coat off yet.

One moment I was an honored guest, which was flattering, and the next, I imagined myself a representative of my kind—a kind to which I ordinarily didn't give much thought, though now that I was here, had suddenly become my affinity group. As if a pogrom might erupt at any moment; not Cossacks this time, but Episcopalians.

Nothing of the sort happened, of course, nor did the problem Noreen anticipate materialize—flak about the two of us sleeping in the same room, in a four-poster bed with dolls and stuffed animals and other reminders of her childhood. And in this old-fashioned, hardly believable fantasyland, I asked her father for her hand in marriage the day before we left. He was delighted to give it.

And why wouldn't he? John Ainsworth knew he could have done worse, what with young people burning draft cards, from what he'd heard within his bubble, when they weren't rioting in the streets. Hippies, yippies, the Democratic convention in Chicago: the world as he understood it had gone haywire. How fortunate that his daughter had found an upstanding young man like myself!

And having so easily fooled him, I found myself wondering whether Ainsworth and his wife knew as little about their daughter.

I met Noreen's sister too, a simple woman who was friendly

enough, but with whom I couldn't find a thing to talk about. She and Noreen had both been adopted, godsends, until their adoptive mother discovered she could indeed conceive, and bestowed two genetic sons on her husband.

An ingenuous man, John Ainsworth. Like his heroes—captains of industry—he had no sense of irony, would not have understood why I blanched when he said his proudest achievement was the work he'd done on the project that produced napalm.

But I liked her mother, Binky, a name bestowed on her by college classmates, though I couldn't bring myself to call her that and instead used her given name: Eleanor. Though her beliefs were without exception his, she at least wore them lightly, and never brought them up unless compelled to defend him. I enjoyed hanging out in the kitchen with her and Noreen, watching mother and daughter gabbing while baking bread and making cookies, the two boys popping in to eat dough and shyly eyeball the guy their older sister lived with in New York City.

*   *   *

In December we returned for the marriage ceremony, the flat landscape now covered with frozen snow. My parents and brother flew in a day later, and my uncle and his wife after that. Another aunt and uncle didn't get to the Chicago airport before the impending blizzard grounded all planes.

Our little clan stayed in the country club, the only one in town, courtesy of my father-in-law. He also offered to pay for the tuxedos my brother and I had to rent, but my father insisted on footing that bill himself. When Noreen and her family weren't doing bridal things, we joined them at dinners and luncheons thrown by friends of the family for the bride and groom, a custom foreign to us. But when it began to snow the afternoon before the scheduled ceremony, we were on our own. It was coming down hard as we ate at Luigi's, the recommended, watered-down Italian restaurant on the edge of town, and there was nearly a foot of it on the ground when we drove into the snow-shoveled country club lot in our rented cars and hurried into the building.

Except for a caretaker, the place was empty. He led us to the dining room and disappeared, the six of us gathering around a banquet-size table as if it was Passover all over again, except without the rituals, or the childhood credulity that made those occasions bearable. My uncle Jack, the family entrepreneur, had bought champagne and two bottles of wine at a liquor store in town on the way back; the most expensive brands they had. It was a good thing too, because we'd said about all anyone could think of while eating our early dinner.

Jack and his wife knew I'd taken drugs, crashed, went to a shrink, got arrested at a draft board sit-in, and, for all I knew, about the job I'd recently lost and the one I had now, which didn't offer health coverage. My parents had enlightened them. A dismal portrait. I always pretended not to notice the resultant vibe when we got together, and now that I was the center of attention—the reason everyone had come to this place—I drew on a college history course to initiate a conversation about nineteenth century politics in America, when the Republican party financed the settling of German burghers into the Midwest, explaining, in my way, the wider world in which we now sat, in an empty country club. But since I was the only one who knew what I was talking about, it became instead a discourse.

Fortunately, by then we were all a bit drunk, and with short-term forgetfulness slipped into the deep past, when all things had a patina of unifying perfection.

Jack told the same story he always did when he got tipsy: about taking me to Ebbets Field when I was three years old. My father recalled the first time I met him, when I was two and he was ushered into my grandparents' tenement living room. My mother had said to me, "This is your father," pointing at him. And I supposedly replied, "No!" and pointed to a framed photo on the wall of a man in military uniform.

Not to leave my brother out of the recollections, my mother remembered how he cried all the time as a baby, and my father added that it took him so long to walk that they assumed there was something wrong with him. They went on for a while in that vein, perhaps making him the foil in order to enhance my standing, since after all I was the man of the hour, and because my brother, a Harvard man now, could hardly care what he'd been like before he even knew his name.

Meanwhile, the blizzard outside socked us in. When my brother and I finally retreated to the room we shared in another wing of the club, the storm had finally ended, leaving a smooth white landscape that came up to the window ledge.

We were so different. What could we possibly talk about? Years later, in the normal course of aging, I'd come to realize that brothers are brothers, no matter what else separates them. They can talk about anything, because there's more between them than words. But that night, to dispel the awkward silence, I suggested we take a walk.

"Your last walk as a free man?" he joked as the two of us, swaddled in overcoats, gloves, and wearing boots we'd found in the cloakroom, set off across the golf course.

It was more a trek than a walk, since the snow came up to our waists and we had to push our way through, huffing clouds of moisture when we finally reached the other side of the course and emerged onto a plowed lane. The nighttime sky was inky black, now that the storm was over, the stars a dazzle of gems, the air cold and crisp. Catching our breath, we set off again, crunching up the road in the absolute silence, past what we'd called "private houses" when we were boys and lived in a project, snowdrifts reaching nearly to the eaves, Christmas lights peeking out.

The unreality of the scene brought out the reality of what it meant to get married, to legally attach yourself to someone else. And echoing his cliché about the last walk of a free man, I said, "Maybe I should just keep walking up this road and not stop until I reach the end."

He laughed, but in that pristine moment of yawning emptiness, it was no joke. I truly felt compelled to walk up that snow-packed road and see where it went. A whole new place, a life I couldn't begin to imagine …

To a town called Alpena, someone would one day tell me, though I'd no doubt have frozen to death first.

And maybe my brother was in an unusual place himself as we crunched up the road. He'd heard disturbing things about me ever since I left home, and then while he was in college. Now, in a serious, eminently reasonable voice, which I'd rarely heard before, he said, "Noreen seems like a nice girl."

"Yes …"

"And Mary and George seem to like her."

"Yes …"

And we left it at that.

*   *   *

The Christmas tree was still in the living room; a nice backdrop, my future in-laws thought, its twinkling lights reflected off the sliding plate-glass doors in the rear of the house, obscuring the backyard. But after the various dinners we'd gone to in people's homes, and the foreignness of that custom, the tree became a problem; not unlike the manger in front of the town hall, which my father had railed about in the country club.

Why on earth would anyone object? my mother-in-law-to-be wondered aloud when he broached the subject. But he knew how to act among strangers, swallowed his outrage and instead made a joke of it;

just as he'd managed not to voice his opinion at any of the get-togethers that there was no objective proof that there'd ever been a man who became Jesus Christ.

Only now my parents, Mary and George, were beside themselves as we waited for the ceremony to begin, whispering to each other, frowning at the little flower girls who scattered petals down the makeshift center aisle as if they were a personal affront. They'd asked me to find a rabbi to administer the vows alongside the local minister, and George suggested as much to Ainsworth. The two of them had hit it off during the celebratory dinners. The former communist and the capitalist pig. Who would have thought? But when George was among strangers, he was an amiable sort—a Sagittarius, like me—and more than that, so far as Ainsworth was concerned, had a Marine's swagger that some men find irresistible.

Indeed, Ainsworth, smitten by George, readily agreed, saying, "By all means, let's have a rabbi too."

Except the only rabbi in the vicinity, thirty miles away, in Saginaw, would only come to recite the prayer for the dead, as custom required when a Jew married outside the tribe. So I shot down that idea.

Someone's aunt, playing an organ that had been squeezed into the crowded room, switched from Schumann to "All You Need Is Love," fumbling with the notes as Noreen walked down the aisle with her father, and then I followed alongside my brother. We had chosen the song, to inject something of ourselves into the ceremony. The Beatles. It's about all the two of us had after everything else had been decided by others. I cringed, hearing it, as the audience whispered in appreciation at the cute touch. The past a plaything, a doodle in the margin of my life.

And then, thankfully, the embarrassing song was over and we stood before the minister, and the blinking tree, said the words, exchanged rings, were pronounced man and wife … and in a whirlwind were shuttled off to the country club; for refreshments, someone had announced.

The banquet hall was lit up when we arrived, and people milled about. But where were the tables? And the buffet? I didn't see any food at all. And there was no music. Just klatches of people on the parquet floor, chatting over champagne flutes.

For chrissake, where was the food?

For my parents, it was the final straw.

No food!

Like we hadn't eaten in days.

They fell upon Noreen and me when we were done shaking hands on the receiving line. For a change George stood in silent agreement as Mary pleaded with me for a Jewish gesture of some sort.

"Like what?" I asked.

"At least break the glass," George suggested.

But Mary, who had not yet conveyed the familial subtext of guilt to accompany her request, felt compelled to add, "Jack and Geri came all the way from Long Island, and in a blizzard too!" Though it hadn't even been predicted when they boarded the plane. My uncle and aunt, who would at least expect a Jewish gesture, even if no one knew what it meant. "And there wasn't even a rabbi!"

"At least break the glass," George said again, turning to me.

By now the Ainsworths had joined us, along with my brother and uncle and aunt, all of us huddled on one side of the banquet hall while the hundred or so guests, the board of directors of the chemical company and their wives, the flower girls and their cousins, the whole *mishpocha*, blithely ignorant of our Talmudic deliberations, continued sipping and chatting.

Again Ainsworth quickly agreed, though he had no idea what it meant to "break the glass." Eleanor, who always backed his decisions, did too, though I could see she was perplexed.

"It's an empty glass," I explained. "We put it on the floor and then I jump up and come down and smash it."

She gave me an odd look, but I could hardly hold it against her. It sounded insane.

"A symbol of fertility," my aunt put in. "Hundreds of years old."

We were all insane.

But these good people whom we'd secretly criticized among ourselves, for the manger on public property and the Christmas tree in the living room, complied, and my father-in-law went to speak to someone in authority.

Minutes later a waiter brought an empty glass wrapped in a white satin napkin on a silver tray.

Our group moved to the center of the room, where my father unwrapped the wineglass and set it on the floor.

"But won't it make a mess that way?" Eleanor asked, displaying her uncommon sense. "When it shatters? What if a flying shard of glass cuts someone?"

So George, who always deferred to women, rewrapped it in the cloth napkin and set it down on the floor again.

Did anyone explain what we were doing? Explain that by breaking this glass I would mark the destruction of the Second Temple, or maybe the Third Temple—none of us knew for sure; we were not observant Jews—in 600 B.C. or so?

But someone must have said something because the entire gathering had turned in our direction, the soft burr of conversation fading and then dying altogether as I stepped up to the napkin-wrapped wineglass, jumped up, and came down on it like the virile man I was expected to be, shattering it; though wrapped up as it was, it made a quiet tinkling sound, hardly virile at all.

The hundred or so witnesses remained frozen in attentive postures, staring at the groom, in his tuxedo; the bride, in white chiffon; at a crumpled napkin in which a glass had been smashed in the middle of a perfectly respectable gathering.

And at what seemed the same moment they all turned away and resumed their conversations, as if nothing inexplicably rude had just occurred.

Back in Brooklyn

Out the bay window the sky was pale, blank. Beneath it, beyond the buildings and rooftops across the way, I pictured streets fanning south through neighborhoods marked by church steeples, elevated subway lines, broad avenues as ugly as those in Detroit, and a few, like Ocean and Eastern Parkways, with promenades as elegant as Parisian boulevards, though now run-down and in disrepair. Neighborhoods I'd heard about or passed through had the aspect of a lost Atlantis, as I sat there by the way window, from the Navy Yard to Sheepshead Bay, Coney Island, the beach, the ocean … the world beyond.

I had a junkie to thank for the expansive view. Rattling the window bars of what had become our cage in the East Village, he chased us from the drug-ridden dystopia Manhattan had become to this slower paced world of exceedingly ordinary charm.

Not that I'd been thinking about moving. Before the junkie showed up, it never occurred to me to move, though it seemed everyone was talking about how dangerous life had become. For some reason, the paranoia never got to me. Perhaps the weeks I'd once spent on the street, hustling nickels and dimes to survive—my own trembling, paranoid era inuring me to this one.

Noreen, however, was a wreck. Her skittishness brought to mind the seizure I'd witnessed, preceded by a crescendo of tension, which now left me wondering whether she wasn't heading toward another fit … for which precautionary reason I'd walk up to Twenty-third Street and meet her at school whenever she worked late in the studio, and then walk her downtown afterward…and why she now often came home in the afternoon, when classes were over, skipping the studio study session that usually went until dark. I could see her trepidation on the walls of our railroad flat, where there were no new canvases. Her work, it seemed, was suffering. Fear can do that to the creative impulse.

With karmic displacement, the widespread fear brought on a social whirl of get-togethers, her school friends popping in more often, to joke about Marcel Duchamp and Dada over pizza and beer. Or we'd go out, meet her crew at bars where artists reputedly hung out, bleak Bowery and Delancey Street watering holes resembling grim Edward Hopper depictions, only less colorful, the art schoolers outnumbering the resident alcoholics.

It was a slumming scene, and rubbed me the wrong way. But what did I know about artists? Or about art? As if, lacking aesthetic awareness, my skepticism was suspect; as if, because I couldn't appreciate their artistic sensibility, there had to be more to it than condescension. I made the same excuse for my boredom as I sat through dull conversation consisting of dropped names—Motherwell, Morley, Jasper Johns, Oldenburg, Rauschenberg, Poons—and mimicking the apparently artistic custom, drank more than I otherwise would have, in an attempt to be part of the unreflective camaraderie.

Then the junkie showed up.

We were in bed in the middle room, me reading, Noreen looking at reproductions in one of her picture books, when he dropped down from the roof to the metal balcony that ran along the rear of the building. There were two windows back there, in the kitchen, and on that hot June night they were open, but with the iron window guards stretched across the openings. The light was on in the kitchen, and you could see the windows from where we lay in the shadow cast by a dresser, which made the junkie's abrupt, bar rattling appearance that much more startling. How desperate was he, trying to shake the bars loose and break in with the light on?

Noreen clutched my arm, eyes wide as I shrugged her off and slipped out of bed. Without thinking, I moved with sudden purpose toward the brightly lit room.

Along the way I spotted a roll of canvas and took hold of it like a baseball bat, bringing it with me into the yellow room. Taking note of the torso at the window, hands gripping the bars, I turned away, toward the front door, as if I hadn't heard or spotted him, and shouted, "Who is it?" supposedly mistaking the rattling window guards for someone knocking, and poised to attack whoever was out there, in the hallway.

Behind me, I heard the junkie clatter away, and turned in time to see his fleeting form. Moving to the window, I listened to him scrabbling down the side of the building from balcony to balcony like a monkey.

Afterward, Noreen pleaded with me to move. There was no subterfuge in it, to ruminate about later. It was clear she was scared.

The next day we looked for an apartment in Brooklyn.

*   *   *

I was working at the housing agency then, as what they called an "independent contractor." But I went to work every day, as at any other job I'd ever had, putting in my time at the office from nine to five. After a month or so, however, I saw advantage in my odd circumstance: except for the guy who hired me, and his assistant, no one knew who I was or why I was there. And they didn't care, as long as I produced an annual report in eight months, which I knew would only take me about a month, so I had plenty of time for other things.

So after my morning coffee and newspaper—comforting tribal habits I'd come to embrace—I would close my office door and work on my stories.

The writing in my recent notebooks was barely legible, with arrows leading to margins filled with text done in different colored inks, which had bled through to the other side and were nearly unreadable, and were further confused by numbers and letters indicating this or that insertion elsewhere, on equally motley pages. I took inordinate pride in their abstract appearance, but knew they had to be typed, if anyone else were to actually understand them. And a superior typewriter came with the position.

The finished or at least more legible result seemed an extension of my own recent self-discipline. If the pages in my notebooks resembled the new crevices and crenellations in my brain—the more creative, expressive person I'd become—the clean, typewritten pages signified the structure and organization of the assimilated person who now did inventory in the morning before leaving the apartment: to remember keys and wallet, notebooks and pens, and not have to double back while halfway to the subway stop, a psychedelic survivor wrestling with the residue of distraction.

Not that my mind didn't still wander as I walked up the quiet brownstone street, feeling so good that I posited the planets in creative alignment, a configuration that explained the surprising perfection of this place where I'd been born, this Brooklyn that was now somehow of a piece with what I recalled and read about …

The tenement apartment of my earliest memories, on a street that slanted down a hill to Eastern Parkway and beyond that to Pitkin Avenue, the shopping mecca of jostling immigrants and wooden pushcarts. Since I'd been so young then, it that if I lived long enough, eventually I might be the last witness to that old-fashioned world; an obituary in the *Times*, if I made it, say, to ninety—the last survivor of the ice box era, living in rooms with tables and chairs that dwarfed him, a place that still loomed in my mind like Plato's cave.

This, before I'd ever met my father, and when my mother was mainly gone, at work, my grandparents substituting as mother and father. I spent a good deal of my later life filtering the sentiments and opinions of those who recalled them as adults, in order to understand who they'd actually been. She was a tough woman, with a hunchback and arthritically gnarled hands, who worked hard in the house and set limits. He was affable and usually unemployed.

In brownstone Brooklyn, I read Camus, *The Stranger*, then the short stories, and was influenced by the existential outlook when I thought about Brownsville and the man I called Uncle Alex, my grandfather's brother, a carpenter from Vilna who lived alone; a Jewish alcoholic, of all things. In my imaginings, Ma, my grandmother, made it clear to her husband that he couldn't visit, that he would be a bad influence—on me. But when she was out shopping, Alex would sometimes drop in to see his brother, bringing me a gift of chocolate covered cherries. I turned that recollection into a story in which she purposely left the apartment at a certain time, because whatever she thought about Alex, he was her husband's brother, after all.

I read *Nausea* too, recalled a day when my grandfather's joints might have been acting up and he couldn't take me on our usual walk: up the steep street, past the ice house, toward the smell of fresh-baked bread from the adjacent Italian ghetto, then around the red brick walls of the girls reformatory and back. But since children needed fresh air, he opened a window and plunked me down on the fire escape in back … where I sat gazing at weeds and brick rubble, a crumbling brick wall, a ginkgo tree jungle of refuse and neglect.

I sat for what seemed a long time, wanted to go back inside. But the window behind me was closed, and I was perched on the second floor, afraid to turn around, crawl to the window and tap on the glass. So I just sat there, staring at the decrepit scene below, experiencing what might have been my first epiphany: that I was alone in the world, even though I knew there were other people somewhere.

I'd have that realization again, more than twenty years later, the first time I dropped acid.

*   *   *

My other grandfather, Benjamin, couldn't find me the day he came to the fourteenth floor of the New York State Housing Authority, intending to take me out to lunch. My father told him I worked there, but with my per diem contract and temporary office, I was anonymous; the lady at the receptionist desk facing the elevators had no idea who I was. Later, when I learned about his attempt to see me—the old man, my grandpa, working as a messenger, to keep busy, turning away a few feet from where I sat—I felt bad.

But then, if it hadn't happened that way, I probably wouldn't have seen him before the police found him dead on the linoleum kitchen floor of his apartment.

This was the grandfather I hardly knew, a slim man with a gentle voice, roughened by the cigars he smoked. I sometimes thought about him when I tasted the woody flavor of my own occasional cheap cigars; the particular pleasure we seemed to share then, and again later, at the bitter end of the smoke.

When we visited back then, his wife, Anna, my grandmother, a heavyset, stolid woman, would be planted in the high-back soft chair in the formal living room as if it were her throne, her legs crossed at the ankles, hands clasped on her chest, glowering in silent, disapproving judgment. She put everyone on edge. Recently, she'd had a stroke, and was now in a facility somewhere in Queens, not far from where my parents lived. Grandpa Ben took two subway lines and a bus from Brooklyn to visit her, nearly every day, to sit in a room where she was immobile, unblinking. Did she know who he was? Was she still passing judgment? No one could say.

When he wasn't visiting her, he was in a building up the block from the duplex where he and she and his children had lived for years, when my father was a boy. Benjamin had been somewhat prosperous then, and for a while even owned a small dress-making shop in the garment district. But somewhere along the way, when his children grew up and then were gone, he lost the shop and he and Anna moved to the tall building on the corner.

The elevator, a tin box, creaked slowly upward, the doors opening onto a somber hallway I instantly recalled. Until I knocked on the door, it hadn't occurred to me that he might not be home. But then I heard him at the other end of the apartment, calling out, "Who's there?"

I loudly announced myself, to be heard through the door as he approached.

"Hold on," he said, just behind it now, unlatching locks. "Just a minute."

Then he stood in the open doorway, shorter than I remembered, looking up at me through bifocals, his small, uneven teeth stained a light, cigar-smoke brown.

"Come, sit," he said, pleased to see me, ushering me into the narrow sitting room in front, rather than the cold, more formal living room where my grandmother once sat in her high-backed chair. This room contained a couch and two armchairs, a familiar bowl of apples and oranges on the low wooden cocktail table between them.

He asked about my health, my wife, my job. I apologized for the fact that no one knew who I was when he'd dropped by, and he waved that away. Yes, of course, it wasn't my fault. Still …

I was nervous. This was my grandfather, after all, who held me toward the sky in home movies, shook me until I laughed. An adult among those whose conversations was beyond my ken. Now, in the shadow of the boy I'd been, I didn't know how to act.

But his lack of pretense and his even-tempered manner soon put me at ease, so much so that I forgot who I was talking to, fell into the easygoing, careless thread of a teenager conversing with his pals, and made a glib remark; a joke, maybe, at someone's expense; a putdown. I'd hardly uttered the foolish remark before it brought me up short and I knew I'd gone too far.

Across the small room, he blinked at me from behind his lenses for several seconds, and then, in a matter-of-fact voice, explained why he disagreed, as if responding to a serious remark uttered by a serious person. I felt both chastened and elevated.

That interchange was the first thing that came to mind when my father told me he was dead—his father's gentle, pragmatic manner of dealing with the world.

"I used to hang out at the poolroom, with guys who had what I guess you'd call a reputation," George told me after his father died. "He never said anything about it, but he knew … and I knew what he thought about those guys. So whatever was happening at the poolroom, I'd be sure to be home in time for dinner.

"But one day I got involved in a game and lost track of the time, and at one point, lining up a shot, I stepped back from the table, looked up and saw the clock on the wall. Always, I'd be sure to get home at five-thirty, six—and now it was seven. Then, a few tables away on the other side of the room, I saw my father, standing by himself. I guess he'd been there awhile, without saying anything. I was surprised—and embarrassed, of course. I said to him, 'Pa, you want me to come home now?'

"You have to understand, my father didn't like everything I did, but he would never embarrass me in front of anyone. Now, with the guys there watching me, he said, 'Finish the game first, George, then come home,' without any judgment or disapproval … then left the poolroom."

*   *   *

I also read Henry Miller while sitting at the bay window overlooking the brownstone street, and his Brooklyn became mine; Williamsburg, where his father, the tailor, lived; and later, the streets of

the *Rosy Crucifixion,* where he roamed. I went to work, and came
home, and read, and under the influence of authors and geography, I
wrote.

Vonnegut, for instance: the surreal world he depicted reminded me
of the army camp behind the Quonset hut, rain rattling on the tin roof. I
went to kindergarten there, first, second, and third grade. This, after my
father came home from the war and we lived in one of the wooden row
houses next to the swamp. Soldiers strolled by the schoolhouse
windows, and there were khaki tents out there, jeeps, and the occasional
tank, raising dust. Did anyone in the government during the so-called
cold war realize that the hastily built camp, with its radar installation to
track Soviet aircraft, would be next to a school? Did the maps the cold
warriors in Washington consulted, which showed Jamaica Bay hard by
the ocean, depict a swamp but not the hastily built housing project for
GIs? Or could it be that they just didn't they care?

But mainly I was motivated by Miller, the old charlatan, who
rendered the everyday life of a casual bohemian so believable. He and
his elusive girlfriend, June, borrowing a roadster in the days when
people went for "a drive"—a journey with no particular destination—
and ended up somewhere exotic, like Long Island … where we went
when I was a boy, to visit relatives who lived in a so-called private
house, with grass and bushes in the backyard, a badminton net, a
barbecue pit … from which we'd return, after dark, to the treeless
housing project in Canarsie, poor relations to my suburban uncle, aunt,
and cousin.

*   *   *

Noreen's father had moved up in the corporate world, become
president and CEO of a different chemical company, which was why
the Ainsworths had relocated to Fairfield County, Connecticut. To get
there, we'd take the subway to Grand Central and then the Metro North

commuter train; a couple of young kids, in the vernacular, leaving Brooklyn and the city behind.

The railroad spur ended at the base of Main Street, where I stared in disbelief at the postcard scene, with its church on a hill overlooking the tidy storefronts. There were no vacant, deteriorating, or boarded-up shops in New Canaan, no failing merchants. Evincing that sorry state, they were no doubt instantly displaced by others, perhaps disappearing in the dead of night in rented moving vans.

The Ainsworths had a ten room house on a few acres, one among the rich family of homes separated by fences and stone walls.

But what I noticed were the trees, hundreds per family, compared to thousands in Prospect Park, for hundreds of thousands of people—a tree for every thousand. Coming home to Brooklyn, emerging from the subway at Grand Army Plaza, with its Arc de Triomphe doppelgänger, I'd spot the splash of green that marked the democratic park, with its trees for everyone, which brought a lump to my throat … for the long-lost Dodgers of the common man and woman; for Coney Island, out there in my mind, a ghost town now; for the gothic bridge that was our Notre Dame …

And then President Street, where my father had been a boy in another neighborhood, and the block we lived on, its stone porches and beige facades indifferent brownstone matrons, welcoming us back.

Young Man Goes West

Noreen's parents precipitated our next upheaval. So far as they were concerned, it was one thing to call yourself an artist, another thing entirely to go to school, which implied a goal. And so as her school term drew to a close, they laid down the law: if she didn't transfer to an institution in the fall that granted a degree, they would no longer pay her tuition.

Since there was no telephone in the apartment—what with her long distance calls in Manhattan, we'd run up a humongous bill, so I went incognito in Brooklyn—she got their edict in the mail. When I walked in, she was sitting on the couch, knees and ankles pressed together, calves parallel lines, conjuring the Christian Science schoolgirl whose father sent her to boarding school to toughen her up—or maybe just to get rid of her, since she was a handful, what with the temper tantrums she threw, which might well have been the warning signs for the seizure I'd witnessed.

It was spring, another glorious day in brownstone land, and I listened with a sinking sense of déjà vu to the ultimatum she'd been given before she rushed on to tell me about an art school she'd heard about in Oakland, California, one that granted a degree and that she was certain, given her portfolio, she could get into.

How many seconds passed before my brain made its empathic quantum leap? Before I stepped over this latest obstacle to my settled state and moved on without a backward glance, embracing a new challenge?

In fact I might have already made that leap while drifting toward the bay window overlooking the street and the stately brownstones across the way, marching up the block to the far corner and the splash of green beyond that was Prospect Park.

I had a few neighborhood acquaintances by then, aside from the familiar faces in the candy store where I made phone calls: people I'd met at the writers' group where I showed up one evening to read a story and went back every week after that.

Fritz, a corpulent poet who sported a cocky beret and rode around the neighborhood on a bicycle, his pant cuffs tied with what seemed red garters ... David, who'd gone to camp in the Catskills with someone I once knew, and now owned a children's toy store on Seventh Avenue, the main drag. He and his wife hosted the group, but though he read regularly—instantly forgettable poems—she modestly made cookies and sat in the living room listening, though I sensed she wanted to read too and lacked confidence ... Irascible Kunzler, who was older than the rest of us and taught a poetry class at Noreen's art school in Manhattan.

"Poetry for visual artists," I said to him once, half joking.

"Illiterates," he replied, not joking at all.

They came to mind as I gazed out the bay window, but by the time I turned back to Noreen, who still sat like an Egyptian hieroglyph, I'd already moved on.

"As soon as my job is over, and we return from Europe," I said, "I'll buy a car and we'll drive out there."

*   *   *

In late summer we loaded the brand new VW station wagon—a gift from my rich uncle's wife—with valises and boxes, a record player and records, books and notebooks, a typewriter, a set of expensive dishes and silverware, pots and pans—marriage gifts—and Noreen's art supplies and rolled-up canvases.

I'd been to California two years before, during the so-called Summer of Love. Four of us drove from the East Village, bound for Haight-Ashbury, in a car to be delivered in Billings, Montana. There, we took to the road, hitching west to Butte, and then on to Idaho Falls, where a bitter fight in a freight yard split us up. Afterward, my companion and I were stuck amidst the buttes and sagebrush, through pouring rain and blistering heat, detained and nearly arrested by a redneck sheriff who took issue with our unkempt appearance, and finally made it to San Francisco a week later.

This trip was nothing like that. Noreen and I stayed in motels, camped one night in the Bighorns and for nearly a week in her uncle's cabin in the Idaho panhandle, jointly owned by her mother, and coasted down to the Bay area in high spirits. She had indeed been accepted at the College of Arts and Crafts, and I had notions of writing great stories while we lived off the savings of my consultant job.

Someday, in the distant future, I would be amused by the short-sightedness of young people, even find it charming. How they never calculated how much they had, nor balanced that against the cost of renting an apartment and buying food. Like them, I had no idea how long we could live off what I'd earned; it merely seemed we'd have enough. After all, hadn't I made more money at my last job than ever before? Forty dollars a day, for eight months!

With the same blithe, unexamined optimism, the hovel we came upon in the Berkeley flatlands after unsuccessfully looking for an apartment for two weeks seemed cozy instead of cramped and gloomy. I wanted to move in right away.

Noreen was subdued as I emanated enthusiasm. Pretending her lack of reaction held no meaning—though by now I could assess the import of her various silences—I said, "So, what'd you think?" with a suggestive upward inflection.

Her response was to tilt her head doubtfully.

"There's a backyard," I said, pointing at a narrow kitchen window with its view of a few square yards of pavement, a fence, and clotheslines.

"It's kind of dark," she eventually replied.

"True," I said, for even an inveterate optimist could see that the ceiling was low, the louver windows stingy and set up high, as in a basement, and that the noonday sun filtered into only one of the three rooms. "But we'll put up some gauzy curtains so the light can come through, and we can paint the rooms, brighten them up."

We'd moved by then into the bedroom, where the mattress the previous tenants had left behind covered most of the floor. "That would help," she agreed, somewhat getting into the spirit of denial. "A fresh coat of paint." I'd said the magic word. Noreen practically worshiped paint; thinking about painting was her own version of imagining a better world.

"Look at this wall," I said, running a hand over the surface. "It's smooth." I still compared everything to the tenements; they'd made a lasting impression.

She ran a hand over it too, said, "Yes, it *is* smooth."

"So what about it?" I asked.

"Well …"

"Your classes start soon, and we've seen a bunch of places already …"

"I'm not sure …"

I said, "C'mon, Noreen. Anytime you face something new or different, it freaks you out. Remember when we got off the plane in Amsterdam? You wanted to stay in the motel next to the airport. I practically had to drag you into the city, but once you did, you loved it."

As if this situation were equivalent.

When I worked up a head of steam, there was no telling what would come out of my mouth, what verbal manipulations I might employ. Sometimes it seemed to me I'd been a more honest person in that period when the affect of drugs rendered me mute.

She forced a smile, said, "All right."

So it happened that, out of my impatience, we came to live in a subdivided house on a treeless street fronted by sere lawns, with the dreary city civic center across the way and the police headquarters up the block.

In Brooklyn, my bay window overlooked the world. Here, a flat sheet of glass wavering with imperfections faced a concrete backyard. I looked for more in the unprepossessing scene outside than could be seen, positing an ashcan lyricism to the empty clotheslines strung out against a drab sky; imagining the bay, San Francisco, the Golden Gate, and the ocean beyond—the Pacific, Japan, China—all out there. But I didn't actually see anything except a wooden fence.

Other things weren't so great either.

When you move to a new place, you don't know the social and sociological story that comes with it. You don't anticipate country music blaring from a record player in an adjacent apartment, for instance, if everything you know about unrequited cowboy love and jilted waitresses emanates from a car radio while you're driving cross-country, dialing for something else. It annoyed the hell out of me.

I strode over there one day and knocked on the door, and when it was cracked open, explained to the girl inside, who had a blackened eye and regarded me distrustfully, that I was trying to work. Would she please turn it down? Which she did, for a few hours, and then blasted it again, either forgetting about me, figuring my appearance was a onetime thing, or that I was something she'd dreamt.

"Stand by Your Man," again and again. I could have beat my head against a wall.

Another day, I caught a glimpse of the boyfriend, shouting at her on his way out. Or maybe at another woman altogether. He looked familiar, though might only have peripherally resembled the stringy characters who hung out on the strip of pavement to wheel and deal and posture in the fall of '67; a reminder that this circumstance was not the worst I'd experienced.

In my own enclosure, a fat cat slunk into the room where I sat with pen in hand, staring at the blank pages of a splayed notebook. The other cat, of the two we inherited from the former tenants, had wandered outside in the rain and gotten lost.

I considered writing about the friendly couple who came by after we agreed to rent the place; in retrospect, probably to get rid of the cats. The guy pointed out the shower nozzle, the refrigerator, the oven, convinced us to take the cats and told us what to feed them. I asked how much he wanted for them and he got upset.

"We never sell animals," he said with indignation.

I was abashed, felt the sting of being politically incorrect—in Berkeley, where I shouldn't have been surprised—and afterward nearly discounted the way he averted his eyes, and the mushy sound of his explanation about moving to New Mexico, living off the land … which was why they were leaving, he said; certainly not because of the dump of a place they were now so eager to flee before we changed our minds.

And then Noreen began school, and I settled into the netherworld of a stay-at-home husband, without a job or any children to give some external purpose to my daily routine. I was free, you might say, until two-thirty, when I'd leave to pick her up at school—which was my idea, seeing how nervous she was in this new, unknown place … a chore I soon looked forward to, because at least it was something to do, an excursion for which I concocted a creative explanation: that it would compel me to write, knowing I only had so much time before having to abandon the effort.

But after dropping Noreen off in the morning and returning to the dank apartment, I didn't write a thing.

Maybe it was the dwindling bank account. The same thing had happened when I was on unemployment. That last check on the horizon, in two months or so, rendered the future a distraction.

Or maybe it was aesthetic deprivation, the concrete backyard, with the dilapidated two-car garage on one side, the wooden fence around it, the empty clotheslines between iron poles sunk into the hard ground.

Meanwhile, I tried to keep up appearances, presumably to impress myself. When I went to pick her up at school, for example, I left the apartment early, brought a notebook with me, parked myself on a bench on the small campus and sat with pen poised, as if I were there to try out a new locale, to be catalyzed by a different setting. An insupportable fantasy as students who had a truer reason for being there moved between buildings with their binders and portfolios.

And I took the notebook with me once a week, when I stood in line for food stamps at a warehouse in the flatlands and gazed up at the hills, as they were called—though they looked like mountains to me—and once actually scribbled something, a line or two from an old Marxist mind-set—never my best creative meme—in which the people up there in the hills, a West Coast version of penthouses, gazed down at the hoi polloi, lording it over us. Later, recalling a line from a poem the crotchety poet Kunzler had recited at the weekly session in Brooklyn, "Class consciousness is false consciousness," I tore out the page and threw it away.

Weekends were a welcome distraction. We'd drive across the bay to San Francisco, and finding one recollected personal landscape or another, I would point out this and that while narrating the details to Noreen, whose own interest lay in whatever attracted the lens of her camera: the facades of houses, storefronts, people in the street.

The tidy gingerbreads in the Haight with fluorescent trim conjured memories that choked me up, of occasional highs and more frequent lows—be-ins, crash pads, begging for food—as Noreen went about snapping what was actually evident.

North Beach, with its strip bars and beatnik coffeehouses, conjuring a trip with a college pal, when we hitchhiked and rode freight trains across the country. After hanging out in that opaque place with a legendary reputation, we began to hitch back, hyped-up beatnik wannabes spending two weeks on the road and one day at our destination.

Noreen and I would eat in Chinatown, at a favorite place we'd found in *Dining in the Bay Area for Less than Five Dollars*, then take in a double bill at the Surf, which showed old and foreign movies, before driving back across the bay to our grim digs.

It was good to get away, when all I had to keep me company the rest of the week was my own sorry self, trying unsuccessfully to write, needing to get out of the house, craving distraction, which now took the form of shopping for dinner.

I'd begin with a few staples in a grocery a few blocks away, which I approached by various routes through the nondescript neighborhood. Then I got in the car and drove up to North Berkeley. I liked the look of it there; like a Japanese garden, to my illiterate gardening mind, with layers of vegetation climbing the hilly streets. And after buying crusty bread and walking around with the loaf tucked under my arm, I'd get back in the car and drive somewhere else, perhaps south of the university campus to a store on College Avenue that sold cheese, and then to the supermarket on Ashby, with its astonishing array of melons, most of which I'd never seen or heard of before moving to California.

Back at the apartment, I'd drop off my purchases, read the flimsy newspaper I bought, then leave again, to pick up Noreen in North Oakland. Or I might try once more to write something down before I left, if only to tell myself I'd done some of what I intended to do before the tediousness of routine sidetracked me.

My notebooks sat on a corner of the desk that came with the place. When we looked at the apartment, its mammoth size, the way it spanned the width of the window it faced, made a stronger impression on me than anything else: the gloomy rooms, the barren view out the window, Noreen's misgivings. But always, when I sat down, stretching my arms in preparation like Jackie Gleason in *The Honeymooners,* then leaned forward and placed my elbows on the scarred wooden surface, nothing came.

After a while things got worse. When you're idle and twiddling your thumbs, they always do.

I finally looked at my bankbook, the nearly depleted savings no longer a distraction, but an outright alarm, which compelled me to check the help wanted ads and line up a job. Having done that, the spare time I hadn't made use of for weeks, despite my efforts to trick myself into creative action, did indeed finally become precious. Finally, I actually wrote something. A piece about a typical morning when I left the apartment to go shopping.

Having spotted a Chicano grocery store in a neighborhood in West Berkeley I'd come across in my meanderings, I decided to find it again and score a jar of jalapeño peppers. Noreen had begun to cook, and the jalapeños I ate on the side enlivened her bland midwestern dishes.

Turning a corner, looking for the bodega, I encountered instead a freeway entrance, with two hitchhikers planted next to it, and while waiting for the light to change, went into a dream, becoming my younger self, thumbing rides … Pulling up to the freeway entrance when the light changed, I offered the couple a lift, thinking to take them a few exits before turning back and resuming my moribund routine.

They clambered in with their knapsacks, a young man and woman; he in the front, to keep me company, she in the back. And then we were rolling along, and talking, passing exits for Albany, El Cerrito, Richmond, as the mature overseer within me who was supposed to be monitoring my behavior forgot to show up. When I saw the sign for San Pablo, I looked at the dashboard clock, did a quick calculation, and announced, "What the hell, I'll take you there. Exactly where are you going anyway?"

Somewhere north of Napa, the boy replied.

Maybe I fell in love with them, or the idea of youth itself, which had slipped past me while I wasn't paying attention. But also, I liked it that they listened when I talked, and more, that they responded; Noreen listened too, but never had much to say. What a pleasure, to actually converse!

I felt both older and younger than myself while tooling along, reflexively negotiating freeway traffic, then the curves of smaller, local roads as the built-up clutter of civilization fell behind us.

Who knows what we talked about? It didn't matter as the scenery flowed past, woods and meadows, fairy-tale houses in cleverly landscaped settings, now and then a ranch on land that opened up suddenly, revealing wide fields … and then, farther north, the vineyards, orderly rows of staked plants marching to a horizon of low hills. This was another California altogether! Not an enclave for students and marginal types like myself, but a whole new scene, an entire country.

"Up there," the boy next to me said, pointing to what seemed a driveway emerging from hills that lined the road to our left, and that's where I turned, climbing a gravel road that gave way to dirt and then tire ruts, which abruptly ended at a corral fence and an overgrown field.

When I stopped and turned off the ignition, the two of them got out, shrugged into their knapsacks, then walked off toward the field. I got out too, watched them reach the fence then stop and turn back, both of them registering my absence at the same time.

"Aren't you coming?" the boy asked.

"But they don't know about me," I replied, gesturing at the field and whatever lay beyond, picturing a cabin somewhere in the wilderness, in a pointillistic scene I recalled from *The Oracle,* the onetime underground newspaper in the Haight, a doctored photo that implied a crew of wizened hippies inside, who would welcome their young friends as I lingered at the door, feeling out of place, situated as I was between worlds.

"It's a big house," the boy said, gesturing again. "There's room for everyone."

I hesitated, then replied, "No, sorry, I can't."

And watched them climb the fence and head into the field, moving toward the distant tree line.

Then got back into the car again and drove down to Berkeley, arriving just in time to pick Noreen up at school.

On Friendship

I'd never had more than one friend at a time, though I might have if I hadn't always stopped at one. This was not by design, but the way my mind, or emotions, seemed to work—that one was enough; any more implied diminishing the friend I already had.

It was a puzzle why I'd become so exclusive, why I couldn't loosen up and pursue friendships among acquaintances, with whom I often had an easy rapport.

Then, abruptly, during my drug period, I had a slew of friends, though in retrospect it seemed less friendship and more confluence with virtual strangers, people with whom I shared a similar head. There was nothing personal between us, our connection dependent on ingesting the same chemicals.

And now I was back to one friend again, Stephen Schulich, with whom I shared old habits and circumstances, rather than the pulsations of a visceral common vibe.

Stephen was younger than me, short, skinny, with an abundance of curly brown hair that formed an uneven Afro around his head, a generational affectation he'd embraced that was now out of date. He had surprisingly delicate features—thin lips and a narrow nose—on a face that tapered to a point at the chin, where a few wisps of hair served as a goatee, which he fingered self-consciously, as if to remind himself that it was there.

We hit it off right away, because he too had landed the marketing research gig incidentally. And because, like me, he was from New

York, his clipped syllables and excited manner of speech a comfortable match for my own. By lunchtime that first day we'd become pals, falling into easy conversation across facing desks … about sports teams we'd once rooted for, though neither of us were actual fans anymore … about childhood and adolescent landmarks that assumed iconic significance as nostalgia, in proximity to high school and college and previous jobs in this or that borough or neighborhood. The easy patter rendered the work of transposing answers from questionnaires to forms of multiple choice boxes an invisible task instead of a chore.

It helped that there wasn't much to the job. Our coded answers, drawn from telephone surveys, were collected every few hours and taken to another department, to be punched onto cards that would be fed into a mainframe computer. The resultant printouts were then brought to our superiors upstairs, to be ruminated over and analyzed in order to parse opinions about purchasable objects with the sales departments of companies that made the products. The relative softness and sponginess of toilet and tissue paper; the preference or lack of it for tabs and screw tops on cans and bottles of beer or soda; the flavor, crunch, and visual appeal of cereal brands; the efficacy and odor of deodorants and perfumes, dishwashing, shampoo, and laundry detergents; the price and convenience of frozen and processed food; the lasting power of painkillers and headache remedies; the tread of tires, comeliness of lingerie, luxuriousness of mattresses, automobiles, and Hawaiian cruises.

Stephen and I need hardly pay attention as we filled in blank boxes, since none of the questions or answers interested us, and because our gabbing required little thought, flowing as it did out of whatever part of the brain produced reflexive camaraderie.

Even when we did happen to remark upon what we were paid to do, the talk rippled out almost mindlessly, and more often than not concluded in self-congratulation because at least we weren't working, say, in the phone room, badgering innocent people who'd been eating, watching TV, playing with their kids, napping, arguing, or hurrying out of the bathroom to get to the ringing phone before an important caller hung up, only to be cajoled instead about choices (a), (b), (c), or (d), and how often, and what smell, taste, texture, longevity, packaging, and so on elicited their approval, rejection, or indifference. Then, in a glass-paneled room similar to ours, these telephone interlocutors would finish up with the stereotyping questions, for marketing purposes, of income, race and ethnicity, and educational achievement. Compared to them, we only had to code answers that had already been recorded, not annoy anyone. Which is to say, we had it good.

We rarely went beyond this, into less comfortable territory. To discuss, for instance, or own complicity in persuading people to buy things they didn't need. Or to admit we were embarrassed by the menial aspect of the job, instead of goofing on it, implying that it was beneath us.

Or did I only assume that Stephen felt as I did? And what did it say about our relationship, and our supposed friendship, that I never asked?

The answer came to me obliquely, when I imagined my wife at school, attending classes and hanging out in between, immersed in a rich, meaningful social life. Not that anything Noreen said confirmed this enviable picture when we ate dinner; she didn't talk much about school. But knowing that she'd spent the day there, while I was filling in blank boxes, was enough for me to affix my own memories to her stray remarks about teachers and studio sessions, to conjure chess games in the student lounge, intense discourses on philosophy, politics, current events, social strife, literature and poetry, and envy her supposed circumstance.

A fantasy that came to life because there was nothing remotely rich or meaningful in the minutiae Stephen and I trafficked in. Trying to put any of it into words when describing my work day to Noreen, it was apparent there was less to it than I'd assumed. Divorced of context and mood, the things Stephen and I bandied about melted away almost as soon as I uttered them, dying like jokes without a punch line. Clearly, whatever transpired between us couldn't be conveyed because there was so little to it.

What could I say, for instance, that would reverberate if I were to tell her that at lunchtime we made epic quests to find a decent sandwich; by which we meant the kind of sandwich we remembered eating once upon a time in New York City during a supposed era of superior, ordinary cuisine. In an ever widening circumference that led farther and farther from the office, we'd look for places that approximated some long ago plate-glass emporium that dispensed free pickles, or butter in dishes instead of in annoying peel-top packets … sought thick-cut bread with crusts and caraway seeds or flecks of dried onion as if looking for manna, aside order of creamy coleslaw, an ice cream scoop of potato salad, instead of chips, a Greek olive whose pulp would dissolve in our mouths, leaving the skin intact …

"Bean sprouts again!" I might shout, critiquing the contents of a sandwich. "They grow lettuce out here, but what's the point if they don't put it in sandwiches?"

"I shouldn't have ordered the oat bread," Stephen might reply. "But I didn't trust what they call rye bread, and they don't have pumpernickel, of course, or bialys either."

"Bialys? Who out here would know anything about bialys?"

"I like a good bialy."

"Well, yeah, who doesn't?"

"And Kaiser rolls."

"Don't remind me. I had one on the way to work the other day, and it was so soft you could squish it in a fist."

"You gotta have a hard crust, that's for sure."

"And tuna fish made *without* mayonnaise! That's my pet peeve. It's not the same at all when it comes out of the can and you just smear a little mayo on the bread."

"Sure, of course. The tuna should be so creamy it falls out in gobs when you take a bite."

Subliminally, it might have been the comfort we both took in eating that led me to suggest that we eat lunch in Chinatown, before I realized that what I had in mind was to elevate the level of discourse between us, to talk about something more meaningful than mayonnaise; that a different venue might set the stage for this elevation.

I chose Sam Wo, where Noreen and I usually ate when we came to the city. After the rambunctious waiter who'd become a local legend took our order in his typically brusque manner, and I explained his crowd-pleasing idiosyncrasies to Stephen, I poured tea into our tiny cups and broached a serious subject—writing, and why it was important to me, though in truth I hadn't written anything recently, merely vowed to do it any day now.

I began as if composing an essay, with my parents, who could not fathom why I wanted to be a writer; and in fact the idea had seemed fanciful to me too. So, in my last year at college, with no clear idea what to do next, I applied to journalism school, thinking I might become a *working* writer, a more acceptable notion.

"Not that I thought about it exactly that way," I explained, "but I come from a workingclass family, and in retrospect it seems it's what I had in mind—to balance my needs with my parents' expectations—and my own expectations, for that matter. I mean, I'd assimilated a lot of what they believed or found foreign, and we're all influenced by our upbringing, whether we recognize it or not."

Stephen sipped his tea and nodded, but then, he was always agreeable, so I didn't know what his nod meant; if he was indicating that he understood, nodding in response to my serious tone, or was flummoxed and had no idea what to say in response.

"You know what I mean," I went on. "The way you and I talk about the neighborhoods we grew up in, the schools we went to. For better or worse, they leave an imprint …"

I paused as the plates of chow mein were placed before us.

As he ducked his head and pronged at the food with his chopsticks, I said, "So writing for a newspaper, a nine-to-five job with a salary, was something my parents could accept, and it seemed I could have my cake and eat it too—do something I liked, and earn a living at the same time … which, like I said, is why I went to journalism school, and incidentally was the first time I lived on my own. My parents couldn't afford to send me to college as an undergraduate, and so I lived at home while going to Queens, which as you know was free."

"I went to Brooklyn," he said, looking up.

"Yeah, I know."

"And it was no picnic living at home, I can tell you that."

"Yeah, I know that too. Anyway, as it turned out, even though I only had a room in a house—in Boston, with a family that took in boarders—living on my own was actually more significant than going to journalism school, which I found a waste of time. I mean, I went there to write, for chrissake, but all the classes—the required courses— were on abstract subjects, like the theory of communications and the history of journalism. Other than a few academic papers, I hardly wrote a thing the first term.

"Finally, the second term, they let me take electives. Writing news stories, if you can believe it, was an elective, not a required course. Who, what, when, and where, in the first paragraph, and maybe, if I was lucky and it was a certain kind of story, *why*. And pretty quickly I realized it was the *why* that interested me, because without it … well, the rest, as far as I was concerned, was uninteresting, superficial."

"The four questions," Stephen said, looking up. He'd nearly cleaned his plate, but had enough left over to hold up a dollop of noodles and roast pork with his chopsticks.

"What?" He'd lost me.

"The four questions," he said, grinning. "Or should I say the *fir* questions?"

"Oh … I see."

"Didn't you have to memorize them too?"

"… Well, yeah," I replied after a moment. "The four questions, sure. I never liked memorizing them. It's similar, I guess, to what—"

"And by the time we got around to eating, we'd all be starving, because my uncle Morris insisted on doing everything in the Haggadah …"

I dove into my plate of food then, which I'd hardly touched, and in disappointment listened to Stephen's recollections and after a while got into it myself, as always, remarking upon the tomato-based chow mein we'd been served.

"It's different than the way they make it on Mott Street."

"And did you notice how they kind of fry the noodles until they stick together? I don't think I like that …"

*   *   *

It was odd to think about Thanksgiving, with the temperature seventy degrees, no autumn leaves changing color, and no family or close friends around. Impulsively, I invited Stephen to come to Berkeley the following Thursday, to celebrate the holiday; he and his girlfriend, whom he'd mentioned but I'd never met.

The invitation surprised him as much as my impulsive invitation surprised me, but he was more than pleased, thanked me profusely, as though I'd done him a great honor. He called his girlfriend up to tell her, and invited me to walk home with him after work, so he could introduce us. And that surprised me too. It turned the nature of my quest for a more significant friendship upside down, since I now had a sense of obligation I hadn't felt before—having thrust both of us into something more personal than I'd intended.

He and Becka lived on a hillside street not far from the office on Montgomery Street, in a typical three-story San Francisco building. Like all the others in the hilly neighborhood, it was set plumb, against the slanting sidewalks, the oddly angled landscape conspiring with my uncertain mood to leave me askew.

He knocked on the ground floor door, and in seconds Becka opened it, as if she'd been waiting inside for the knock. Still, a flicker of uncertainty crossed her face as her glance darted to me, then back to him. She was short, which made Stephen appear taller, and the way he calmly introduced us, putting her at ease, bringing on a shy smile, enhanced him even more. I'd never seen him as a reassuring figure, which was a minor revelation as Becka leaned forward and offered her hand to me, setting it limply in mine, applying no pressure. She had a mane of frizzy hair, not unlike his, and the same innocent look but even more so, which brought Stephen back into perspective as I'd come to see him: as someone only theoretically living in a grown-up world.

When we were inside, she said, "Stephen has told me so much about you," and I could tell, from her deferential tone, that he had. She apologized for the mess—though the small apartment appeared reasonably neat—offered to make tea, and when I accepted, asked if I'd stay for dinner.

"I'd like to," I replied, "but Noreen, my wife—"

"Yes, Stephen mentioned her."

"She'll be expecting me."

The tea ceremony enabled us to somewhat bridge the awkward mood, as we slipped into a New York groove, recalling where we were children and went to school. I asked Becka where she worked—she was a secretary, a temp position at an accounting firm—and Stephen, a protective presence, expanded upon her answers. Between the cup and the lip, and a second round of the now tepid brew, we managed to pass enough time to assuage our nervousness and avoid incipient embarrassment before I finally was able to leave.

The awkwardness did not bode well for Thanksgiving, and when I told Noreen about my impulsive invitation, it got worse, since she acted put upon, which in turn put me out, because I'd never copped an attitude about her friends, and in fact always welcomed them without reservation. And then, during the week, she kept it up, complained about shopping for food as if I'd needlessly made her life difficult, though I went with her and pushed a shopping cart down aisles, lugged groceries into the kitchen, helped put them away, made myself useful.

When Stephen and Becka showed up on Thursday, Noreen was still in a peevish frame of mind, greeting them with a false, overly wide smile and a syrupy graciousness that grated on me.

I showed our guests around the three room apartment we'd recently moved into, inanely pointing out the leaded glass window over my desk and the canvases tacked to the walls, as if they wouldn't have noticed them otherwise. They couldn't help but notice, had in fact been staring, agog, at the abstract canvases, as well as the piles of books and notebooks on my desk, and now stood speechless before the strokes and blotches of color on the walls.

When we sat down, Noreen remained on her feet, bringing out plates of appetizers; olives, hummus, cheese and crackers, an eggplant dip, a pyramid of vee-cut slices of pita bread, almost too much to fit on the cocktail table. And that bothered me too, as if the food was meant to compensate for and excuse her absence. Clearly, so far as she was concerned, these people I'd invited not only weren't creative types, but didn't know enough to even appreciate the arts. And as if I'd long since sold my soul without realizing it, noticing that Stephen and Becka appeared lost, I wondered if I too didn't think less of them because of it; if Noreen's elitist attitude had become mine as well.

As we nibbled cheese and crackers and the other hors d'oeuvres, and made the smallest of small talk, Noreen finally returned to the living room and sat down. Perhaps she'd just been nervous; she was never good with strangers, after all. And then, when she was the one to suggest that we all drive up into the hills and take a walk before dinner, lightening the heavy mood, it seemed I'd indeed misjudged her, that out of my own discomfort I had found meaning where there wasn't any.

So we drove up into the hills as dusk came on, got out of the car, paired off, and began to climb toward the pine forest above. Noreen and I, each a head taller than Becka and Stephen, had the look of guides; Becka safe with Noreen, just as Stephen was safe with me as the two of us pulled ahead, the two shorter, younger people seemingly in our care.

Emerging from the trees into a clearing near the top of a hill, Stephen and I paused and looked down, at the women making their way up, at the giant puddle that was the bay far below, lights now limning the bridge spans in the semidark and marking the city of hills on the other side …

Always, when Stephen and I sat across from each other at work, when we walked the lunchtime streets in nostalgic quest for a memorable sandwich, when we sat eating in places that fell short of our standards, we talked. We were never at a loss for words. And now, for a change, as we stood up high, taking in the panorama, we were silent. Two people who somewhat knew each other, saying nothing.

Yet as uncharacteristic as that silence was, I knew it's how I'd remember him, for I was already fashioning my recollection of that moment … and would indeed recall the   companionable silence between us when Stephen was laid off a few weeks later. Instead of talk, a sense of unspoken communion as we stood there on top of the world, each of us knowing it was as far as he and I would go.

Suburban Artists

Alan and Mary Benveniste lived in a Marin County suburb and commuted to the art school in Oakland. Wind chimes and hanging flower pots adorned their porch, as it did others on the street. And when Noreen and I visited, I liked to sit out there, on the beach type chairs and the chaise longue, taking in the tidy shingled dwellings flowing across the San Anselmo hills.

Having found their way out West from the suburbs of Long Island, they had the New York custom of fashioning the inside of their house as if to hunker down through a cold winter. I pointed this out to Alan, but he shot it down, noting that they were artists, an identity never far from his lips, though to me it seemed they were channeling the acquisitiveness of their upbringing into collecting things that were pleasing to the eye.

There were tie-dyed sheets tacked to the walls, bonsai trees on end tables, an Oriental rug that looked like the real thing on the floor, Turkish pillows on the cushy couch. A humongous double-pump fish tank full of colorful tropical fish bubbled softly beneath the constant soundtrack of an expensive stereo system that had made Alan's father a well-to-do wheeler dealer. And, amidst this plenitude, were the things they'd made themselves; Mary's woven shawls and hand-built ceramic sculptures, Alan's school assignment paintings and the canvas he was currently working on, which sat on an easel in the living room, hidden by a towel.

We visited nearly every other weekend, liked their laid-back style and sense of comfort; Noreen, perhaps, because she was no stranger to the moneyed vibe, or hadn't been until she moved in with me; while I always had liked being a tourist in a cushy environment, knowing I wasn't responsible for the upkeep or burdened by its presumptions. Their digs reminded me of my Long Island cousin, whom I'd visited as a boy—an only child conditioned to comfort. Like him, the Benvenistes also seemed incapable of questioning what they'd always had, or of examining the attitude that went with it.

When we arrived, they would first of all show us their latest purchases—a new piece of art, a record, a woofer or tweeter, a tropical fish with neon markings—offer us some exotic juice to drink, lay out hors d'oeuvres from the gourmet grocery in town, and then, when we settled in, they began to complain. Often about the instructors at school, a sorry lot because they didn't worship what went on in the so-called art world back East; an assessment with which Noreen readily agreed.

Or Alan might bitch about the long drive to school, down the peninsula, through the no-man's-land around San Quentin, over the interminable bridge to the East Bay and then the aesthetically deprived boulevards of Richmond, the insane freeway … It was awkward then, being a guest, when my inclination was to disagree or point out unpleasant truths—that they'd chosen to commute to school in order to live in comfort amidst the comfortable.

But mostly the Benvenistes doted upon money, in the form of checks they received from their parents for tuition, and that Alan got from his father for rent, food, and miscellaneous expenses like rugs, plants, and tropical fish.

"He'll pull the plug any day now," he said once, playing with his ponytail, which he had a nervous habit of stroking, when he wasn't tugging at his mustache. "I see through him. I know his game. He wants me to slink back there with my tail between my legs, to work for him and take orders from my brother. Like the world has more than enough artists! Like what it needs is more turntable salesmen!"

"So what'll you do then?" I asked.

He looked at me with puzzlement, not exactly forgetting his point so much as losing the drift, what with the lingering effects of the marijuana he casually smoked.

"If he stops sending you money," I explained.

"Oh, I see …" And he made a gurgling sound and fluttered his fingers at his throat as if he were going down the drain.

Another time, after I'd asked what he would do if the money stopped coming, he shocked me by saying, "I'd get a job, I guess."

"You mean, out here?"

"Yeah, sure. Where else? I tell you, man, I can't go back there and sell turntables. I did it one summer. Never again. My brother's a slave driver."

I had a job myself by then, with the marketing research firm in San Francisco, and made enough so we'd been able to move to a new apartment in another subdivided house, in a better neighborhood, on a quiet street.

"What kind of job?" I asked, unable to imagine where a prima donna like Alan would agree to work.

"Well, not a *job*, actually. I've been thinking … maybe I can sell a few paintings."

"Your paintings?"

"Yeah, of course *my* paintings," he replied with annoyance, thinking I was attacking his work, and thus by extension his way of life.

Not that Alan's paintings were bad, just that I'd only seen the few color exercises he'd done at school, some notebook ruminations that resembled doodles, and occasionally the canvas he had been working on forever, the one hidden by a towel, which he only revealed when he was feeling good about himself.

"Well, okay," I said. "You want to sell your paintings."

"And Mary's kachina dolls. We can sell them on consignment … You've seen 'em. They're beautiful. There are shops in Sausalito where you can make big bucks, selling to tourists."

Alan was a Sephardic Jew, tall and swarthy, with dark hair, a floppy mustache, and that swooping ponytail. Mary was Irish, pale, diminutive, with blond hair that flowed down her back to her waist. Where he was excitable, she was phlegmatic. But they were both spoiled, and when their present sinecure came up in conversation, they could be vitriolic about their situation.

"The old bastard's cheating on my mother," Alan said about his father, then spent some time mocking the old man for wearing a toupee. "To hide his age."

"The randy old goat," Mary added, sewing faster; she always had material in her hands, was always working on something.

"He's got a cute little tootsie tucked away in the city," Alan said, "and when my mother finds out, she'll tie his balls in a knot."

"He'll have to support *two* harpies then."

Alan groaned. "Oh Jesus, am I screwed!"

"One will take him to the cleaners, while the other picks his pocket."

"If he's hit with a big alimony bill," Alan said, more plaintive than infuriated, now that his generic complaints had assumed actual narrative form, "what's gonna happen to us, Mare?"

I said to him once, "If you're so worried about getting cut off, why don't you buy less things?"

He regarded me with disbelief. "These are not just *things*," he finally replied with disdain, gesturing at the room, with its layers of color, texture, and shape. "They're *art*!"

And there it was: the snobbery of artists.

Though in fact Alan was more dabbler than artist, lackadaisical rather than driven, unlike his wife, or Noreen and the art students I'd met through her in New York, whose lofts were cluttered with canvases, raw materials, found objects; who lived in spaces that had the feel of a work in progress, not an exhibition gallery, like the Benveniste house in San Anselmo.

It seemed the only painting Alan had been working on since I met him was the one hidden on the easel in the living room. Sometimes weeks passed before he'd take off the towel draped over the easel to show me the progress he'd made, and then only when we were halfway out the door, as if anticipating criticism, he waited until the usual friendly greetings were exchanged, a critical response unlikely. It consisted of mainly blank canvas with a dense foliage of exotic flowers in one corner, where tiny, microscopic buddhas perched on tendrils and branches.

Suddenly nervous, he'd tug at the ponytail while I studied it. And then, in deference to his self-consciousness, I'd say something like, "You're on to something," or maybe, jokingly, "When you worked on this, were you on anything?" instead of saying, "If you didn't smoke so much grass, Alan, maybe by now you would've have moved across the canvas instead of spending weeks on one six-inch corner."

"Okay," I said now, as we discussed survival, "I see that all these things—excuse me, this art—is important to you, that you can't function without it," taking a leaf from his book and trying to get under his skin. We had that in common; a New York needling thing. "That doesn't mean you can't move to a less expensive, more affordable place … Berkeley, for instance, or maybe North Oakland, near the school."

Pissed off, he replied: "You know what your problem is, man?"

"That I don't have a rich, compliant father?"

He grinned. I liked that about Alan—that he could take a putdown. "No, I wouldn't blame you for that—it's not your fault. Your problem is, you don't know how to live successfully."

"What the hell does that mean? I eat, I go to work, and once in a while, when I can carve out the time, I write."

"I mean, you worry about where you can afford to live, instead of living *as if* you were successful."

That stopped me for a moment. "Clearly, we have a different definition of success, Alan."

"I'm not saying there's a formula. Everyone's different. But whatever your definition, you're not successful if you're just getting by, just scraping along."

I gestured dismissively. "Look, if you want to make art, or write, or do whatever, you have to make some sacrifices. If having possessions is so important to you—"

"No, man, no! You're missing the point. It's not the possessions— they're only a facade, the *trappings* of success. The point is, if you lived *as if you were a success*—like a famous writer—people would treat you differently, and that might lead to actually getting published instead of just putting your stories in a filing cabinet."

"You don't know what the fuck you're talking about," I said with annoyance. "It must be your hothouse upbringing. If you don't have money, then you don't have it. It's that simple. I know what I have and what I can afford, and I live within my means. You, on the other hand, think you're entitled to what you've always had, what you were brought up with, but maybe that embarrasses you, so you create this fiction in which you've somehow fashioned your own circumstance. You haven't. It's just a twist of fate, like you said, when you didn't blame me for not having a wealthy father … and—here's the punch line—he could pull the plug on you any day, as you also said."

"Okay," he replied, sitting back. "But what would you have me do instead? Live among junkies, people on welfare, poor white trash—"

"Are you serious?" I said with amazement.

"Sure. It's not dangerous here. Mary and I are safe."

"Safe … " I was flabbergasted, didn't know what to say. They considered themselves artists, and I liked to believe that had something to do with transcendence. As if making art were intrinsically spiritual.

A sappy notion.

"You're right," he went on. "I've always lived in comfort. The well-to-do life is the only one I know—or want to know." He fingered his mustache, regarded me with amusement. "You'd feel the same way in my shoes, you just don't know it."

*   *   *

Still, I liked Alan's company, despite his cantankerousness, or maybe because of it, and he also reintroduced me to pot, which I hadn't smoked in a while, and that was okay too.

Now, as the four of us headed south in my car, toward L.A., he said, "You take everything so seriously, man. Why can't you just relax and enjoy yourself?"

"What? I'm just sitting here driving."

"Yeah, but I know you're thinking a mile a minute? Tell the truth. You can't just sit back and enjoy the scenery, can you? You always have to explain things. Like those fields over there, why they look dry, or the clouds in the sky, what kind they are. C'mon, man, admit it."

We were rolling through the flat, ocher San Joaquin Valley, Alan in the passenger seat next to me, Noreen and Mary in back.

"You remind me of my brother," he went on. "He thinks everything out, has a reason for everything, so of course he thinks there's something wrong with me for drawing, for making pictures, that it's something you're supposed to grow out of … that it's okay to play with crayons when you're in first grade, but when you grow up it's time to do *serious* things, like make money."

That was why he and Mary were going to Los Angeles: to buy Indian rugs at a trade show, so they could sell them for a profit in Sausalito. Noreen and I were in the mood to travel, so when Alan brought up he trade show, I suggested that we all go together. Then he suggested my station wagon, because his VW bug was so small, and I agreed.

Mary passed a joint up front. Alan took a drag and offered it to me, said, "My father thinks I should be more like Joel," squeezing the words out as he held his breath, smoke escaping between his teeth. "He thinks when I get art 'out of my system,' I'll become one of his salesmen, too."

Alan was never what you'd call psychologically secure, but I'd never seen him as loopy. Perhaps he was smoking more dope now because his parents' divorce, and what it implied, was imminent.

I said, "What about the rugs?"

He eyed me suspiciously. "What about them?"

"Well, you're gonna buy them in order to sell them, right?"

He looked at the joint, said, "I should've seen that coming. You think I'll be ripping off the Indians, don't you?"

"What? No. That never entered my mind. Why would you think that?"

He made a guttural sound, nodding to let me know he'd answer in a second, when he released his breath, and then, in a burst of expelled smoke, said, "Let me tell you something—the Indians are more than happy to sell their rugs. That's why they're for sale! And the people we sell them to will be more than happy to buy them from us. That's called capitalism, in case you didn't know. It's the system we live under."

"Listen, Alan—"

"And you don't like that, do you? But it's a fact of life, no different than you going to your job—"

"What's no different?"

He had to think about that a moment. "Dealing rugs."

"Listen, your premise is wrong. I was just saying—"

"Me and Mary are in the middle. We're the 'middlemen,' or the middle people, between the seller and buyer … no different than the summer I sold stereo speakers, when you think about it … except I love art. So sue me."

They had three thousand dollars with them, their savings, to buy the Indian rugs. It might have been the first time Alan had invested anything he considered his, in hopes of making money.

"If it works out," he was saying, "it has to be better than moving back and working for my father ... and my asshole brother."

But as we climbed into the San Gabriel mountains a hundred miles later, and the effect of the pot wore off, he became less combative, said, "Maybe I've been looking at this the wrong way," sounding philosophical. "Maybe I *should* go back and sell turntables, and work for my father for a year, like he proposed. I mean, what's a year in a person's life? Bupkis. He told me, y'know, that he'd find us a nice place to live, in the West Village, and if I hold out, maybe he'd even buy me a car—he charges all that to the company anyway, so why should he give a shit? And if his business keeps growing, he might expand to the West Coast, open an office in San Francisco, and I could be his regional sales manager."

It sounded like his father the salesman had worked him over good. But I just said, "What about school?"

He shrugged. "No big deal. We can go back later, and artists don't need to go to school anyway. That's a racket. Mary can make kachina dolls and shawls, and I can paint—"

"But you'd be working full-time."

He thought about that a moment. "I wouldn't have to give it up. I could paint at night, and on weekends ... Well, okay, you're right, maybe not as much as I'd like to. I'd have to make some sacrifices— but just for a year. And if he opens an office out here and makes me regional manager, I'll have people working for me ..."

And a bit later, as we wound down out of the grapevine, coasting toward the L.A. basin: "But yeah, you have a point ... Who needs his money? We can come down here every few months, and other places too—they have these shows all the time—buy rugs, bring'em back and sell them to tourists up there … I know something about rugs, you know—which ones are valuable and which aren't. I showed you that book, remember? I don't know why I didn't think about doing this months ago."

*　　　　　　　　　*　　　　　　　　　*

The Great Western Arts & Crafts Show took place in an exhibition hall in East Los Angeles plunked down amidst industrial warehouses and auto salvage yards. At nine o'clock in the morning traders were still hanging rugs on walls and partitions, laying out precious stones and crafted silver on black velvet in display cases, arranging leather belts, boots, saddles, wood carvings, a panoply of the Old West.

Alan was subdued on the ride from the motel; more concentrated than usual, less diffuse. After entering the hall, he and Mary split up and went in different directions, moving methodically down separate aisles, from one rug booth to another, assessing and appraising. An hour or so later I came upon them at the rear of the massive hall, comparing notes before moving off together.

By then I'd bought Noreen a jade ring, intending to surprise her with it back in Berkeley, and, perhaps recalling the ragged cowboy shirt I once had, she led me to a booth that sold them and had me pick one out. Then the two of us agreed to buy a small Indian ceremonial rug.

In the parking lot several hours later, Alan and Mary displayed everything they'd bought, Alan tenderly unfolding the rugs one a time and draping them across the car roof and hood, pausing between each to await our reactions.

"They're beautiful," Noreen said.

"Terrific," I said.

He beamed. Unlike showing his own work, he had no self-conscious doubts about the rugs. "This one only cost five hundred," he said, carefully unfolding another.

Five hundred? I hadn't thought about the sums involved until then. It seemed an enormous amount for a rug, no matter how beautiful.

"And I'd say we can get fifteen," he concluded.

But after they were folded up and put away in the back of the car, and we'd eaten—reveling in real, barely digestible Jewish food, which we couldn't find in the Bay area—and were driving north, up through the grapevine, Alan began to rethink his sales strategy.

"Out of town tourists," he said derisively from the backseat, where he sat with Mary. "They won't appreciate these beautiful rugs. I know it! If I could, I'd keep them for ourselves."

"Alan!" she nearly shouted. "We are *going* to sell those rugs!"

"Yeah, yeah, of course," he replied. "I said, 'If I could,' didn't I?"

"And *we* can't," she said pointedly.

"Yeah, of course we'll sell them, Mare. That's why we bought 'em, after all."

"Damn right," she said.

Mary always seemed the more practical of the two. She had a wry smile, sometimes even rolled her eyes when Alan got carried away. But now, looking at her in the rearview, I could see that she was not amused.

"Except maybe the one with the green and red geometric design— no, no, just hear me out, Mare!" he said quickly, before she could interrupt. "We'll just jack up the prices a little bit on the others and make more than enough anyway. Y'see what I'm getting at? We can afford to take one for ourselves, can't we? I mean, look at all the trouble we went to, doing the research, coming down here. We deserve a little something for ourselves, don't we?"

"Well … the green and red one *would* look good on the long wall," she admitted.

After a moment, he said, "I also love the small white one, with the square heads."

"Alan …"

"Be realistic, Mare. How much could we sell that one for, as small as it is?"

"But that would be two that we put aside for ourselves, out of only six."

"Yeah, but the *smallest* two, and the tourists—you know as well as I do, when you think about it, to them, *big* is beautiful. So how much do you think we'd get for the small ones anyway?"

"Not much, I suppose … and it is a beauty."

"It's gorgeous."

"And that'll still leave five rugs."

"Four."

"Right, four … big ones, though."

"Well …"

"And look at it this way," he said. "With the profit we make, we can always come back down here again and buy more."

Writers and Poets

Brilliant morning sunshine suffused the kitchen where Colin Shay and I made a fetish of soft-boiling eggs, striving for the perfect result, cracking them open to eat the liquid yolks with tiny spoons and slivers of toast. We'd chase it with coffee while discussing poetry and writing, the goings-on in the writers and poets group, then move to the beat-up couch and chair in the minuscule sitting room, to play a game of chess.

That room had its own charm, bookshelves crammed with dog-eared paperbacks and chap books, an Oriental rug so frayed the design was a blur. I liked it: the beat-up furniture, cheap paperbacks, chap books, old records; a generational aesthetic of simple possessions and available culture, a scratchy Neil Young record accompanying us as we played and talked some more.

From there we'd descend a narrow spiral staircase to the bowels of the two-story house, move past cardboard boxes stacked against fake wood-paneled walls beneath the low ceiling. The bathroom was a dank cement cell with sink, toilet, and iron stall shower, reminiscent, in its minimal way, of our mutual tenement days in the East Village. Colin and I had belonged to different tribes then but prowled the same obscure bookstores, ate in the same Polish and Ukrainian restaurants, hung out in coffeehouses in that mecca of utopian expectation.

Across the hall, in another room, was the printing press, with its inebriating inky odor, circular platen, raised foot pedals. It seemed a magic contraption, one that situated my poet friend in literary history. He was quick to laugh and denigrate his self-publishing ventures as quixotic, but I could see that my admiration pleased him. And beyond the typesetting cases, an adjoining room where two mammoth desks sat side by side, the adjacent desktops nearly covered with the latest series of poems he was working on.

His smiling, self-effacing mood would shift then, become serious, and I'd get quiet too, tempered by the vulnerability I knew he had to feel, however many poetry anthologies he'd been published in. When you present your work, it's like baring your persona to critical inspection.

The first time I came to Colin's house in the flatlands and we moved from the kitchen to the threadbare salon upstairs to his inner sanctum workroom, I caught that shift in his mood, and approaching his work in progress, hesitated. He gestured me closer to the desks, to lean over the quilt of neatly arranged typewritten pages and margin inserts done in his calligraphic handwriting. I might have been intimidated, aware of the poets and writers he knew: McClure, Snyder, Creely, Bly, Bremser, Burroughs.

"So what do you think?" he asked, assuming I'd already read what I was hovering over. In fact there was too much on the pages to focus on all at once.

"I'm not much of a critic," I replied.

"C'mon, Peter," he said, chiding me gently. "I've heard you comment at the workshops. You always have *something* to say."

"Maybe so," I replied, "but if you notice, I pretty much confine myself to prose."

"Poetry, prose, what's the difference? They called Whitman a 'prose poet' because of his long lines, which were revolutionary at the time, but no one takes that seriously anymore. Writing is writing, whether it's poetry or prose ..."

He'd brought up Whitman before. I'd read him years ago, the way I read Byron, Keats, and the rest of those old-timers in college—as an assignment; not as actual people who'd experienced life. The only poets

I approached as if they had something to say to me were those popularized by the drug subculture: Ginsberg, Ferlinghetti, Blake.

"Or Mayakovsky," he said, and looked at me. "Do you know him?"

"Except that he's Russian, no."

"Just read as if you were reading a story," he said, gesturing at the poems, "and tell me what you think," and, grinning, poked my arm like a tough guy picking a fight. "Go on, I can take it."

So I started to read, carefully, conscious of him backing away, giving me room. After a while I said, "It flows beautifully from line to line ..."

"And ..."

"And nothing." I said, and looked at him. "I like it."

He frowned, disappointed, then softened, perhaps deciding I merely needed further encouragement. All that, communicated in a glance.

"Well, okay," I said. "It seems to me it falters here," and I pointed at the desktop surface between two pages set side by side.

He moved up next to me and leaned over, though no doubt knew what he'd written and typed; like me, Colin was meticulous.

"I mean, the shift between them is abrupt," I said. "Here, in 'Lotus Glow,' we're inside your head when you're into the drug rush ... and then you come down and look around and eviscerate the straight world you're now in, because of its pettiness and hypocrisy—which I like, by the way. But abruptly, in the next poem, 'Resignation,' you're reborn— a different person, embracing the world you've just derided."

We were standing side by side now, staring down at the pages.

"You see what I mean? It's still what it was—so far as the reader can see—only now you accept that world you'd dismissed—no more than that, you seem to embrace it ... so I'm left wondering, what happened—in your head—between this poem and the one before, to get you from here to there?"

Abruptly he straightened, said, "You're right. There should be another poem here," and tapped the desktop between pages. "I began to work on it, then put it aside."

I said, "Why?" He didn't answer, and I added, pointing at the gap, "Were you going through withdrawal at the time, between this one and the other?"

He didn't agree, but said instead, "You sensed the missing poem," and looked at me with as much appreciation as he'd evinced disappointment before, when I'd tried to avoid commenting.

It emboldened me, and I went on. "Maybe it was too painful to look at, so you put it off. I mean, I've done that myself … left a hole in the middle of a story, walked away from it knowing it was incomplete."

"Maybe …"

At the first Wednesday night meeting I'd attended, Colin read a poem about being a junkie. Everyone knew it was one in a collection he was working on; they heard some of the others. The collection arrayed over the adjacent desktops. And soon afterward we became friends, met over soft-boiled eggs at his house, critiqued each other's work. I'd met a few addicts in the East Village and avoided them afterward, the notion of sticking a needle into my vein unthinkable, and more than that, because of the things I'd heard about junkies—that they were dishonest, manipulative; that you couldn't trust them. But having crashed myself, on other drugs, and then pieced myself together, it seemed I had more in common with him than anyone else in the group.

"When I try to write about the bad times," I said when we went back upstairs, "I come up with other things to do to avoid getting into it."

"Like washing the dishes," he said, and smiled. "Or mopping the floor. The other day I even got down on my hands and knees to clean the toilet, if you can believe it."

I laughed. "My own way of distracting myself is grocery shopping. I get in the car and drive halfway across town for a container of milk, and then go somewhere else for vegetables, and somewhere else to buy a chicken—"

"But why fear the images our minds create?" he asked, as if questioning himself. And then to me, in a tougher tone: "It's no excuse. We have to let the images penetrate, to batter us—if it comes to that. Anything else is cowardly."

*   *   *

A smattering of people—featured readers, friends, acquaintances—circulated among the coffeehouse tables. It seemed that I might be the only outsider there, having read a flyer tacked to a telephone pole, as I sat self-consciously sipping coffee. Then a guy with a biblical beard called the room to attention, everyone sat down at the tables or on the lip of the raised platform that served as a stage, and the reading began.

A grizzled-looking character, an abundance of hair held out of his eyes by a bandana, stepped to the podium to recite a few short poems. Fittingly, since he had the look of a prospector, he wrote about the Wild West, as if that world had abruptly disappeared when he went away for the weekend, returning to find crowded freeways, housing tracts crawling over the hills, huge supermarkets fronted by massive parking lots filled with cars. He was an affable type, and I liked him right away; a misplaced person looking for the best in things, no matter how screwed-up, wandering the aisles of canned and packaged food, standing on the tarmac of a cheap motel watching the sun rise as trucks dopplered past on the highway.

A woman with piercing eyes and jet black hair read next, in a dramatic, self-assured manner, the loose, billowing sleeves of her blouse swaying like the crow in her poem as she flew through the night on a recriminating mission to find an old lover somewhere in the density of San Francisco. With her bird's-eye view, she saw solitary men and women masturbating through open windows, took in a

squabbling couple, the woman on the verge of murdering the man—
portraying it without emotion—before glimpsing her intended prey,
entwined with someone other than her as she swooped past, superior
and disdainful.

Next came a computer programmer with a placid countenance, He
stepped to the podium, looking businesslike in a sweater vest, shuffled
his papers as if about to present a paper at a convention, then
declaimed, in short, declarative sentences, a haphazard get-together at
the water cooler, lunch in the company cafeteria, the contents of his
briefcase, and concluded from these disparate elements an underlying
emotive state that affirmed life.

In sharp contrast, the teenage girl who stormed defiantly to the
podium after him took in the room with darting, distrustful eyes, as
though the place were full of hostile strangers. Men, it turned out, as
she clung to a rag doll during her first period, excoriating a callous
masculine world incapable of understanding her.

And then the bearded spokesman again, who paused long enough to
create a silent space that drew everyone in, and in his deep voice read a
short story that left me disappointed, in light of his authoritative
manner. There was always that, at these things: the delivery that
persuaded, trumping words and meaning. It's why I'd always preferred
reading off the page, where words are on their own.

After nodding to the applause, the moderator announced a break,
and as people got up and milled again, I milled too, introducing myself
to a few readers, asking about their group, when it met and where,
returning to my seat after the intermission, though I'd heard enough and
had by then exhausted the pretense that brought me there. I'd been in
Berkeley several months and knew almost no one; my wife, a few of
her art school friends, a fellow worker at the job in San Francisco. In
truth, I'd merely come to find a few people with whom I might
converse.

Another prose writer moved to the podium, tall, with black-framed spectacles, a Vandyke beard, and hair trimmed close to the skull. Politically, socially, I didn't want to be competitive, but that's the way I am, and now I listened to this other wordsmith as a competitor, picking the components of his piece apart. His writing was sparse, which I couldn't fault, but he employed psychology to explain too much, yet only dwelled on the surface of things, which enabled me to criticize him both coming and going. But I had to admit that he had an ear for dialogue and at least knew when to end a paragraph.

An older woman, past thirty, read a poem about giving birth, taking her daughter to kindergarten on the first day of school, reading her a bedtime story at night. It humbled me, as people who learn selflessness as caretakers often do, rendering those of us who know nothing about being parents essentially limited.

Then a college student bounced onto the stage and exuberantly read several short pieces I couldn't follow, full of metaphors and references to the Persians, Hammurabi, Mayan temples, restoring my superior attitude.

And finally Colin, long hair pulled back in a ponytail, hairless face smooth. He moved languidly, looked younger than his age, except for a downward tug at the corners of his lips when he smiled, as if he knew something he chose not to divulge, holding himself apart, however gracious he otherwise appeared.

He read without affectation—in contrast to the lilting delivery of some others—a poem about a woman whom he resisted losing himself to amidst sensuous pleasure, maintaining the same distance that characterized him in the coffeehouse; a declaration of integrity.

*   *   *

In the kitchen, Colin looked up from the piece I'd given him to read, said, with enthusiasm, "You captured him, with all the contradictions you didn't convey in the last version ... It's great, Peter. Fantastic. You answered every criticism—in the group, and your own. I wouldn't change a word."

His approval had the usual effect on me; not good at accepting compliments, I attempted to deflect it, took a gratuitous sip of coffee, cold now, after sitting awhile on the tabletop.

"No, really," he said, as if seeing through me, tapping the typewritten pages before him. "It amazes me how much you notice ... the microscopic details, the nuances and subtleties. I wish I had that gift."

An odd comment, since we had just that sort of detailed perceptivity in common. But then, at the Wednesday workshops, Colin doled out compliments with the same hyperbole; though he could be touchy at times, particularly after he read his own stuff, when he looked up and emanated defiance.

I said, "But you do have the gift of detail, Colin. It's why we're friends."

"But one thing puzzles me ..."

I put down the cup. We'd been discussing each other's work long enough for me to recognize his oblique way of introducing criticism.

"You capture Patrick's egotism, his brilliance ... why he captivates you. You don't miss a thing. So what's the 'mystery' you mention here ... You see what I mean? Either you're an omniscient narrator or you're not."

"Well," I said, "though I write in the first person, and the *I* character is also me, the narrator and the character aren't the same." It surprised me that I had to explain it. "I didn't see then what I see now ... What my character found mysterious—the *me* I was then—the narrator, looking back, might have figured out."

"'Might' have figured out?"

"Well, yeah ... I'm still not sure I've entirely nailed Patrick."

"It's interesting," he said, leaning back, "that you see him as a mystery to be solved."

In fact, I saw Colin that way too. He moved fluidly, gracefully, a physical reflection of how adaptable he was, quick to laugh at himself and to encourage others. But he could be cool, listen and observe without reaction, and then respond with that downward tug of a smile that hinted at a private assessment.

I said, "And I want Patrick to be a mystery to the reader as well, which is why, as the narrator, I withhold certain things. I don't want to reveal everything the narrator might know … Like when Patrick and I meet that first time and he gestures me into the back room and tells me I'm the smartest person there, except for him—"

Colin laughed.

"I was taken aback by his egotism, but flattered too … and the narrator, not the character—not yet at any rate—knows that my lack of self-assurance is why I came to mythologize Patrick."

Colin nodded. "I see … Still, you don't want to sell your character short. Your younger self. He has to be believable, and with all that he notices, I wonder why the person you were doesn't see more. You see what I mean? It seems you're playing a game."

I could have responded to that, but it would have meant reiterating what I'd already said, turning a critique into an argument, defending myself. So I sat back and picked at the toast crumbs on my plate, the two of us falling into companionable silence in the bright kitchen, with its egg cups, broken shells, and coffee mugs on the table before us.

After a while I said, "I've been thinking about Patrick in connection with the other stories I mentioned … a collection of sorts, three characters, each seeking truth in their own way, given their personalities—"

"Patrick, Manchild, and …"

"Carl, though so far his story is just snippets and notes. They overlap, the three of them—that's the way it was, or the way I saw it—

so I'm thinking if I combine them into a longer piece, stretch out beyond my usual eight to ten pages, I'll be able to say more, show them interacting, better describe the scene—"

"You mean a novel."

I hesitated. "I don't know if I'd call it that … a novel. That's … I don't know …"

"Then don't think call it anything. Just do it. When you're into it, it's the work that counts, not what you call it."

I sighed. "The thing is, you put in four hours a day, every day, like clockwork. I admire your discipline. It's different for me. Sometimes days go by and I can't bring myself to sit down and write a thing. If it weren't for the group, it would be even worse, since that at least compels me to produce something so I won't feel like a slacker. It creates a deadline, of sorts, and I've always operated well with deadlines."

"Don't worry about how you work," he said, "whether in spurts or methodically. What difference does it make? When you get older, like me, you'll get more economical. That's what happens."

I laughed. "What're you? Thirty-one? Thirty-two?"

"Thirty-three," he said.

"Holy shit! An old man!"

"And you're in your late twenties," he said seriously. "Old enough to begin your first novel."

We went downstairs then, to what I now thought of as the poetry room, where the latest version of his collection was spread out on the desktops. I scanned the poems I'd read before, which were mainly the same, except for a few new handwritten insertions in the margins, then focused on the most recent version of what had been his missing poem.

Maybe I'd drunk too much coffee upstairs; I had trouble taking it in. Colin's poems seemed to flow like water, moving and shifting, with solid objects appearing suddenly, like boulders in a stream, and as quickly left behind. In this latest poem there was a stream of apparitions with only an occasional word—most often *masks* or *props*—amidst inchoate impressions. It seemed to me he was drowning in his own sensations.

"So what'd you think?" he asked after a while.

"I was thinking how sensory it is," I said.

When I didn't go on, he frowned. "Yeah, and ... ?"

"The masks ... explain that to me."

"False faces," he said.

"And the props ... ?"

"Also false ... crutches."

"And you felt you had to smash them."

"Yes."

"And you turn that anger on yourself," I said, leaned over and read aloud, "'Caught in the web of self-justification.'"

"Yes," he said, still waiting on me, expecting more, all business now.

I plunged on, said, "The web of self-justification ... is that your own complicity in the world of masks people hide behind?"

"Yes ... that's what I was getting at."

"The phoniness became your justification to keep shooting up—and recognizing that the world you scorned became your excuse—your prop—you were able to leave the drug behind."

"Yes," he said. "That's it exactly."

I thought to leave it at that, but added, "Maybe you could add some physical detail, solid material things like fire escapes, tenement facades, something to indicate a sense of place ... It would be a fitting contrast to the false facades and the props ..."

After a moment he said, "I'll have to think about it," with a finality that precluded further talk.

Colin and Maggie

With her pale complexion and diminutive features, Maggie personified ethereal poetry, an anomaly in the overly bright room, with the remains of spaghetti and meatballs on mismatched plates on the kitchen table, along with an array of antique-looking wineglasses tinted green and brown. They were hardly large enough for the half bottle of Chianti she was imbibing, filling her glass again and again while the rest of us sipped from the dainty vessels.

Holding her latest unsteadily in one hand, she caught herself on the edge of the table as she leaned forward. "Your writing," she said to me, "the way it moves from observation to harsh ... *assessment* ... discursive and then so suddenly ... *serious* and ... *neutral* ... " She paused so long, I thought she was through, then concluded, "It's quite *surreal*, isn't it?"

Surreal. It brought Salvador Dali to mind, that image of a melted clock.

She turned abruptly toward Colin, who was pushing leftover spaghetti around his plate with a fork. "Don't you think so, Cole?"

"Don't I think what?"

"That Peter's writing is surreal?"

He flattened his lips in a poor semblance of a smile and shrugged.

Abruptly, she turned the other way, sloshing wine onto the table and her plate. "Noreen, you know him better than anyone. Is Peter as ... *detached* as his writing indicates ... ?"

"He seems all right to me," Noreen replied, trying to make a joke of it.

I'd always been uncomfortable around people who were drunk. But Noreen's discomfort derived from something else. This wasn't her kind of gathering; she'd been on edge all evening, before Maggie began to pause over her words. Literary allusions meant nothing to Noreen, and the semblance of a theme, and the hint of deeper meaning waiting to be plumbed, made her restless; more intense than the lighthearted talk about art and pop culture that characterized her bull sessions with friends.

In New York, before we settled into our current mode as a couple, she'd welcomed my friends and acquaintances, made dinner for them, hung around as we talked, though she had little to say. And after a while she'd duck out of the room, with the excuse that she had something to do; make coffee or tea, arrange cookies on a plate, wash the dishes. In response to her evident discomfort, I eventually stopped inviting friends over, met them elsewhere, and then not at all, eventually allowing former friendships to dwindle and dissipate.

Which occurred to me now as she played with the fringes of her place mat and I reflected on Colin and Maggie's relationship. Like the poem he'd read in the coffeehouse when Colin first caught my attention—asserting the distance between himself and a lover, who might have been Maggie—they shared a life while maintaining separation. The two of them seemed unconcerned about their differences or in pleasing or appeasing each other. Even when it came to poetry, their most significant affinity, they coexisted; Maggie into nineteenth century idealism, Colin embracing Whitman's common rolling-stone man, and the beats.

She poured herself more wine, and sloshed more into her plate while trying to hold herself erect, her head wobbling on a slender neck like a wounded swan. Noreen looked at me aslant, conveying an appeal to leave. And out of habit I was almost about to comply when Maggie's head snapped up and she said, "So, Peter ... when you look at all of us, in this room, what do you see? Do we seem … *grotesque*? You don't *seem* alienated, but … it's difficult to tell …"

I was about to dismiss her question, out of annoyance, but said instead, "Grotesque? Is that what you meant by 'surreal'?" And before she could formulate a response, I added, "Because I don't think of my writing as surreal, Maggie. I think of it as realistic."

Her chalky cheekbones flushed pink. "Oh, Peter, *come on*! How can anyone know what's *real*?"

"Maybe we can't, absolutely," I replied, "but we're capable of seeing things the same way—maybe not objectively, but as Orwell says, we can strive for neutral fact—while observing our associations so our emotions don't blindly determine our conclusions."

"Emotions," she countered passionately, "are not merely an *impediment* to what we conclude! They're at the heart of it!"

"But they can also get in the way."

"In the way of *what*?"

"What we see, what we think."

"But surely what we *feel* is as significant as what we *think* …"

"I don't disagree with that."

"Oh, Peter!" she blurted, falling back in her chair and flapping a hand at me. "You're such a *sophist!*"

Surrealism, sophistry … it bothered me that I had only a vague notion what some of the terms she used meant. I'd come across them in college but hadn't paid much attention. Only recently—reading books on my own, rather than because they were assigned, and less dismissive of what I didn't know—had I begun to challenge the lockjaw mind-set that what I knew was all I needed to know. But my self-education had been haphazard, which left me feeling obtuse around people like Maggie, who even drunk seemed to know more about what she was talking about than I did.

Colin had begun clearing the table. Taking it as a cue, Noreen got up too, brought dishes to the sink and offered to help wash them; an excuse to busy herself. As if sensing her ploy, he pointedly rolled up his sleeves and said with a grin, "It's my house, Noreen. If I want to wash the dishes, that's my prerogative."

She looked chagrined, and then Maggie managed to stand up too, leaning against the table for support, imploring Noreen—"As an *artiste*," she said with exaggerated respect—to examine the sketches and paintings in the house and tell her what she thought. Noreen threw me a beleaguered look as she followed Maggie out of the room.

At night, with its bare bulb illumination, the kitchen was a different place than in the resplendent morning sunlight as Colin and I indulged in our soft boiled egg ritual. The cracks in the plaster walls were more prominent, as well as the stained linoleum floor and breaks in the wooden molding around the room. I'd wondered how he could afford to rent a whole house, with no apparent job or means of support, even with Maggie working part-time as a waitress. But seeing the room now, it was less puzzling; the place looked dilapidated.

His back to me, Colin rinsed and washed dishes, and over his shoulder asked, "Anything new on Patrick Malone?"

"You mean—"

"Has your narrator figured him out yet?"

"Actually," I replied, raising my voice to be heard over the running water, "it's funny that you ask. I think I might have spotted him last week, in Golden Gate Park."

He turned around, holding a dish. "You *saw* him? Patrick Malone? Out here?"

"I'm not sure, but I think so." I was about to say more when he turned back to the sink. I didn't want to shout. One of the things I'd learned during the period that obsessed me was to wait for people to pay attention when I had something important to tell them.

Maybe Colin had learned that as well, or was good at reading me. When I didn't continue, he turned off the faucet, wiped his hands on a dish towel, and turned around to face me, leaning against the counter.

"The thing is," I went on, "I'm not sure it was Patrick. Not that it matters anyway, because seeing whoever it was that I thought might be him left me thinking about Patrick in a different way, crystallized something that I guess I'd been ruminating about all along." I grinned. "You said I notice a lot—and I do—but sometimes it takes years for me to figure out what it meant."

He said, "So, what did you figure out?"

"Well … Noreen and I went to the museum in the park—the De Young—and when we took a walk afterward, we heard music wafting through the trees, which brought to mind another be-in, years ago, that I stumbled across the same way … and just like then, when we got there, I was astonished to see so many people sprawled over the open field.

"It was the sheep meadow, and we went down and sat in the crowd—I was amazed at how many hippies were there, though a lot of them were young kids and might have just dressed the part. We were focused on the band up front, on stage, and since I've never been able to get into the music in those settings, I looked around, took in the people around us who were sitting and wandering here and there, which was when I spotted him."

"The guy you thought was Patrick."

"Yeah."

"So, why didn't you just go talk to him?"

"Well … it's like that poem you put off doing—and the writing I put off doing. Sometimes this queasy feeling comes over me when I think back on those days … the bad times, the things I don't want to remember … it seems they might overwhelm me, so actually going over to speak to the guy I thought was Patrick … well, I just couldn't do it."

Colin nodded. "I understand."

"He was in the thick of the crowd—Patrick, or his doppelgänger— tossing a football to a teenager who stood about forty feet away … the two of them standing there, playing catch amidst the seated people, and this guy who looked like Patrick was throwing with extreme, almost excruciating care, because if he threw too long or short or too far to either side, the ball would've hit someone.

"That's what struck me. He could've gone to the side of the field with the kid, or to the back, where the crowd petered out and there was plenty of open space. But instead he chose to stay there, surrounded by people … and I realized it was something Patrick had always done, that it wasn't accidental or haphazard. It was purposeful."

"You had an epiphany."

"Yeah, I guess you say that … and afterward, I went back and redid my piece-a lot of small but essential details—in order to add that aspect of him to my portrait, because it explained a lot … Patrick always put himself in situations where he had to be hypervigilant, where he had to be alert …"

"That's fantastic," Colin said, and turned back to the counter. As he scooped coffee grounds into a pot, he added, "To so clearly see what you have to do … I wish that would happen to me more often. Instead, I flounder around to try to get there."

I said, "But that's not all. Wednesday night, I learned something else about Patrick—it must have been astrological or something, one thing after another …"

"What happened Wednesday?" Colin hadn't been at the weekly workshop.

"Well, I read the new improved version of 'Patrick Malone,' who now more clearly sought to live on the precipice, and afterward, Maureen—who had never heard the piece before—took me aside, told me she recognized the Eighth Street commune from my description of it and said she'd known Patrick."

Colin was placing mugs and spoons on the table. He took a step back, surprised. "Maureen *knew* your Patrick Malone?"

"Yeah, and she told me she didn't like him much."

He shook his head in wonderment. "How could anyone not like Patrick Malone? He's a terrific character, a force of nature."

"Yeah, well of course there's a difference between reading about a character and knowing one. And Maureen doesn't like anyone that much anyway. Not that a lot of people back then didn't feel the same way about Patrick. But here's the thing—she said that Patrick was out here for a while, living in a commune of some sort in a warehouse on the Embarcadero, and that when she ran into him, he was into junk."

It felt odd to say that. I'd read Colin's collection of poems and even made suggestions he'd found helpful. But it was one thing for him to talk about being a junkie, another for me to broach the subject. It seemed it might offend him. What did I know about being a junkie anyway?

He didn't say anything for several seconds, then asked, "So, how does that change the way you see him?"

"Well … I don't know, to tell you the truth. Patrick wasn't a junkie when I knew him. He liked to think he was the king of the acid heads, and as you know, indirectly he introduced me to Buddhism, and other things. It's hard to jibe that with, y'know, this …"

"All kinds of people become junkies," he said. "And Patrick lived to get high. I'm not saying that one drug leads to another, but that compulsion is a thing in itself, no matter what the drug."

The women returned to the kitchen then.

Maggie, who appeared steadier now, plopped down into a chair. "Cole," she said, "Noreen *loved* Dahlia's print—the one of the Orthodox church with the graceful onion domes. She gushed over it!"

Noreen rolled her eyes at me as she sat down. Neither of us had an affinity with or appreciation for the theatrical or overly dramatic, but her private communication to that effect annoyed me.

"And she made some *marvelous* suggestions about redoing the downstairs rooms, to make them more spacious."

"Oh?" Colin lifted an eyebrow and feigned a smile. "Did she say how I could pull that off with a two ton printing press and a carload of type-setting trays in the room?"

He'd moved back to the stove, where the coffeepot was percolating. And it struck me that he was not just indifferent toward Noreen, which I'd assumed, but flat out didn't like her.

"Oh *c'mon,* Cole," Maggie said. "You know you never give any thought to … *aesthetics,* unless it concerns typefaces or paper stock. But there *is* something to be said about appearances."

"Yes, I've heard that," he said.

"Is there any more wine?" she asked.

"I'm making coffee, Maggie," he replied pointedly.

I said to Noreen, "I was telling Colin that someone in the poetry group heard that Patrick was living in San Francisco for a while …"

"Really? Then maybe that *was* him in the park."

"And that he was a junkie when she ran into him."

Noreen tilted her head to one side in a shrug. "That doesn't surprise me. Patrick was into junk years ago, on the lower east side."

"Is this someone you know, Cole?" Maggie asked, trying to keep up.

I hardly heard her. I was thinking about what Noreen had said, and disconcerted by the way she'd said it—casually, as if it was of no significance that someone we'd both known had become an addict. She'd offered the information casually, the way she talked about art and artists with her friends: who was good, who was bad, who was overrated, as they blithely moved from one subject to another, without reflecting on any of it. Except what she'd said so offhandedly about Patrick—someone who had lived in my head for months now—sounded not merely superficial, but callous.

I said to her, "Are you sure? He was a junkie back then, when I knew him?"

"I saw him shoot up once, in an apartment we were in."

"I'm flabbergasted ... I mean, Patrick never said a word about it, or ever acted as if he was on junk."

"How do you think a junkie acts?" Colin asked from the stove.

"Well ... I guess I don't really know."

"I don't think he was actually a junkie then," Noreen said. "He told me he was just experimenting."

Her words hung there in the too bright kitchen as Colin took the coffeepot off the burner. Then, in a deceptively mild tone, he shot those heavy thought balloons down, saying, "That's how most prospective junkies put it," carrying the pot to the table. "'Just experimenting.'" And moving behind Noreen, he held the pot high and arched the dark brown liquid into her cup in a thin, hot stream just over her shoulder.

Immigrants

We'd begun to miss the changing seasons when we fortuitously happened upon Phil and Doris's house in North Oakland, New York hangout on Friday nights, a respite from California; usually agreeable, often contentious. Right away we felt at home.

Phil had been editor of an art magazine in Manhattan, so Noreen was quick to embrace the weekly free-all-for all, despite her usual aversion to intellectual conversation, which allowed me to enjoy the pleasures of intellectual talk without concerning myself with her usual reticence in such settings. In that speakeasy of familiar inflections and contractions, she'd sit at the oval table in the wood-paneled dining room, rarely saying anything, but clearly at home, surrounded by the framed geometric pieces Frank Stella had exchanged with Phil for his collection of books on art history and criticism.

The evening we walked in and were introduced by Phil's niece Carole, who had a pottery studio in West Berkeley where Noreen fashioned pots and bowls, Phil was expounding on the influence of technology on art. He went on for a while until Julian, his wife's brother, lost patience and interrupted.

"Art isn't life," Julian declared. "It represents life."

"And how does that contradict anything I said?" Phil countered.

"Life *happens,* whether or not it's captured by a camera or a painter or a writer. It doesn't *derive* from them—they derive their work from it."

"It's not so simple," Phil said, with what Julian took as a

condescending tone. "Life influences art, and art influences life. The contours of time and place, conveyed, for example, by socialist realism, are representations, but in turn the style of it affects the style of other work, as you can see if you study the period."

"I'm not interested in 'style,'" Julian replied, as if it was a dirty word. "Style comes and goes and is affected by all sorts of cross currents. I'm talking about *life* ..."

Which led to a counter response, as coffee and Danish and other snacks were brought to the table, and new people popped in, to add their opinions on the topic at hand, which shifted or changed with each new addition.

... The pyramids as architectural achievement, the Gothic churches of medieval France-crowning moments of particular aesthetic histories. But what about the slaves and peasants who constructed them? Julian asked. Were ends more significant than means? Does beauty trump the cruelties that bring it about?

... R. D. Laing and creative schizophrenia, Timothy Leary and LSD ... Julian, who'd been a dancer with the Living Theater, threw in Nijinski, as idiot savant; I added Bobby Fischer and Prince Myshkin; and Carole, who had a passion for naif art, added Grandma Moses. A ragged debate that culminated in the conundrum: Does psychotherapy and its adjustments ruin unique artistic expression?

... Alfred Hitchcock's severed hand. Salvador Dali, Bunuel. Black humor as genre, style as distinct from substance—

"Aesthetics is no excuse for immorality!" Julian heatedly declared, he and Phil eyeing each other across the table, battle lines drawn.

And that was interesting too—the interplay between them. Did it reflect a family dynamic? Personal animus displaced into opinion? Or maybe the two of them were just different types: Phil cerebral, driven, an iconoclast from an era that rebelled against conformism; Julian ethical, fair-minded, of a generation when disagreement was the norm. Though Phil went off by himself at times and smoked pot, he could be counted on to deride hippie utopianism, which Julian would defend.

"I've read Marquez and Borges," Phil said, "but that doesn't mean I buy into magical realism, or the fictions of Don Juan and his Yaqui shaman."

I could have sworn he'd said the opposite earlier in the evening, or on another night, while making a point about Malraux's *Anti-Memoirs.* But it didn't matter. It was the adrenaline that carried the flow of conversation that made it a lively place to be.

At some point the Lasker children wandered in, the boy, before he went to sleep upstairs, the two teenage daughters later. They'd pull up chairs and snack on cake and cookies as the table was replenished with coffee and tea, the evening seemingly taking a breath as small talk took over. Julian and I might move to the adjacent room for a game of chess. The younger daughter, who was musical, often gravitated to the upright piano in the front room, to play Scott Joplin rags. And Doris Lasker's friend Harold, who lived up the block, would always make an appearance, precipitating an irritable reaction from Phil; between art critic and college administrator, a different typological clash than he had with Julian. And out of that spark the night's next debate might well erupt, seemingly out of nowhere.

Only now, fatigue and the jitter of caffeine and sugar altered the mood, lowered the civil barrier between opinion and emotional subtext. Then Doris Lasker might step in, diplomatically scoff at her brother's exaggeration or at Phil's certainties, or in a pinch disappear and return with a new treat, a surprise she'd withheld for just this circumstance, jostling the clutter of empty dishes aside to set down a platter of carved cantaloupe and watermelon, grapes and strawberries.

Or, depending upon the vagaries of the night, the late break might bring on a bout of nostalgia.

Autumn, when the weather turned brisk, encouraging work and renewed creativity, as if ushered in by the school schedule … and not long after, the leaves turning color, Halloween and Thanksgiving, pumpkins and turkeys, all of which were dissociated from their seasonal meaning here, in California, where it was sunny and seventy degrees every day.

Winter, with stark, bare branches silhouetted against the sky, and snow, of course, transforming the city into a wonderland, before it was ground to slush, stained by pollution, then pockmarked and frozen, resembling dirty styrofoam.

One night, miffed by something or other, I described a scene I'd witnessed in a local parking lot on a rare hot day when atypical clouds built, followed by thunder and lightning, then a storm that dropped buckets, for all of five minutes, as I stood beneath an overhang, marveling silently at the spectacle when a transplant from a different foreign land who stood next to me shouted, "I didn't come out here for this!" and shook his fist at the sky.

Visible change. That's what was missing here, where the weather was never an obstacle, except for a few bleak months of gray skies and rain.

Phil and Doris had come West first; because of their children, I supposed. He resigned as editor of the prestigious magazine to open a gallery in San Francisco, which soon failed; collectors preferred to buy art in New York or Los Angeles. So now he flew down to L.A. at midweek to teach a class in art history at a university, and flew back two days later.

Julian had been a dancer, and left it behind to live a simpler life. For a while he'd done a lot of drugs, but now—Phil confided in me—he seemed to lack ambition and wandered aimlessly, as if expecting some perfect thing to fall out of the sky.

Carole might have immigrated because Uncle Phil, and Doris, were already here, and because she'd heard about the pottery community in West Berkeley, where Peter Volkos had a studio. But none of that would have mattered if not for an unhappy break-up and divorce she still couldn't talk about.

Harold, from up the block, landed a job with the university and relocated with his family. A few months later he'd gone through a divorce too, his wife moving back East with his daughter. He tried to hide his sorrow with false cheer, but doted over the Lasker children when he popped in, particularly the older daughter, in junior high school like his own daughter.

Noreen, in contrast, had few regrets. She hadn't been in New York long enough to miss it, and disliked the company town in the Midwest where she'd grown up too much to be nostalgic about it.

And I was there because of my go-with-the-flow approach to life, following circumstance out to the coast. Why not be here? Why not go anywhere? My job was boring, but I was writing, meeting poets and other writers, living life instead of merely observing it.

But there were times when I felt displaced, and at the Lasker speakeasy one night I fell into a rant about how different things were in California, how unreal it was.

When I wound down, expecting a sympathetic reaction, Julian said, "What does that mean, 'unreal'?"

What was I so worked up about? I had to think a moment, come up with something concrete. "You know, the whole laid-back thing … people aren't as intense, aren't as passionate about what they do."

"So you're just saying it's not like New York."

"Well … yeah."

"But why should it be?" he asked.

"Well, it doesn't have to be, of course. I just get put out about a certain … I don't know … Like, I never see anyone reading … books, magazines, even newspapers, which strikes me as odd."

"Why?" he asked. "What makes you think reading is any more significant than anything else?"

Put that way, my diatribe sounded silly, but I plowed ahead. "It's part of something more—an attitude. People here don't want to wrestle with ideas, much less differences of opinion. On the surface, everyone is agreeable, smiling, saying, 'Have a nice day.' But what they're really doing is avoiding anything that might be challenging or more significant."

"People say similar things everywhere," he replied, his calmness in the face of my vociferousness getting on my nerves. "In New York they ask, 'How're you doin'?' Do you really think they care how you're doing?"

"But here it's more than just an expression. *Everything* is on the surface, Julian. *Everything* is superficial."

"*Who*, exactly, are you talking about?"

"*Everyone!* They're tossing Frisbees, sunning themselves, jogging, walking dogs, *doing* things—"

"What's wrong with that?"

"Of course they're entitled to do whatever they want," I went on doggedly, "but it galls me, sitting in a park, reading a book, surrounded by all this robust activity, feeling like a freak and wondering if I stay out here long enough whether I'll be smiling and nodding too, saying 'Have a nice day,' losing all sense of curiosity, of passion, of—"

"That will never happen," Phil said.

It brought me up short. "Well, okay, probably not. But—"

"You could live here the rest of your life," he went on, "and you would never lose your *vermigeh*." He'd been quiet, and now he was adamant, as Phil always was with notions he'd been contemplating.

"My *vermigeh*?"

"Your *menschedicke vermigeh.* It isn't something you can lose."

I had a vague idea what that meant; *vermigeh.* Yiddish for "the spirit of things," and *menschedicke,* a humanitarian outlook. And I understood why he said it wasn't something I could lose—since I hadn't chosen it, but carried it within me—and in fact took pride in it, though it didn't feel like mine so much as a sense of obligation inculcated in me.

Like Doris, when Phil and Julian threatened to spiral out of control, turning intellectual disagreement into something personal, She'd interject herself obliquely, poke fun at her husband or brother, as if their manner of expression was a comic quirk. A *menschedicke* thing to do.

Later, thinking about it, the pride I'd taken in Phil's characterization—that I had a humanitarian mantle-turned upon itself, since it seemed I had no choice in the matter. It precluded other possibilities, set me apart. My *vermigeh* was predicated on my awareness as an outsider, which denied me entrance to a less claustrophobic, more spacious world. Feeling like an immigrant, I imagined invisible gears at work, and imagined that if I could only see them, glimpse the mechanism, I might be able to move with the unselfconscious ease of a native.

Walking down the street, my *vermigeh* seemed a bubble that separated me from the seductiveness of California. I walked through the room temperature weather in a state of perpetual contraction, as if it were winter.

*   *   *

Gary Higgins peered in the open doorway one morning while Noreen was making breakfast. I looked over my shoulder and was startled by a blond stubble-bearded face, which broke into a smile in response to my surprise.

"Hello," he said, as though it was the most natural thing in the world to pop into a stranger's kitchen.

"Hello yourself," I replied, and couldn't help but smile back. "Whoever you are."

"Gary," he said, sticking out a large hand, which I shook.

An unusual introduction, and that much more impressionable for reminding me of Patrick Malone, never far from my thoughts as I tried to capture him in writing. He had introduced himself to me with the same ingenuousness.

"Come in, Gary," Noreen said from the stove. "Jilly told me all about you, how wonderful you are."

He grinned at that as he entered the room. "She sent me for eggs …"

"Sit down, sit down," I said, gesturing.

" … since she hasn't gone shopping and there isn't much in the refrigerator," he finished. He was tall, had trouble arranging his legs beneath the table.

Jillian Norris and Noreen had met at boarding school, and I'd seen her several times since then: when she visited us in Manhattan, then Brooklyn, and a week ago, when she moved into the vacant studio apartment, which Noreen had told her about.

"You want some coffee?" I asked him.

"I never refuse coffee," he replied, smiling, as affable as anyone I'd ever met.

"Eggs?" Noreen asked.

"I won't refuse that either, he said, and she set the plate of sausage and eggs she'd been making for me in front of him. By then Gary had poured coffee from the glass pot, the sleeve of his frayed flannel shirt, too small for him, riding up his forearm.

"Jilly told me you met in Carmel," Noreen said, back at the stove again. "Actually, she gushed about it."

He looked up from his plate of eggs and grinned; of course. "She gushed?"

"Maybe I wasn't supposed to tell you that."

"It's an interesting story," he said, leaning back. "How we met. Kismet, you might say." He looked at me. "Is that right? Kismet?"

"I don't know. Fate?"

"Yes, fate. I'd been on the road for weeks, hitchhiking from Alaska, heading for L.A., where my parents live, but in no rush … taking time to read, to think, staying away from towns. And then I saw a sign for Carmel—"

Noreen leaned over a put a plate of sausage and eggs before me.

"But wasn't this for you?" I asked.

"I'll make some more," she said. "Go on, Gary."

He'd poured himself another cup of coffee. "As I said, I was avoiding towns, staying away from people, but when I saw the sign for Carmel … it's strange, I know, and you'll probably doubt my sanity—"

"We don't do that," I said lightly. "We reserve our intolerance for pillars of society."

He laughed. "Well, okay then … When I saw that sign, something told me I should go there, so I did, then wandered the streets and eventually came upon a little coffeehouse, exactly the kind of place I was hoping to find, with just a few people inside. I went in, ordered coffee at the counter, and seated myself at a rear table, so I wouldn't be near the man and two women up front … I'd been on the road a long time, and didn't want to speak to anyone, to answer questions. I preferred to be left alone. But I overheard their conversation in the empty room, not the words, but the sound of it, which was like German, but not exactly, and while I thought about it, I felt a tap on my shoulder. It was the man from the group up front, and he told me, with an accent, that it was the custom in his country for a man and woman to share coffee and cake with a stranger after they were married …

"In my fantastic state of mind, his invitation seemed … prescient." He hesitated before saying the word, as if unsure of it. "That I was destined to join them. So I did, and when I sat down, Jill and I made this incredible eye contact, staring at each other. I felt this surge between us, as if I'd left my body and entered hers, and as if she had entered mine … that we were making love to each through our eyes, possessed by one another …"

Jillian had entered the kitchen while Gary was telling his story, and now, when he paused and looked at her, their eyes locked, as if to illustrate that moment.

She had a narrow face with high cheekbones, and usually—at least when I was around—a pinched, disapproving look. But locking eyes with Gary, Jillian seemed transformed, her countenance softer, gentler.

Gary shook his head. "I know it sounds hopelessly romantic," he continued, "and ordinarily I distrust anything romantic, but—"

"Gary!" she said.

"—it truly did seem that we both knew we'd been drawn to that place to be with each other."

She softened again, and they stared at each other some more as Noreen rolled her eyes at me. Neither of us were big on rapture; but then, it had been a while since she'd locked eyes on me, transfixed.

I said, "I never heard of that custom—to share coffee and cake with a stranger."

"It's Swiss," Jillian said, resting a hand on Gary's shoulder. "Mark and Christina had just come from their wedding." She said this to Noreen, not me. Then in a louder voice declared, "It's true!" startling Gary, who looked up at her in surprise.

Her thin lips were a tight line, like the Jillian I knew, then he reached out, took her hand and squeezed it, and for another moment they were in their own world again.

Jillian sat down at the table, playfully scolded him for forgetting the eggs, and Gary joked back, then Noreen brought her and herself a plate of food, and the two women talked as Gary and I paired off at the other end of the table.

After a while Noreen offered to take Jillian to the pottery studio in West Berkeley. They left as Gary and I continued our discursive conversation.

From the outset I was taken by his lack of pretension, and we both had strong convictions about spiritual matters, had heard and read similar things. Something else was in play too; whatever it is that precludes instant friendship.

We hardly engaged in small talk, were soon exchanging insights and tossing ideas back and forth. Gurdjieff and Ouspensky, Casteneda, Krishnamurti, Steiner, Keyserling, Buddhism and Taoism ... By the time we moved to the living room we were concluding each other's thoughts, losing track of time in the flow of talk. Drinking more coffee, sampling each other's rolling tobacco, we speculated and sometimes knew something about exotic places we'd read about or, in Gary's case, had visited.

He'd dropped out of high school in Los Angeles to see the world— "seeking something more than knowledge," as he put it—become an apprentice seaman on a merchant ship to the Philippines and Japan; later wandered through Scandinavia, trekked across Norway on cross-country skis; watched the whales surface from a skiff in Baja California; settled down eventually with a wife and child, in Juneau, Alaska—

He broke off there, apologized for talking about himself too much, and I took over, telling him about taking drugs and afterward dealing with a limited attention span, relearning how to talk and make myself understood, then beginning to write again ...

Gary sat in a wing chair, which, like the table he'd had trouble arranging his legs beneath, seemed too small for him. Occasionally he'd take a pen and pad from a chest pocket of his faded flannel shirt, hold up a hand to stop me, apologize for interrupting, and ask me to repeat a word I'd used, so he could write it down.

"To broaden my vocabulary," he explained. Having never gone back and finished high school, he was educating himself.

When the women returned in late afternoon, Jillian went to her apartment to take a nap, Noreen prepared the batch of cookies she planned to bring to the Laskers' that evening, and I impulsively said to

Gary, "You should come," unwilling to relinquish the good feeling we'd established … and because I'd hastily concluded that since he liked to talk, he'd enjoy the Lasker salon, where talk was the common denominator.

*   *   *

The usual crew was there, along with a few other Lasker friends or acquaintances from New York. And right away I knew I'd made a mistake.

Standing in the arch to the dining room, Gary looked too big for the place, and the place too crowded, with people elbow-to-elbow crowded around the table with its cluttered array of food. Everyone paused, seemingly all at once, as Gary stood looming there. I introduced him, and in response names were thrown at him, too many to be remembered, and when that ended, his perfectly reasonable response, "Pleased to meet you," sounded too polite, not quite believable, not a New York thing to say.

He took a seat, squeezing in, and within seconds someone asked him what he did; a typical question, the kind New Yorkers always ask each other, which at the Laskers' often meant: What are you working on? I was tensely alert, felt protective, projected myself into his discomfort, which in fact was mine, anticipating what he might say. I hoped it wouldn't be "seeking something more than knowledge."

But Gary was a sociable sort, and easily replied that he wasn't doing anything at the moment but had recently been a fisherman.

Which captured everyone's attention. Where did he fish? someone asked, and he described the channel in the bay off Juneau, he and his partner in their small boat, beneath the looming decks of larger, commercial boats that went out in fleets and brought their catches to the filleting sheds …

This elicited even more questions, exacerbating my nervousness, until, to divert attention from him, I inserted myself, said the first fish thing that came to mind, about catching one at Montauk as a boy and how it lay there in the sand, flapping around, then blew up to twice its size, scaring me away.

"A blowfish," someone said, nodding. "I caught one too, in Rockaway."

"They're poisonous," someone else said. "You have to cook them just right."

"To the Japanese, they're a delicacy ..."

And by then Gary was indeed off the hook, receding into the background as talk moved on to other things ... at which point, after helping himself to coffee and cake, he retreated from the table to the adjacent room, watching the gesticulation and talk from a distance. With him sitting there, apart, I felt removed as well. A detached observer. How fast we all spoke, trying to get it all out before being interrupted, jumping in order to be heard, like cutting in and out of dense traffic, elbowing into the subway at rush hour ...

When Gary stood up, thanked the Laskers for their hospitality, and left, I felt relieved. But I couldn't get back into the garrulous flow, with its disparate juxtapositions and assertions. A comment, a remark, an idea surfaced, to be confirmed or riposted. Yes, this was talk, but not at all like the communion Gary and I had earlier that day when we moved from thing to thing in a spirit of creating something mutual. I felt overwhelmed by this talk, disloyal too, because I was still here. Having invited Gary, it now seemed that I'd abandoned him.

Which didn't make sense, of course. It was my *vermigeh* talking. But I couldn't shake the feeling, and a few minutes later slipped out too, leaving Noreen, who was having a perfectly fine time.

We lived a few blocks away. Coming up the block, I spotted Gary sitting on the brick steps that led to my apartment door. He looked up as I approached, and before I could say anything, said, with a slight smile,

"It was too much for me." And left it at that.

*   *   *

But I couldn't leave it, thought about it all week, and as Friday approached, told Noreen, "Let's do something different for a change."

She was surprised, said, "I thought you enjoyed going to the Laskers'."

There were things we never talked about, and as we got to know each other, things we chose not to bring up. My *vermigeh* was one of them. It might have explained my tendency to cede to her, but we didn't talk about that either. So I merely replied, "Yeah, I do enjoy going there, but that doesn't mean we have to show up every week. Let's do something else for a change. We can go to Chinatown, North Beach, the Haight …

And then, the following week, I suggested we go back again, maybe splurge at the Cliff House for dinner, then catch a movie at the Surf. "They're showing Konchalovsky's *Uncle Vanya*, and I'd like to see it again."

But while we were there, I was acutely aware that it was Friday and we weren't at the Laskers', which might have been the impetus to drive up Geary to what I'd heard was a Jewish neighborhood; as if I were homesick for corned beef and pastrami, though it never interested me when we lived in New York. I parked the car on the wide, busy boulevard and we looked for a delicatessen, but couldn't find any. We were about to give up when Noreen spotted a gallon-size jar of sour pickles in an otherwise empty grocery window, looking like an exotic exhibit.

"Imported from Chicago," the shop owner said seriously.

The following week we brought it to the Lasker house, showing up, as usual, unannounced.

The two weeks we'd been gone seemed like a month.

Carole was there with a companion, a man, for the first time, a brusque character who'd grown up in Israel and just moved out to the Bay area, from Queens, to open an import-export business. People cringed when he spoke, presenting himself as an expert on everything. Fortunately, he was unaware of the impression he made: his mawkish pronouncements followed by uncomfortable silence.

Julian and Doris's parents, Ida and Sam Friedman, were visiting their grandchildren, which might have explained the less combative mood between Julian and Phil that night. The Friedmans had brought several platters of lox and smoked whitefish from the Bronx, and when we arrived, the food was on platters on the table, to which we added our giant jar of pickles.

Phil, excited about Picasso's Blue Period, outlined a series of lectures he would deliver at Cal Arts that might lead to a book. Doris had upholstered a chair, which sat up front, in the living room, and was planning to do the couch next, a more difficult project. Even Harold showed up in a rare good mood; his daughter would be visiting that week.

Later, the children popped in, as usual, to be doted upon by their grandparents. The younger daughter went through her Scott Joplin repertoire, and the son came downstairs at eleven with the plot from the latest episode of *Columbo*, which he'd been watching.

At midnight the lox had been devoured and the whitefish stripped to skeletons. We were picking at the golden skins, idly talking about this and that, when out of nowhere Harold said, "It's a good life, isn't it?"

And I could see, in its way, that it was.

Backyard Guru

The lights of the Tudor house next door, beyond the trimmed hedges, had gone out, as well as blasting music from the low-slung apartment building up the block, when Gary and I returned from our late night walk and talk past the shuttered stores on College Avenue, down Ashby to Telegraph, up to the university and back. But I could still see candlelight through the gauzy fabric in the glass-paned door, and so sat down on the red brick steps, rolled another cigarette, and tried to extend a faltering conversation, at least until Noreen, Jillian, and Jeremy tired of their session; hopefully before Gary and I ran out of things to say.

Jeremy was the problem; the reason we were out there.

After moving into the renovated shack in back, he'd undergone a spiritual awakening, and was now no doubt imparting his newfound wisdom inside. Gary rolled his own cigarette too and listened to my frayed thread of recycled talk, not questioning why we were out there at three in the morning. But now that we were no longer moving, the air felt chill, so it wasn't long before I got up, and with mutual unspoken agreement he followed me inside.

Jeremy and the women were sitting cross-legged on the floor. I sat down on the couch, and Gary moved to the fireplace and leaned against the mantel, the two of us overlooking the overly solemn gathering. Our entrance momentarily impinged on Jeremy's spiel. He paused as we settled in, reshifted his haunches—meaningfully pressing his index fingers against each thumb, forearms resting on his thighs—before picking up where he'd left off, his soft cadence seemingly casting a spell over the compliant women.

"... And then we'd gather in the meadow for the afternoon satransana ..." He paused again, nodding in agreement with himself until Noreen and Jillian to reflexively nodded. "And after satransana, we'd walk to the pool at top of the hill, to take the ritual cleansing baths ..."

Jeremy was slight, with a sparse beard and hair just long enough to pull back into a tight bun, shaping his head like a Brazil nut. He wore a white robe with a curlicue design on the chest that might have been a Sanscrit inscription, and billowing sleeves resembling the blouse worn by Charlton Heston in *The Ten Commandments*.

The day he dropped by to introduce himself, after moving into the shack, he'd looked like an ordinary person. He was from a suburb of Kansas City, he told Noreen, sitting down to tea at the kitchen table, a midwesterner like herself, and with the ingenuousness that went with the territory. Afterward, it became his custom to drop by whenever the door was open.

Though always polite to me, it was obvious that Jeremy came to see Noreen. Seeing that my presence appeared to unnerve him, in an attempt to put him at ease I was less outgoing when he visited, which I sensed he found threatening. Instead, I sat quietly, nibbled cookies and sipped tea while they talked, which was all right, since I preferred listening to them commune over the conditions of their upbringing, the cluelessness of their parents. My own father and mother were clueless too—we all shared a generation gap—but their recollections struck me as more naive, more American, than my own.

And then Jeremy cultivated the beard, and not long after that put on the robe instead of blue jeans, and moccasins instead of sneakers—as if to personify two kinds of Indian at once. When he pulled his hair back in the painful-looking ascetic style, the unconvincing transformation was complete, accompanied by dollops of clichéd wisdom and soft-voiced pronouncements. And because I distrusted his one-size-fits-all version of happiness, his presence became a drag.

But even then I might have been able to shrug off his spiritual bromides if not for Noreen's abject reaction to them. Perhaps she was the one I actually had a problem with, and I held Jeremy responsible for revealing her gullibility.

"What're you talking about?" I said now, from the couch, my voice abrasive in the subdued room, in contrast to his soft, lulling speech.

Noreen shot a glare at me from her spot on the floor. "Jeremy just spent three days in a Zen retreat."

"Gathering in a meadow to chant, taking ritual baths," I said to him. "That doesn't sound like any Zen I've heard about, where they clobber you to bring you to your senses."

"There are many different sects," Jeremy replied, beginning the infernal nodding routine again, which I cut short:

"What's this one called?"

"If you didn't interrupt," Jillian snapped, "you might find out." And then: "We were doing all right before the two of you barged in."

Gary sat down then, in the wing chair by the window, took his tobacco pouch from a pocket and began rolling a cigarette.

I said, "Yeah, well, it was getting cold outside … and I do live here."

"Go on, Jeremy," Noreen said solicitously, after throwing me another look.

He exhaled deeply, maybe to drive out the bad spirits, before resuming. "Well … after the sauna, we'd participate in a group massage, walking on each other's backs—barefoot, of course. You can't imagine how much good it does," he added, perking up, like the boy from the suburbs of Kansas City. "It relieves the tension, harmonizes the energy within us with—"

"Let's do it!" Jillian said, perking up as well.

"You mean right here?" Jeremy asked uncertainly.

"Right here, right now, like the chant you recited."

He wavered, flattered at being cited, then glanced at me, with reasonable reluctance to subject himself to a heckler.

"I've been tense all day," Jillian said, "and I have a splitting headache."

"Yes, I can sense that," he replied.

"Maybe if you walked on my back, it would help."

He hesitated again, but only for a moment—he wanted to do good; I could see that—said, "Okay," and stood up in a practiced motion, like a beach chair unfolding itself. Gathering his robe, he parted it and girded each half around his legs with impressive aplomb, as if he'd taken a course on robe girding.

Gary, who'd been quiet till then, said to him, "I've heard of that technique. Are you sure you know what you're doing? If you put pressure in the wrong place, you can snap the spine."

"I'll be careful," Jeremy said, working on his loose sleeves, folding them over his elbows. "We were tutored in it." Then, all trussed up, he said to Noreen, "The floor feels cold beneath my feet. We'll need a blanket."

She went into the bedroom to get one.

"Okay," he said when she returned. "Spread it out, right here … that's right. Now, Jill, lie down on your stomach … Noreen, come stand next to me so I can lean on your shoulder."

Gary finished his cigarette, crossed the room and sat down in the chair by the desk, farther from the preparations on the floor. In fact, everyone was moving around now, doing Jeremy's bidding or reacting to it, except me. I continued to sit like a curmudgeon on the couch.

Jillian lay facedown on the floor, hands at her sides, body rigid.

"Just relax," Jeremy said, looking down at her.

"I don't know what's wrong with me," she said. "I hardly ever get headaches."

"You're tense, but we'll soon change that … Don't think about anything at all. Make your mind a still pool, without the ripple of thought," and he reached out with a bare foot and touched her back with a toe, as if testing the temperature water, then gripped Noreen's shoulder with a hand, boosted himself onto Jillian's back, and began kneading it with his feet, leaning on Noreen to keep his balance.

With the three of them poised in the middle of the room, the candle on the floor threw Jeremy and Noreen's combined shadow on the walls and ceiling.

"It hurts there!" Jillian blurted.

"Don't talk," he said. "Don't talk, and don't think about anything. That's the cause of all tension. It's in your head."

But it was in the situation too, in the expectation of healing, and in the supposed healer's presumption.

The room was stuffy, and I got up to open a window. The cat, curled up in its usual spot on the hot air vent in the floor, woke up and began tearing at the couch with its claws. The candlelight flickered, animating Jeremy's outstretched arms, too obviously rendering him a puppet master as he maintained his balance, his shadow looming as Jillian moaned.

I lit a cigarette with a loud scratch, watched the flame flare up in the incendiary atmosphere.

"Don't talk and don't think," Jeremy intoned again, his voice nearly a whisper. "Repeat silently to yourself, 'Satransana om ibiditsit, satransana om ibiditsit …'"

I reached over and swatted the cat, who bolted from the room with a squawk. Gary got up, moved back to the fireplace, his eyes fixed on Jillian as Jeremy dismounted and I sighed in relief, not realizing I'd been holding my breath, afraid he'd snap her spine. Then Noreen went into the kitchen, to make tea, and turning on the overhead light, dispelled the candlelight setting in the living room, ending one onstage scene as another abruptly took its place.

Everyone appeared to have forgotten about Jillian … except Gary, who watched her slowly get up off the floor, then lean over, press her hands to her head … and fall back down to her knees.

"My head is killing me!" she shouted, drawing us all back to her.

Jeremy, who'd turned away to ungird his loins, was startled. He took a step toward her, but Gary was there first, standing over Jillian as she knelt on the floor. He gripped her shoulders and said, "Get up, Jill!" for some reason angry.

"I can't!" she said, frantically massaging her temples now, kneading both sides of her head with her fingers.

"Get up, Jillian!"

"I'll get some aspirin," I said, and bolted for the bathroom, returning as Noreen appeared from the kitchen with a glass of water.

Jillian was on her feet now, hands clamped to her head like a vise as Gary held her steady; Jeremy, bewildered, on the periphery.

"That won't do any good!" Jillian snapped, slapping my hand away as I offered her the aspirin, sending the pills flying.

"You have to calm down," Gary said, still holding onto her.

"That's easy enough for you to say!" she shouted, pushing his hands away too. "It's not an ordinary headache!"

"Jill—"

"Leave me alone!" she yelled, looking up. "All of you, leave me alone!" And with that, she ran out of the apartment.

Gary hesitated a moment, then went after her.

*   *   *

The clock tick-tocking in the kitchen accentuated the underlying silence as Jeremy sat down at the table, slipping into a chair as if to go unnoticed. He took a slice of banana bread from the plate Noreen had set down, nibbled at it, sipped his tea with bowed head. I sat down at the table too, prepared my tea, ate my slice, and pretended he wasn't there.

A hint of smudgy daylight filtered through the curtains in the other room when Gary returned, without Jillian. He poured himself a cup of tea, took a piece of cake, and back up to a wall.

Jeremy looked up at him, said, "Jill mentioned that you lived in Alaska …"

A non sequitur, in context; it took Gary a moment to reply. "Yes. What about it?"

"I wonder … what's it like up there? How did you earn a living?"

"I was a fisherman."

"Really?" Jeremy was impressed. "Can anyone go up there and do that?"

"Sure," Gary said. "Why not?"

"How would a person go about doing it? … I mean, how would I do it, if I went up there?"

Gary didn't respond for a moment, perhaps still trying to orient himself to the conversation after what had happened in the next room. Finally, he said, "You might write a letter to the chamber of commerce … or go to one of the local bars and pick a fight with the biggest man you see." I laughed, and he glanced at me, surprised; apparently he'd been serious. "Or challenge him to a pie-eating contest."

Jeremy was incredulous. "A pie-eating contest? You're kidding, right?"

"No … it happens. People up there like to compete. It doesn't matter what the competition is."

"That's wild," I said.

"Yes, that is wild," Jeremy said, nodding. "Sounds like the Wild West—not that I'd mind that," he added quickly. "Being on a frontier, I mean. I want to live a simpler life."

"People there want everything people want here," Gary said. "A car, a house, a washing machine and dishwasher, a color television set … what they think of as prosperity."

"But it's so big. There must be places that are undeveloped …"

"If you go inland."

"That's what I'd like to do … but it's not so easy for someone like me. I'm used to a certain way of life, certain … conveniences …"

"There are a lot of people like you in Alaska," Gary said. "Educated people who come from California and elsewhere, wanting to live what they think is a simpler life."

"But … what would small-town people think of me?"

"What do you mean?"

"I mean … how difficult is it to be accepted?"

"You seem friendly enough," Gary replied, shrugging.

"No, I mean, are there any freaks up there, people who aren't straight?"

In an instant Gary lost patience. He finished his tea all at once, pushed off the wall and plunked his empty cup on the table. He looked at Noreen, standing by the sink, holding a cup in both hands as if to warm herself. "I've got to go," he said to her, then nodded at me, at Jeremy, and left.

For a change I felt sorry for Jeremy, his childlike ideas left in the lurch. He appeared lost, embarrassed, ate what was left of the banana bread on his plate, reached out and awkwardly shook hands with me before getting up. Then he embraced Noreen, thanked her for her hospitality, in that midwestern way they had in common, and left as if fleeing from embarrassment, his robe billowing out the door.

With everyone else gone, the room felt both enervated and tense as Noreen cleared the dishes from the table and put them in the sink. I waited for her to turn around, dreading what might come next; nothing about that night had felt right. When she finally did turn and face me, her anger did not come as a surprise.

"I know you don't like him," she said accusingly, "but can't you just once in your life give someone a break?"

"Wait a minute," I said, suddenly angry. "You got me wrong. I don't dislike Jeremy when he's the sweet guy from the suburbs, which he used to be. It's when he puts on airs that he drives me up the wall."

"What are you talking about?" she asked, louder still.

"I'm talking about the Jeremy who talks about his rigid parents who don't approve of him, and you can see—even while he's putting them down—that he wishes it weren't so. Or the simple Jeremy—and he *is* simple, which I don't mean as an insult—the guy bares himself when he says he'd like to lead a simpler life, which in fact would suit him. Not the guy who postures as if he's something more than he is ..."

"That's what I like about him too," Noreen said, somewhat mollified, leaning back against a kitchen counter. "He's honest, and sincere. All right, he can be silly at times, but—"

"So what're we arguing about?"

"I can overlook when he's silly—but you can't, can you? You want him to be a certain way ... You always want *everyone* to be a certain way!"

"I like the guy when he's vulnerable," I said, "not when he poses as a guru. What's wrong with that?"

"And you sure let him know it tonight, didn't you?"

"Me? He set himself up for his own fall when he went into his guru act."

"That's not for you to judge!" she shouted, unable to stand still, walking into the living room. "Who do you think you are, God? Who gave you the right to come in with your judgments and act as if—"

"You judge too! All the time! Only you come to different conclusions—and keep them inside like a clam! And as for coming in," I was shouting now, following her, "Gary and I sat out there till three in the morning!"

"You were talking," she said turning back, sounding less sure of herself.

"Yeah, but we couldn't talk forever. If you ask me, you and Jillian precipitated the whole fiasco by encouraging him, by going along with his pseudospiritual routine. Jesus, the guy literally walked all over her!"

"There you go again, always judging everyone!" she shouted, returning to the kitchen, moving mindlessly, propelled by anger.

"God forbid I should indulge in brainlessness!" I yelled, following her again.

"There!" She turned on me. "You're doing it now! Why is it that every time I try to tell you what you do, you accuse me of—"

"And why is it," I bellowed, "that whenever I express an actual opinion, you criticize me for expressing it?" And lowering my voice, I added in a mocking tone, "Can't you take me as I am, or do you want me to be a certain way?"

"Damn you!"

I saw the cup coming and ducked. It hit the wall behind me and shattered. I clenched my fists and stepped forward, and Noreen backed to the sink, hands up to ward me off. We stared at each other for a moment, as I fought with my fury, then abruptly turned and stomped out of the room.

"Peter!" she cried when I was at the front door.

"What?" I shouted, turning back, staring across the kitchen.

She was clutching herself, her face tight, drawn. "Don't leave," she said in a small voice.

"What'd you mean, don't leave? You just threw something at my head!"

"Please don't leave …"

Her anguish got to me. "I'll be back," I said in a softer voice, "but right now I need to get away—"

She moaned then, hands clawing at her shoulders and chest, and gasped for air. Startled, I bolted toward her as she began to spasm.

Grabbing her arms, I tried to twist them behind her back, to keep her from hurting herself as her nails dug into my forearms. Then her eyes rolled up into their sockets and she went limp, slipping from me to puddle on the floor.

*   *   *

It all came back to me, Noreen bolting out of the tenement apartment, me pursuing her downstairs and up the block, wrestling with her as she clawed at me before collapsing to the pavement. More than two years had passed, and the impression that seizure made had governed aspects of my behavior ever since, constraining me ... until, as the event receded, it became less influential.

And now, as if no time had passed at all, I was back there again, settling her onto the mattress in the bedroom, bringing her tea—as I had while nursing her through a bad trip even longer ago—drawing the shades and locking the front door, protecting her from the world, ministering to her as to an invalid.

And then, listening to her more attentively than I had in a while, I realized that she'd lost her enthusiasm for making art.

It came as a surprise, but now that she confessed it, the evidence was all around me. The color field watercolors and gargantuan canvases in the living room and kitchen had been on the walls of our railroad flat in Manhattan, and the few recent pieces she'd done were derivative, imitative, of an earlier style.

"They're just exercises," she said with a shrug when I asked about them.

As long as I'd been living with Noreen, art had grounded her, put her life in perspective. I sometimes wondered if that was true of my writing, but hadn't done it long or often enough to know.

I said, "If you don't care about what you're doing, why not do something else?"

"Like what?"

"I don't know ... weaving, ceramics ... " She'd taken classes, carded wool, worked on a simple hand loom, spent hours at the pottery studio.

"I like all that, and I'll still do it, of course. But they're not a replacement for painting, which was my first love."

"You don't want to paint anymore?"

"I don't feel the same way about it ... It's not *immediate* enough," she said, and looked at me. "I've been thinking about photography ..."

"Okay ... I can see that. You've always taken pictures ..."

"But my camera's old, and clunky … I need one with more versatility, with better lens attachments. And then there's darkroom equipment and supplies … paper, chemicals, a printer—the ones at school aren't available on weekends or at night, and I need to work at my own pace, to set my own schedule …"

"You're saying we can't afford it." Just like that, it was *we*, not *you*. It came out of me without hesitation. I was either a prince or a schmuck. Or maybe both.

She was sitting on the sofa in the living room now, her legs aligned in parallel lines, hands folded in her lap. I'd seen that posture before—the schoolgirl speaking to a parent; it meant she wanted something. "It will be very expensive," she said.

"What about your parents?" I asked, though I already knew the answer.

"They're already paying for school, and they weren't thrilled about that."

I bristled, thinking about Ainsworth, the sixth wealthiest man in Connecticut, according to the copy of *Forbes* her mother had sent. Who, in a fit of anger when Noreen was a child, told her she wasn't really theirs, that she'd been adopted. It explained why she was reluctant to ask for what would only be given grudgingly, if at all.

But telling her it was reasonable to ask more of her parents was not something I could point out in the wake of her seizure.

*   *   *

"But why do *you* have to get a job?" Colin asked. "Why doesn't she get one?"

"Well, for one thing, my job is about to end—they've been hinting as much for weeks. For another, Noreen's in school and can't do much, really, and I could make a lot more working for the post office … "

He lifted his shoulder in a shrug that indicated a lack of sympathy. I couldn't hold it against him. Maggie was a waitress, after all, and he didn't feel he had to alter his life because of her.

"I took the civil service test back in Brooklyn," I told him, "and I'm on the list."

Colin leaned back in his chair. "I don't think you're being straight with yourself, Peter. I think you believe that what Noreen does is more important than what you do."

"No, that's not it," I said, and in fact I didn't think it was; or maybe I didn't want to believe it. "Sometimes, you've just got to go in whatever direction life takes you."

"That's true … but what if you're reading it wrong? Maybe this isn't one of those times." He leaned forward: "Your book is important, Peter. I think it's a mistake to stop now, just when you're getting started and have momentum."

"Getting a full-time job doesn't mean I can't write," I said, and recalled scoffing when Alan Benveniste told me the same thing—that he could still paint pictures while selling turntables. He accepted the job, and he and Mary had gone back East; I had no idea how much painting he was doing.

Colin sat back, his movement away from me a seeming rebuttal. Then, abruptly, he changed the subject: "And how is our friend Patrick Malone doing?"

I was relieved by the shift. "I'm through with Patrick—at least for a while. I started thinking about another character, the one I call Manchild."

"The alchemist."

"Yeah, and he's even harder to decipher than Patrick. He was scientific, detached, taciturn—less like me than Patrick was … He was an epileptic, you know …"

Colin waited, expecting me to continue.

But though it had always been my inclination to reveal my sources, to explain my thinking, I said nothing more, keeping Noreen's seizure to myself.

Life on the Deadline

At five in the morning, when the alarm went off, Noreen slipped out of bed, letting me sleep an extra ten minutes while she made coffee. She put my favorite Mozart violin concerto on the turntable while preparing lunch—a sumptuous sandwich of thick homemade bread, tuna fish or egg salad smothered in mayonnaise, the way I liked it—the lovely music wafting into the bedroom along with the odor of fresh-brewed coffee as I rolled off the mattress and pulled on the blue-gray pants, the pale blue shirt, the matching postal jacket.

It was still dark outside when I emerged from the bedroom, reflected in windows mirrored by the kitchen light; one of the little things that brightened the long day. In accordance with the union contract, as a so-called substitute carrier I had no choice but to accept mandatory overtime if the supervisors ordered it.

The fog rising off the unseen bay was otherworldly as I drove to work on the empty elevated highway; not unpleasant, obscuring the routinized day to come. And then I'd pull into the station lot, with the early morning sun glaring off pavement, jeeps and half-ton trucks waiting to be loaded, and the workday would truly begin, a treadmill that wouldn't let me off for nine or ten hours.

Civic Center, as it was called, was my first assigned station; in fact, the downtown Oakland building housed three stations in its cavernous back room, already bustling when I punched in … rows of metal cases where mail was sorted by the eighty or so carriers, canvas bags next to each case—the day's allotment, supplemented by more mail when a bell rang, indicating that the second dispatch was ready to be cased, added to the rest, bundled up and moved out.

By then the so-called regulars, who worked the same easily cased routes every day, had gathered in the aisles, to talk, smoke, or take a morning break in the swing room—coffee, packaged cupcakes, and candy bars from vending machines—while those of us who'd been screwed by the union and were bounced from route to route continued to labor at the cases, trying to catch up. Casing mail wasn't a skill, after all, but a mechanical chore, the mind-numbing repetition that automatically moved fingers and hands to this or that mail slot at the glancing sight of an address an advantage.

My first week, however, was what you might call a honeymoon. I was assigned to a mentor, Bill, who'd just returned to work after being out several months with a heart attack. He had two more years until retirement, he said while helping me case the unfamiliar addresses and routing the magazines and newspapers, then recounted his medical history, a catalogue of strokes, blood clots, and ulcers; the aged mailman's norm. He went on to describe a future fantasy of sitting in his backyard in Walnut Creek, reading the newspaper, playing with the dog, shopping with the wife, basking in a life when he didn't have to punch in anymore—breaking off when he saw me fumbling with a stack of cased mail I'd just pulled out of address slots to lecture me on the advantages of using old-fashioned string to newfangled rubber bands.

"Always wear your cap," he counseled after we punched out a jeep and left the station. "If an inspector sees you without it, you'll be written up."

I'd put it on, out of respect for him, forcing it down over my bushy mane, because Bill was a conscientious worker, a good guy, doing the best he could; though eventually, when I went out on my own, I would never wear it. None of the younger substitute carriers did; our daily rebellion against the regulations.

After that first week, Bill went on vacation—he planned to spend it in his backyard for a week—and I was assigned his route, a sinecure I would only appreciate in retrospect, when they bounced me all over the place from one day to the next.

That solo week gave me the wrong impression; leaving the station at almost the same time as everyone else, packing the jeep with mail trays not long after they did, driving off as the morning sun threw nine o'clock shadows across the tarmac.

Even so, my first stop informed me of who and what I was: a man in uniform, in the service of strangers.

*   *   *

They were well-to-do at 1200 Lakeshore, the building overlooking Lake Merritt; a few of them even idly rich. Like a feudal peasant toiling for my betters, I recognized them from their mail as I began casing all over again, this time divvying up the letters and magazines intended for the building into apartment slots in the walk-in closet of a mailroom off the lobby. The owner of the city's largest jewelry store. The local furniture emporium mogul. The self-important society columnist of the *Tribune*, the city's daily newspaper, the note he'd written in bold letters to Bill taped beneath his cubbyhole slot: **DO NOT WRINKLE MY MAIL.** And, of course, Charles Finley, insurance magnate from Chicago, owner of the Oakland A's, who had won the World Series the year before. Despite the size of his opening, Finley's mail hardly ever fit; I had to shove it in with both hands: magazines, newspapers, letters.

It made me seethe, to labor there while tenants gathered in the lobby, opening and closing the gang-box doors, complaining loudly because the mail hadn't magically appeared, wondering aloud to one another what was taking so long.

At some point, that first day, the doorman peered into the little room and looked over my shoulder, as if his uniform cap and epaulets conferred an authority greater than my blue-gray uniformity. But to give him his due, at my backward glance he asked, "How's it going?" a momentary blow for equality, both of us equally answerable to the babbling idiots out there, he essentially no less subservient than I.

"Not bad," I replied, turning back to my mail tray. "A few minutes more."

Which was a lie. No way could I get it all up before ten, and by then there'd be an angry mob out there slamming those little gang-box doors in my unseen face.

The doorman probably didn't believe me. He'd seen Bill in action, and in comparison had to know exactly where I was at.

But when he popped back out and I heard him in the lobby, he lied as well, adding his own embellishment: "Just a few minutes more … very heavy delivery today."

They were overgrown babies at 1200 Lakeshore, too spoiled to be placated for long, and soon enough one or two with more gumption than the rest, or who were needier victims of habit, breached the class barrier and peered into the open door to the little room to see what the problem was.

And there I was.

"Where's Bill?"

"On vacation," I said that first day on my own, and then, glomming to the daily harassment, I changed the story, saying, "He's out sick," thinking that might elicit sympathy, buy me some time before they turned hysterical.

"Oh … not another heart attack, I hope."

"No, no, not that. Maybe his ulcer is acting up."

"Oh … oh, I see."

No sooner had that interloper receded, like the first wave of an oncoming tide, than the deluge began, the gang-box doors on the lobby side opening and closing in a mounting clatter, the same nitwits looking for their mail every few seconds, and after each look exclaiming in surprise at the continued failure of the well-known magic trick whose delightful result clueless children feel they have a right to expect.

I heard: "Has he done the seventeenth floor yet?"

And: "I don't understand how this can happen …"

"Is he here yet? I don't see him back there."

"Where's Bill? It's not Bill back there, is it?"

When the mail was finally up and the clacking doors silent, I sat back with a sigh, opened my lunch box, unwrapped the gooey sandwich and began to devour it in big gulps, mayonnaise dripping onto my uniform shirt and spattering all over. It must have been eleven or eleven-thirty by then, and I'd only managed a banana, at eight a.m. while casing in the station.

Without Bill to guide me, I assumed the scrutiny was over, now that I'd fed the beast that clamored for its mail; that since I was not needed anymore, I was invisible.

Except, of course, I wore a uniform.

As did the doorman, who peered into the little room again, only this time with a different, more entitled attitude, because I was no longer necessary. "Take all the time you want," he said with a tilt of his head, the epaulets on his crimson jacket those of a generalissimo, his smile a flat line.

It said: "Fucken deadbeat. Brings the mail late, takes more than two hours to get it up, and now has the nerve to eat lunch in my mailroom!"

On the bright side, this brutish life would sensitize me. Soon I'd be able to read minds, or at least guess what people were thinking by their twitches and inflections. Not so different, when you think about it, than my Proustian associative awareness of Mozart and fresh-brewed coffee when I woke up. Except to appreciate this sensitivity I would have had to overlook the mean-spiritedness it revealed. And I wasn't there yet. For all I knew back then, I might never be.

I thrust what was left of the sandwich back into the lunch box, glugged what was left of the coffee, and got the hell out of there.

Just as well. Six blocks of mail to deliver, and it was almost noon.

*　　　　　*　　　　　*

The uniform was a lightning rod for rich and poor alike.

On Check Day, people scrutinizing me from behind drawn curtains and through venetian slats as I sat in the half-ton truck; infuriated when I took a coffee break; lingering at the curb as I stepped onto the street and hefted the fifty-pound burden to my shoulder; actually shaking fists at me as I moved off in what they considered the wrong direction, shouting, "Where's my check, Mr. Mailman?" as though I were personally, maliciously, withholding it. "Hey, Mr. Mailman, where's my check?"

I'd be anticipating this harassment at the station while casing. Check Day, and I wasn't anywhere close to being out on the route because, goddamn it, tomorrow was Election Day, or Columbus Day, or some other kind of irrelevant day, and all the so-called dated material, as the post office called it, and that ordinary people rightly considered junk, had to go out. The political and other sales crap was so thick as I labored at the metal case, it obscured the important green envelopes with brown checks showing in the see-through window.

On Check Day, in the humongous back room, there was no banter. All was quiet except for the shuffling sound of mail being cased, the air of shared purpose palpable. Mutual dread united us, even the usual bitchers and bickerers. Like soldiers preparing to move out of trenches, we knew the check people were out there, waiting. They'd been there since eight o'clock and now it was nine and every passing minute ratcheted the tension up with more vivid imagery of an enraged citizenry multiplying and getting meaner and, *goddamn it, if we didn't get out on the street soon, the fucken routes were gonna be mine fields!*

No doubt there were some sane sorts out there, patient if not understanding souls. And some philosophical types who actually didn't care if the check came at noon, or one, or even two, because they knew it would be gone by the end of the day anyway, appropriated by the landlord, the grocer, or some other agent of indebtedness. But according to a magazine article I read while scarfing down a sandwich in the truck after leaving the station, criminal sociologists had calculated that a

troublemaker population of six percent—the malcontent threshold—
would undo any society, which would eventually dissolve in chaos. A
paltry percentage compared to what awaited me outside as I cased the
mail, envisioning a waiting army of watchers, pointers, threateners,
Kalikaks and Smerdiakovs.

And then it was nine-thirty going on ten, according to the big clock
overlooking the gunmetal gray cases, the older guys with routes in
Grand Lake already gone, because few so-called patrons in that zip
code were on welfare. But the rest of us, from middle age on down,
lacking seniority to land the cushy routes, or lacking even a regular
route, were still there; the youngest and least experienced casing West
Oakland, where it seemed every person with an address lived from
check to check.

Maybe I had it wrong. It might have been the anticipatory
psychology of Check Day that rendered those tense morning hours in
the station more fraught than what ever happened out on the streets.
Maybe no one was scrutinizing me behind drawn shades as I made my
way from ramshackle house to ramshackle house, past cyclone and
picket fences, barking dogs, treading on broken pavement or gravel or
dirt. And it could be that the guy up ahead on the corner had not been
glaring at me, merely squinting against the bright glare of the sun on
those treeless streets with names like Oak, Cypress, and Willow.

But like the rich people in the lobby at 1200 Lakeshore, they were
indeed waiting, whether with violent intent or not. Which provides its
own psychology.

I saw them on the steps of dilapidated houses or the row-house
project, or gathered in groups, watching me when I stopped to eat lunch
in the jeep or half-ton truck, before I learned better and didn't stop at all
until finishing the route, loading my bag again and heading out on the
next loop, no matter how hungry or in need of a bathroom. I didn't even
pause for a smoke.

God, I hated those fucken furniture stores owned by that asshole at
1200 Lakeshore, with his Columbus Day flyers to be delivered at every

address in a neighborhood where everyone was on welfare, disability, or received a check for dependent children. Who among them could afford furniture, even on the installment plan? It was the checks they desperately wanted, not the crappy flyers.

Or the politicians running for office! What was the point of voting when the potholed and unpaved streets were an advertisement from the last election, when Reagan had become governor? I'd approach a house where an old man sat on the porch steps and feel like a fool, handing him a political flyer, which he'd throw away in his haste to get at the brown envelope containing the green check.

Still, the divine principle of contrast applied to the poor streets as well as anywhere else when I finally did finish the route. I'd drive away with heavenly relief, looking for a peaceful spot to eat my long forestalled lunch in the metal truck, inhale my gooey tuna fish or egg salad sandwich, wash it down with a quart of chocolate milk I bought at a corner grocery store.

I remember one day in particular, finishing lunch in sight of a small park. A band was playing, batons spinning in the air against a clear blue sky. Some local holiday. The Reverend Something-or-other Jubilee Something-or-other. A festive scene. On the heels of my frantic delivery day, it would have been another of those rare, perfect moments I entered in a journal, had I kept one, if only I could have found a bathroom before my bladder burst.

Workingclass Hero

Just when I knew most of the routes at Civic Center well enough to do the job in eight hours, orders emanating from the mysterious Concrete Slab near the navy yard transferred me elsewhere.

The winter season was now upon us, and the day's dire, low-hanging clouds opened up, as usual, when I pulled into the barbed-wire lot behind Temescal Station, where mail handlers were unloading the early dispatch from an eighteen-wheeler amidst the downpour.

Following the other slickered and peak-capped carriers inside, I punched in and checked with the clipboard supervisor. Two dozen people were already busy at four rows of cases in the cramped back room, trays, mail bags, satchels, and parcels cluttering the two aisles. I'd been told to case one route, deliver it, then return to pick up a section of another route whose carrier had an afternoon doctor's appointment. It would amount to a ten hour day; ten and a half, if you counted the unpaid lunch hour the union had neglected to fight for during the last collective bargaining agreement.

"That Lily leave early *every* Check Day," the boulder-sized woman casing next to me said, obliquely addressing while intoning to everyone else in the close-knit room. "Lily be the one you come back for," she explained in a softer aside.

"Okay," I said agreeably, following the counsel of Confucius to be politely invisible in newly arrived settings.

After a while she glanced at me as I fumbled with a stack of mail and scanned the address labels on the unfamiliar case. "You best be speeding up," she warned, "lest the customers out there be ripping you limb from limb."

I nodded as if this were helpful advice, though I was casing as fast as I could.

The carrier on my other side, another hefty sort, with a thick, impressive mustache, loudly addressed the far aisle: "I hear you be planning a disability claim. Ain't that right, Lily?"

"Mind your own damn business, Norman," Lily replied from beyond the row of metal cases, a remark met by a chorus of oohs and aahs.

"You got no quarrel with me," Norman said. "I think you got the right idea."

Nearby, a new voice: "They got inspectors look into that kinda thing."

"Don't be a chump," someone else put in. "What they gonna find if they take a X ray of the woman's back? No way they can prove otherwise if she say she can't walk good enough to carry a satchelful of mail."

The heavyset woman next to me leaned in my direction and said, in a chiding tone, "You best not be listening so hard if it slow you up, baby."

"Really," I replied, "I'm casing as fast as I can."

She snorted. "Then you be the slowest mailman ever."

Half a dozen carriers laughed, and I realized they were all listening to everything, and had no doubt been eyeing me all along, sizing me up. The new white guy in their black station. The others who shared my complexion—a few older guys and several younger substitutes, like me—had said nothing, steering clear of the morning dozens, whose putdowns could be tricky without the proper, accompanying attitude.

"You got a way with words, Clarise," one of the snickerers said.

Clarise leaned her bulk toward me again and in a near whisper said, "You be gettin' that mail up, and when I finish here, I hep you with the flats," by which she meant the canvas bags bursting with circulars and magazines.

"Thanks," I replied, which seemed inadequate, since helpfulness was not a typical post office trait, and this humongous woman for some reason had decided to take me under her wing.

The talk went on around me as I struggled to match addresses to mail slots. Snippets about sports to ease the boredom—who might beat Ali, now that Frazier had lost the belt; whether the Raiders had a shot at the championship; about Snitch, the wiry type casing earnestly down the aisle, who rarely spoke and was thought to be an informer; about Rosie, the light-skinned supervisor, and Oswald, her ambitious white-skinned assistant; about who might be elected union rep, and if there would be a strike in the spring—this in softer, more circumspect tones, given the proximity of the supposed snitch and the ambitious assistant supervisor; and whether Juan would be allowed to bring his German shepherd with him on his route, which I gathered was a subject of heated dispute every morning.

"He sit right next to me in the jeep," Juan called out from the next aisle. "He don't bother no one, and he guards the mail while I'm away."

Several people hooted. "Who gonna bother to steal the *mail*?"

"You be surprised, man. Lot of miscreants out there."

"Mis-what?"

Clearly, the beige Chicano had been accepted into the coal black to nut brown group.

Clarise had by then moved to my flats case and was rapidly flipping magazines into the proper openings. "If Juan can bring his dog with him," she declared loudly, "then I can too!"

"But you don't have no dog, Clarise."

"Maybe not," she replied truculently, "but you wait—I might go out and get one after work today."

Both aisles erupted in hoots and catcalls.

I still had half a tray of letters to case when the others began to pull down. "Here, let me at that," Clarise said, elbowing me aside. "You route them flats."

I began to fumble through the magazines, putting them in

consecutive address order as she fluidly flipped letters into openings. "You know this route?" I asked.

"I be the floater on these here," she replied, sweeping a heavy arm at the row of cases on our side of the aisle. "I got Grady's today, Johnson tomorrow, Ruby, Norman, then yours Friday. You here 'cause Earvin, the reg'lar carrier, be ill."

"He always be ill on Check Day," someone down the row said, again making it clear that everyone listened to and heard everything.

"Can't rightly blame him," the stocky carrier on my other side said, and grinned at me. "Last Check Day, Earvin nearly dropped dead on that long route you on today."

"Don't you go scarin' the boy!" Clarise snapped, and to me said, "Doctor say it just a mild heart something."

"An *infarction,*" Norman said, and grinned at me again, not at all pleasantly, with a hint of challenge, as if to say he knew a thing or two about words, so I'd best not underestimate him.

The Oakland post office had the material for a monumental tract on race relations, from guys like Norman—hyperalert for condescension—to white college-educated carriers who adopted blackspeak to mimic their way into acceptance; from black-over-white and white-over-black supervisors, in primarily black or white stations, to outright rednecks who worked in the hills, ate and drank and stoked their common resentments together; from angry black carriers who lived in mixed neighborhoods and worked in segregated ones, to black mail handlers overworked by variously hued foreman at the Concrete Slab who competed to rise in the pyramid whose faceless executives issued orders to guys on the bottom, like me.

Norman leaned closer, and with a smile not meant for me, but for the inside joke he was making with himself, said, "What with Lily's route on top of this one, you be makin' a lotta money today."

"You leave him be, Norman Brown. Not everyone be as greedy as you, thinkin' 'bout money allatime."

"Watch out for dogs," he said to me. "That route known for vicious breeds."

Clarise glared at him. "Leave him *be*, Norman. He got a bad day ahead of him already without you ruinin' it further."

Indeed, it would be a bad day. Wherever I parked the jeep, people descended on me out of nowhere, demanding their checks. I wasn't required to give them out, and wasn't supposed to without identification, but being who I was—burdened with a noble notion of public servanthood—I'd stop and delve through stacks of bound mail anyway, as slanting rain dripped down my neck and back. But at least the downpour kept the dogs away, I thought, while lugging the satchel up and down unfamiliar streets. Finally, at three, I finished the route, returned to the station, grabbed the canvas bag by Lily's case, and, with adrenaline propelling me at the prospect of finishing sometime before it got dark, checked the soggy map and sped out to deliver the portion of her route that would complete my day.

I dumped the contents of the canvas bag onto the floor of the jeep, stuffed two numbered stacks of letters and flats into my satchel, and took off into the first loop. It was raining even harder now, pen-written addresses blurring on envelopes as I plowed ahead, skim-reading the mail, oblivious to puddles, my feet moving with their own volition down watery sidewalk culverts and across slick lawns. I went down several times and had to crawl around, retrieving spilled letters; often, I had to stop to seek out a cleverly camouflaged mailbox or slot as rain splattered my face.

Following the flow of mail, expecting to find myself back at the jeep—routes were fashioned by the regular carriers into loops—I instead ran out of letters two blocks from my umbilical source and had to trudge back through the deluge. There, I fell inside the vaporized metal and glass vehicle, wiping water from my face, taking a good look at what still lay scattered in the jeep.

"Fucken Lily," I muttered, understanding now the quips and meaningful silences that had accompanied all mention of her name in the station that morning. She'd given me nearly her entire route to deliver.

Still muttering to myself, I stuffed the next batch of numbered bundles into the satchel and headed back out into the cataclysmic rain. By the time I returned to the jeep again, I'd put in nearly ten hours, and there was still enough mail to consume another hour and a half or two.

It had happened to me before, was customary, in fact, that the so-called regulars took advantage of the substitutes-in-name-only by unloading a hefty chunk of their routes whenever the supervisors okayed it. But on this more than usually miserable day, with the cold rain chilling my bones and saturating my shoes and socks, I'd had enough of the usual.

It was gloomy twilight when I got back to the station lot, where all the jeeps but mine were lined up, and my car sat alone. Inside, there was only one clerk up front, selling stamps, and a janitor in back, pushing a broom. The other carriers had long since finished their routes and gone home. Even the supervisors were gone. I dragged the canvas bag to Lily's case, dumped the remaining bundled mail onto the tabletop, and punched out.

*   *   *

When I walked in the next morning the chatter in the aisles instantly died, highlighting Lily, glaring at me as I punched in. That was the whole story, right there. I walked to the infarction victim's case in the extended silence, aware of the unfriendly scrutiny, and began casing the day's mail. Even Clarise, my former benefactor, now working two cases over, would only glance furtively at me, as if I were contagious.

An hour or so of this silent treatment ensued, underlined by soft talk among the carriers—no playful or insulting banter on this day—before the supervisor called me up front, and then even that small talk stopped, rendering a remark in the next aisle suddenly audible: "Unreliable." It was the most critical thing one carrier could say about another, and followed me from the back room through the cage partition separating the carriers from the clerks and supervisors. It seemed I'd broken through the color barrier all at once, unifying the cantankerous station.

Rose, the gentle, olive-skinned supervisor regarded me sorrowfully. Oswald, her puffy, narrow-eyed assistant, frowned at me, and spoke first, saying: "What you did yesterday is grounds for suspension."

The idea of a week off, even without pay, didn't sound bad. "So suspend me," I replied.

His beady eyes nearly popped. It was a reaction I wouldn't comprehend until a few weeks later, when I saw a carrier break down and cry in another station after being suspended for a week; for bringing a shotgun to work in his satchel. For all their complaining, these carriers were thankful to be working at one of the better jobs available to them.

Taking a different tack, Oswald wagged a finger at me, saying, "There are people out there who were expecting their checks, and I've personally been on the phone all morning, trying to explain—"

"Ozzie, let me handle this," Rose said.

Oswald did a poor job of trying to hide his annoyance—at her now, as much as me. He didn't like being interrupted by a woman, who, on top of that, was also black. In his perfect world she would at best have been his assistant, rather than the other way around. Swallowing his resentment, he nodded brusquely and lurched away.

Behind me, in the rear of the station beyond the cage wall, I heard the riffling sound of mail being cased, but no conversation; everyone listening.

"What happened yesterday?" Rose asked in a reasonable voice. "Did you get sick and have to go home?"

She was such a fine, well-meaning sort, I almost took the out she offered. But I said, "No, Rose. I just decided that after ten hours, it was time to quit."

She didn't mind me using her first name. "But Mr. Weissman—"

"Peter," I said.

She smiled, which, given the context, then doubled back on her, creased her lips downward into a frown. "Peter … maybe you haven't been a carrier that long and don't know that substitutes have no choice but to work overtime—"

"But I do have a choice, Rose, if I'm willing to accept the consequences. You can suspend me, if you want, and I'll accept that, but I won't be dumped on by other carriers, and I won't work more than ten hours, no matter what the regulations say."

She regarded me a moment, then briskly said, "All right, Mr. Weissman. You can return to your case."

So I went back, amidst the silence, and resumed casing.

"That one got a lot to learn," I heard someone in the next aisle say, and then heard nothing at all.

*　　　　　　*　　　　　　*

It turned out that Rose didn't write me up, but I was now a pariah in the station. Still, I was never assigned Lily's route again, and the portions of other carriers' routes I delivered were merely unreasonable rather than outrageous. Having made my point, I now kept my mouth shut, hoping I might eventually be accepted back into the community of my fellow workers if I remained anonymous long enough. It was not a strategy that worked. No one wanted anything to do with me.

And then one morning when Rose was off for the day, Oswald Beamish summoned me up front, handed me a slip of paper on which three addresses were scrawled, and said, "Pull that mail for me, Weissman."

The three addressees had the usual bills and department store advertisements, along with a newsletter from the Farm Workers Union, an English edition of the *Beijing Review*, and a copy of *Organic Gardening* magazine. I brought it all up to Oswald's desk and, curious, asked, "What's this about?"

"Never mind," he replied, flicking me away with a fat hand. "You can return to your case."

After a while he brought the mail back and I finished casing. As usual, I was running late. I pulled down, punched out, loaded everything into a jeep, and began my always frantic dash through the first few loops. I paused for coffee and half a sandwich from my lunch box, then continued working ... and almost immediately came across the farm workers' newsletter.

A thin young man, about my age, opened the door to a modest brown-shingled house and blinked at me owlishly, as if he'd just woken up. "Yes?" he said.

I handed him a bill and the newsletter and told him, "I'm the substitute on this route today and thought you might want to know they're checking your mail down at the station."

His mouth fell open and he stared at me for several seconds. "But ... why?" he finally said. He had medium-length hair, a new mustache, an unprepossessing appearance that my announcement had transformed into bewilderment and then fear.

I said, "I guess they think you're a dangerous revolutionary."

A joke, intended to lighten the mood, but it had the opposite effect. He looked over his shoulder and shouted into the dim interior, "Sarah, come out here, will you?" Turning back, nervously fingering his slight mustache, he said to me, "A revolutionary? I don't understand. It must be a mistake. I— We—" He looked at the woman who had joined him in the doorway and was regarding me quizzically through bifocals. He said to her, "He says someone's checking our mail."

Her eyes widened, four of them, one pair atop the other. "Why?" she asked me.

Seeing the king-size poster of Cesar Chavez in the living room behind them, and knowing that we lived in America, I was almost as surprised as they were: that they could be so naive. Speaking softly, as if to nervous children, I said, "Maybe it's because you're involved with the farm workers. Anyway, I didn't mean to alarm you, I just thought you had the right to know." I turned to leave, but the woman reached out and grasped my arm.

"What should we do?" she asked, her four eyes searching my face for an answer.

"Why don't you call up the station, ask them what's going on, and why."

"What station?" the young man asked.

Some revolutionaries. When it came time to seize vital buildings, they wouldn't know where to find them. "Temescal," I said. "It's in the phone book. If you call, ask for Oswald Beamish—he's the guy who looked at your mail."

A few blocks later the *Beijing Review* went into the gang box of a run-down stucco apartment building. No one answered the bell, so I scribbled a note, dropped it in with the subversive publication, and moved on.

In the final loop I came to *Organic Gardening*. It went to an aluminum-sided cottage in a cul-de-sac. The woman who appeared behind a locked screen door looked to be in her seventies. She stared at me without expression as I repeated my news three times, then thanked me tonelessly and brusquely closed the door.

I'd just punched in and sat down in front of the case with that day's mark-ups when Oswald bolted into the back room. He pointed at me with a trembling finger, shouted, *"You!"* and jerked his thumb toward the front of the station.

Ever since bracing Lily a few weeks before, I'd been the invisible man. But in fact everyone was always watching me, just as they always watched each other. And listening too, as they were now, in the silence following Oswald's imperious summons.

"What do you mean, telling people I've been reading their mail?" he demanded when I stood before his desk. Trying to keep his voice down, in his repressed fury he produced a quavering squeak.

I said, "I didn't say you were reading their mail—"

"What's said in this station stays in this station!"

"Why?" I asked. "Are you afraid of something?"

He stared at me a moment, blinked ponderously, then a sudden cautiousness came over him. I could almost hear him think, *Is there something to be afraid of here?* In the measured voice of a public service announcement, he replied, "It's no one's business what goes on behind—"

"People have the right to know if you're checking up on them."

His fat cheeks puffed up even more, with indignation. "I'm not checking up!" he shouted, then caught himself and looked around, as if again wondering, *Is there something to be afraid of here?* Maybe, maybe not; he wasn't sure. Softly, with calculated reasonableness, he said, "Look, Weissman, some mornings I get a call from downtown"— he pointed at the phone on his desk—"and they tell me to look at the mail going to a certain address. I don't know anything about it. They—"

"Do they have a list?"

He looked befuddled. "A list? How the hell should I know?"

"But you're the one who's doing their bidding. Don't you *want* to know?"

"It's not me, it's them!" he said plaintively.

"Who?"

"I don't know who! A voice, different voices, not always the same one. It doesn't matter. The point is—"

"It does matter," I cut in. "You should find out."

He sighed, chest heaving in frustration and dismay. "You don't understand. This happens all the time—it's *routine.* I can't do anything about it. It's just my job."

I knew something about history, so of course I'd heard that before. "Do what you want," I said. "In the meantime I intend to give your name to anyone whose mail you examine on the routes I deliver, because as far as I can see, you're responsible."

Oswald looked unhappy. I almost felt sorry for him: caught between his invisible superiors and what the post office flatteringly called its postal patrons. "I could put you on report," he said, but without conviction.

"Go ahead," I replied.

What a grand troublemaker I'd become.

The following morning, talk stopped as I punched in and moved to my assigned case. At least five minutes elapsed before anyone spoke, the shuffle of mail the only sound. And then it was that ball breaker, Norman, obviously picking up a conversation that had been cut short when I arrived.

"They pay me to deliver the mail," he said, loud enough to be heard throughout the station, "not to be no gov'mint spy." And then added, "They don't pay me nowheres near enough for that."

Several people laughed. I turned and looked at him, but he kept an impassive face and purposefully looked straight ahead as he continued to case.

"You gonna tell them what Norman say, Snitch?" someone in the next aisle asked facetiously, and a few people snickered.

"I just do my job, that's all," Snitch replied gruffly, working stolidly at his case.

Norman said, "I hear you thinkin' 'bout running for union rep, Snitch. How much they pay you to do that?"

In the next aisle, Earvin, the union rep, interjected in a booming voice: "I don't get a penny, Brother Norman."

"But you don't work for the kind that *Brother* Snitch do," someone remarked.

Snitch hunched his shoulders, presented his back to the aisle.

Clarise, working the case behind me, leaned toward my shoulder. "How you doin' on that route, baby?" she asked, speaking to me for the first time in two weeks. "You need help?"

"No," I told her. "I think I've finally got this one down."

We were speaking softly, but as usual, everyone heard. "You think you finish that itty-bitty route before sunset, then?" she asked.

Several people laughed.

"Not if he be stopping to tell everyone what the post office up to," Norman announced. "He do that, be too much to *ever* finish."

The Communists Upstairs

Before the drug dealer moved in, the communists lived upstairs: Dick, who worked at the Concrete Slab in West Oakland; Judy, secretary at a public interest law firm in San Francisco, which she proudly described as the foremost defender of progressive causes in the Bay area.

Occasionally, when I was assigned to collections—picking up the mail people deposited in steel blue boxes on the street and bringing it to the Concrete Slab—I'd see Dick on the loading docks; me in mailman blue-gray, Dick in the street clothes the loaders wore, a laminated photo ID pinned to his shirt. We'd exchange a quick greeting while being pulled in different directions by the time clock. On those days, coming home earlier than usual, empty leather satchel looped over my shoulder, Judy might be reading on the front lawn. She'd put her book aside, look up to greet me, and we'd talk for a few minutes, though she mainly did the talking, bringing up the latest political outrage against the common people, while I stood there on aching feet, eager to break away, to flounce down in the apartment and take off my shoes.

From Dick's grandiloquent manner of speech and neatly trimmed Lenin beard, and Judy's pride in the legal firm she worked for, I should have suspected they might be communists. But the newspapers were so full of crap about so-called radicals fomenting this or that, nefarious agents of revolution, Black Panthers on the loose, the notion that they were actual communists—the old-fashioned card-carrying kind—would have struck me as fiction. A few graying diehards, sure, who no one but the FBI took seriously—if in fact even they did. But who among people our age could be in thrall to party doctrine?

I knew, however, that many once had been. My parents, for instance, though I'd never seen any of the membership cards you heard so much about. And from the circle of friends who were their affinity group when I was a boy, I knew what communist apartments typically looked like, or at least what was on the walls: the Charles White print of a black tenant farmer with a hoe, or an old black woman looking tired and dignified, or Abraham Lincoln with a prominent wart on his nose. Or all of them, in my childhood living room.

So I was startled to see one of those prints in Dick and Judy Lindner's apartment. "When I was a boy," I said, staring at that familiar old black woman, "this one used to hang on the wall."

Judy stood beside me, where we admired it side by side. "It's a beauty, isn't it?" she said.

"We had one of Abraham Lincoln too," I told her, which brought to mind the needlepoint my mother had made and framed.

> *As I would not be a slave,*
> *So I would not be a master,*
> *This expresses my idea of democracy.*
> *Whatever differs from this,*
> *to the extent of the difference,*
> *Is no democracy.*
> — *A. Lincoln*

I could recite those verses before I knew what poetry was, and still could. It always brought to mind the wooden row houses, the whitewash that rubbed off on your hand like chalk, the barrel of kerosene heating oil in front, perched on four wooden legs—a horse I pretended to ride, kicking the barrel to move it faster, reprised in home movies. The kerosene heater inside, with its distinctive smell …

Except for the Charles White print, nothing else in the Lindners' apartment conjured those hardscrabble days. A polished wood-plank cocktail table, bookshelves and leather chairs … it was a comfortable setting. But the old black woman sparked a sense of kinship in me toward these upstairs neighbors with whom I'd never felt comfortable.

And then Noreen and I sat down to dinner, and as the four of us went at the spaghetti and meatballs, the circumstantial memory that predisposed me toward our hosts was soon dissipated by a relentless barrage of opinionation.

First it was Dick, then Judy, then Dick again. They took turns: the war in Vietnam, poverty, joblessness, racism, the plight of migrant workers ... I'd heard it all before, in fact did not disagree with any of it, shared the same conclusions and even the same outrage. But the predictability of it all, and the implicit expectation of agreement, soon made it hard to concentrate. How could I listen carefully, seriously, when a key word or phrase would telegraph what would inevitably come next? Before I knew it I'd eaten half a loaf of garlic bread, out of pent-up frustration.

For Noreen it was a different story. She'd been brought up in an archetypal American family; Mayflower descendants, my father-in-law liked to tell people, though impossibly at the same time swelling with pride over his German, landowning forebears; her mother a descendant of a Spokane timber baron. And Noreen the family misfit, given away at birth by a Montana schoolteacher, displaying an artistic inclination, breaking away during the generational upheaval, then coming to New York to live with me. Though essentially apolitical, she identified with left wing causes, because that was part of the outsider zeitgeist, and now she sat quietly amidst the staccato of opinion; immune to intellectualizing, yet seemingly smitten by the didactic pronouncements the Lindners specialized in.

Her misconception was still another reason for my annoyance at feeling put upon as a guest to be agreeable, while silently dissenting with the expectation that I had to agree with everything said. Ironic, that my take on it had more to do with Noreen's artistic freedom than she apparently understood. Following the party line—any party—can never lead to good art.

Not that I had to contribute much to the one-sided conversation as we ate. Our hosts didn't need my input, appeared to get along fine without me. A nod or a humming sound not unlike the noises I made out on the route to placate stray dogs was enough, as twined the spaghetti on my plate into yarn-sized balls and stuffed them into my pasta hole of a mouth.

At one of the Friday night get-togethers, Phil Lasker, amidst a political conversation, said to me, "We were formed by Marxist opinion," in a commiserating tone, as if confessing to a disability. "It was our weltanschauung." I knew what he meant, though it wasn't something I'd thought about: my reflexive dislike of the well-to-do and their attitudes, and my cringing reaction to the politically committed types I encountered, a supposed affinity group from which I recoiled, as I silently recoiled now, while restlessly stuffing my face.

But my surreptitious reaction wasn't as hidden as I'd thought, when Dick's recitation about something or other shifted, became even more persistent, as though in response to a recalcitrant vibration that belied the agreeable humming sounds intended to mask me from his radar. I'd been found out, which stirred my interest for the first time since we sat down: that he had an intuitive faculty, and that it could still operate while his mind was clogged with superficialities.

I was more fortunate than Dick, I supposed, or Judy. My own schooling in politics was salubrious, having less to do with beliefs than the communal aspects of my upbringing. As a child, I knew nothing about communism, but sensed the familial bonds of the trade union community to which my family and others belonged. The husbands— my father and his pals—worked in the garment shops; the wives played pinochle and mahjong; the children, like me, went to camp together and saw each other on long weekends at rooming houses in New England and upstate New York where fellow travelers without much money gathered. A familial reality in which I knew most of my parents' friends better than I knew my own uncles and aunts, and their children were closer to me than my cousins.

Later, as the sixties approached, when prospering families went in different directions—like everyone in America—and the workingman's circle dissipated, it seemed in retrospect that I'd had a taste of socialism in the unpretentious world of camaraderie … which was presented in college as something else, quite specific, derived from Marx and Hegel and a host of others we read about and whose names I mostly forgot, a catalogue of people, definitions, and ideas only vaguely related to what I'd experienced.

Now, as Dick talked at me and I played with the cold spaghetti in my plate, arranging it in designs, cutting the strands into smaller and smaller pieces, I almost sighed, or perhaps I actually did when he said, "The brothers have it together. They know we'll all have to get down and do it," as if he were exhorting the black workers on the docks to join the picket line when the strike that was always imminent finally occurred—the true believer's High Mass of longed for confrontation.

The flat inflection of his appropriated black vernacular jolted me, and without thinking I interrupted, saying, "It's not just an issue of workers and bosses in the post office. There's race too."

"Yes, of course there is," Judy put in, sounding relieved that I'd finally said something.

"I mean," I went on, "at Temescal—where I've been assigned recently—there's tension between black and white carriers, and between the assistant supervisor, who's white, and the supervisor, who's black—in addition to which she's a woman and he, of course, isn't. There's all kinds of things going on, not just class conflict."

"It's the fault of the carriers," Dick said, pushing back from the table with two hands, putting distance between us. "Your so-called union is more of a guild than a true workers' organization. It's elitist. When routes in a lily white neighborhood like Piedmont come up for bid, who gets them? You know as well as I do that it's the white carriers, because they were hired first and have more seniority. It plays the bosses' game, divides us from one another."

The bosses. My father's vocabulary, coming home from work, complaining about working conditions.

"But how is that the fault of the white carriers?" I asked. "I mean, they've been working longer, at an awful job. They *do* have seniority. So why wouldn't they bid on those cushy routes, which will make what time they have to put in easier? I've been at Piedmont. There are no welfare checks to deliver there, and no one, black or white, wants to deliver on Check Day."

After a few seconds Dick frowned. "It's not at all like that on the docks," he said. "Black and white, Oriental and Chicano, we're all together. There's no division. We know we have a common enemy. We know there's strength in unity. We know that if we don't stick together, the company will pick us off one at a time …"

A funny story occurred to me than, a bridge, it seemed, between politics and race; something that might leaven the atmosphere. Without thinking it through—though humor is always a tricky thing; you never know what someone will find funny—I said, "Do you know Rick, who moved into the shack in back?"

Dick stared at me without comprehension, at the quick shift.

Judy said, "Oh yes. He's living with Martha, isn't he?"

"Right. That's him. He told me a story about a friend of his who works on the loading docks up in Richmond, a white guy who was being ostracized by the guys he works with, who are all black. He worked alongside them every day, lifting and heaving the sixty-pound bags—you know what I mean, Dick—and the black guys never said a word to him, gave him the silent treatment. He assumed it was a matter of race, and it bothered him, so after work one day he asked a friend of his—a musician, who had black friends—what he might say to convince the guys he works with that though he's white, he's all right— that he wasn't a bad guy. And his friend told him that the next morning when he went to work, he should greet them with the expression, 'What it is, brothers?' You know it. I'm sure you hear it all the time: 'What it is.'

"So the guy went home and repeated it to himself: 'What it is, what it is.' He practiced different ways to say it. 'What *it* is, brothers? What it *is*, brothers?' And the following morning, after punching in, he walked down the loading dock toward the guys, who were pretending not to notice him, as usual, and when he got close enough and they finally looked at him, he blurted out, 'Hey, brothers, what is it?'"

The punch line hung over the table like a frozen word balloon. Now both Dick and Judy were staring at me, and I could imagine their own thought balloons: What's the joke? And: What's he getting at? And: Is he a racist?

"And of course that was it for him," I went on quickly, regretting that I'd emerged from my nods and humming sounds to tell a joke that might make a point. Why had I bothered? And then I added, "If they didn't have anything to do with him before, they certainly didn't now," also to no effect.

One afternoon in the mail truck I came across a mainstream progressive magazine, and while eating lunch read an article entitled, "Red Diaper Babies: Where Are They Now?" According to the piece, they were academics, lawyers, psychologists, white-collar professionals. Many of them were do-gooders, involved in social causes. I didn't recognize my own background at all. There was reference to the working class, but no blue collar workers.

I thought about that now. Dick's father had been a scientist and a college professor. He might even have been black-listed in the McCarthy era, when my father got rid of all the copies of *The New Masses* that I used to look at in the closet, in my hiding place behind the fall of coats, as any kid would look at comic books: the cartoon depictions of fat tuxedoed capitalists smoking cigars, resembling the caricature I would come across years later on a *Monopoly* board. And Judy's parents, who were part of Hollywood society and had to keep their heads down too.

We all emerged at the same historical time, if not the same socioeconomic place: fathers returning from war, mothers doing housework, an explosion of children. The fifties, an era when the desire for security shaped opinions. If you were a kid growing up in that atmosphere, revisiting it later in college, the oppressive conformity might have seemed a plot. But if so, what a fantastic counterplot it spawned, when the fearfulness of one generation begat the rebellious upheaval of another, during what we called, simply, the Sixties.

And in fact I could imagine the enthusiasm of my parents coming of age in their own era, with a notion of changing the world ... too soon undercut by the actualities of history and the need to earn a living. I'd been old enough back then to recall that we had things we'd never had before, and then to recognize that with prosperity—even distributed unfairly—the necessity of a workers' state became superfluous. The revolution was not supposed to be a utopia of the poor, after all. There were bigger apartments, helpful appliances, better cars, more leisure time. And so, like almost everyone else, my parents slipped away from the cause.

Yet Dick and Judy were proud, self-confessed communists. I found it bizarre. An anachronism. They spoke of equal distribution of wealth as if it had never been tried before and failed, albeit for reasons that excused the failure. With similar naiveté they believed that environmental degradation would end and all technology prove beneficial if only the means of production were shifted from the few to the many. They considered art—if not the creative urge itself—valid only in the service of politics, and had somehow managed to overlook the fact that young people like ourselves were now more concerned about gaining time—to write and paint, to travel, to do everything or nothing—than about seizing the means of production.

In the wake of my story, Dick had begun expostulating, and still was, ignoring Noreen altogether now, focusing solely on me, with an unexamined psychological desire to turn me to his way of thinking. And I was back to nodding, though not as often, and only to politely indicate that I was listening, though it was hard to concentrate, given his toneless cadence.

But I was thinking about the intellectual construct that underlay the subject that consumed him: the working class. And the circumstance that informed my own approach to the same subject: guys who worked with their hands, who labored for a paycheck and for the most part did not like what they were doing. For them, solidarity was a tangible thing, not a means to an end. It was a measure of self-worth to be part of a community, with its wives and children, summer camps and weekend getaways to rooming houses where we all ate at the same big table.

Judy, uneasy now with her husband's seemingly endless diathesis on the labor movement, eventually cut in and the talk turned small; a discussion between her and Noreen about art, of all things. And I got up and moved to their bookshelves to scan the titles there, mainly sociopolitical paperbacks that had been popular in the past decade. My eyes skimmed them as I sought something more evocative, trying to recapture that ambient moment when I walked in and saw the Charles White print; perhaps an out-of-date political novel, like those that still collected dust on my parents' shelves. I didn't find any.

Turning back to the table, where the dishes had been cleared and Judy set down a cake she'd baked and cups for coffee, I spotted the Black Panther newspaper on the cocktail table, and its blaring tabloid headline: **SEIZE THE TIME!** And briefly inspired by that sentiment, I had an urge to sit down again and tell Judy and Dick about my parents, about the rooming houses and the summer camps and all the rest ... to alter the present by conjoining it with that past, in order to bring about something that would connect us.

Instead, I settled for a piece of cake.

Delwood Ray

Delwood Ray, in training to become a post office supervisor, was shuttled from station to station. And as a full-time substitute carrier, dispatched to wherever I was needed or bureaucratic whim placed me, I occasionally ran into him. At Temescal, for instance, where he was working under the eye of Rose, the local supervisor, and Oswald Beamish, her resentful assistant. A few times, he'd assigned me to this or that route, looking as glum as if he'd have to carry the load himself.

"He'll never make it," one of the carriers confided to the aisle of casing workers. "He's not tough enough."

A brutal assessment that surprised me, since I assumed the black carriers would take pride in one of their own trying to work his way up. But then, the interracial subtleties eluded me: that this young, educated man did not speak or joke like his so-called brothers and sisters, and thus stood out almost as much as I did; except, where I might have been excused for being different, Delwood was summarily dismissed from further consideration.

It seemed cruel. But it's easy to romanticize an underclass, and in truth, a sophisticated psychology informed the black carriers at Temescal, who had a way of recognizing power relationships I'd begun to glimpse in the exclamatory put-downs, elevating one above another, often peppered with laughter and complaint to save face, or to preempt being cut to pieces by the more assertive among them. In which convoluted sense Delwood Ray might have been the only black man in Temescal Station who suffered because he wasn't white.

"Then how come he there and we be here?" another carrier replied, to the assertion that the supervisor-in-training wasn't tough enough for the job.

My fellow carriers eyed me, the white carrier, as I kept my eyes focused on the case, rendering myself invisible. After a moment conversation resumed as if I weren't there.

"I mean, he won't *keep* the job. You see what I'm saying? He don't have the stomach for it."

Even Rose, who liked and got along with everyone, was uncomfortable with the new trainee, calling him "Mister Ray," a formality at odds with her usual friendliness.

A few months later I ran into Delwood Ray again, at Civic Center. In his subdued way, he stood out, being too well dressed in a crisp suit and tie, which he never loosened. It was in his posture too, head tilted forward as though he were about to ask a question, his smooth, caramel face vaguely troubled.

When I checked in at the front desk, which he shared with several other supervisors and assistants, since three stations were housed there, he asked me in his soft voice, "What about taking Route 617, Mr. Weissman?" then regarded me for a moment, and absent an immediate response, quickly added, "Or Route 629 … ?" Again, when I didn't speak up instantly—having no idea what those particular numbers portended, except that they were in West Oakland—he cited another available route, with even more urgency, hoping I'd accept one of them and put him out of his misery. Then, before I could respond, he thrust his clipboard into my hands, as if to say, "Take it! I give up! Give yourself a route!"

Clearly, Delwood Ray was uncomfortable giving orders.

Every substitute, white or black, who lined up for assignments, underwent the same ordeal. His discomfort called for sympathy, which was disconcerting, since we were his underlings in the setup; an inequality, it seemed, that unnerved Delwood. I came to realize that it was what made him tick.

Benny Cadwaller, for example, was more than comfortable dispensing orders, and he expected them to be obeyed immediately. He doled out AWOL reprimands without hesitation, and would write you up for insubordination if you looked at him the wrong way.

At the multistation Civic Center, Benny was akin to a lieutenant in charge of several barracks, the other supervisors his sergeants, Delwood Ray merely a recruit from officers' candidate training school. I heard him tell Delwood, "You got to show 'em who's boss," holding a fist under the younger man's nose, gold gem rings on four fingers, gaudy showpieces. "Got to assert yourself!"

This was the Benny Cadwaller who wore an orange and fuchsia sport jacket to work each morning, or something similarly hideous, and whose conked hair formed deep waves on either side of his head, with a coxcomb pompadour on top. The Benny Cadwaller who clicked across the floor on three-inch platform shoes, summoned the other supervisors to the front desk one morning and led them out of the huge room as we labored under the deadline-prodding Big Clock. None of us knew they'd left the building until they returned and Benny, in his booming voice, shouted: "The danger is past! The bomb has been defused!"

Yet for some reason he took Delwood Ray under his wing.

What could Benny Cadwaller have had in common with the self-effacing trainee?

Maybe it had something to do with race, but then, that hadn't mattered to the carriers at Temescal, or if it did, only as a negative. Perhaps Benny wanted something less tangible from Delwood, who exuded an odd gentility; maybe to vicariously connect to his thoughtfulness an attendant air of respectability, in return for schooling Delwood in the ways of the post office world.

"Give orders firmly!" Cadwaller told him. "Never back down or show doubt. The minute they step out of line, write 'em up."

Delwood squirmed under this tutelage, cringed at the inevitable slap on the back that would follow. But Benny seemed oblivious to his pupil's reaction. Given his strutting, preening vanity, it might never have occurred to him that someone he'd chosen to befriend wouldn't feel privileged and grateful in response.

"Benny's much smarter than you think," Wayne Hooper, one of the subs, said when a bunch of us were putting him down one afternoon on the shore of Lake Merritt. It had been a light day, the routes easily delivered, our jeeps and trucks lining the curb. "Benny plays the clown, but he knows what they notice downtown—how much overtime gets handed out, and whether the checks get delivered. Benny knows how to take care of business."

In fact Benny Cadwaller was a terrible supervisor. When he sat at the front desk commanding, threatening, ridiculing any carrier who had the temerity to complain about being overworked, stacks of fourth-class mail—also known as junk—would proliferate beneath the metal cases, and in the rush to deliver ten hours of work in eight—because he never approved overtime—misdelivered mail would spawn a deluge of complaints ... which, of course, he blamed on the carriers.

"Me and Benny share an understanding," Hooper went on as we lounged by the lake, several of the young white guys passing a joint back and forth. "The checks are the only complaints that matter, man, because that's government mail."

And who could say he wasn't right? A whacked-out hippie type who looked like a dissipated Buffalo Bill, Hooper himself was an example. Like most subs, he usually worked a route for a day or two, then moved elsewhere, and being a fuck-up, he always left as much mail to the next guy as he could. Except recently Hooper had been assigned a route whose regular was on leave after a heart attack, and the undelivered mail beneath, around, and on top of his case had expanded like a wild fungus: misaddressed letters brought back to the station and never marked up; sloppy stacks of letters held together with rubber bands; magazines, flyers, catalogues, Mickey & Goofy fun kits all over the place. Benny Cadwaller would click down the aisle in the morning and pause at Hooper's case to tell him he was a disgrace, but never ordered him to clean up the mess.

And then, for some reason, probably an impending visit from postal inspectors to clock the routes and measure performance, Benny changed his mind one day, told Delwood Ray: "Get that route cleaned up."

Of course, as with any job, those in charge don't actually do the work. But Delwood was not the type to accept the managerial metaphor. He knew the difference between accomplishing a task and delegating responsibility, and when Hooper's shirker instinct led him to take off sick on the day of his route's reclamation, there I was, standing before Delwood in the morning, awaiting orders.

I think Delwood liked me, or maybe just respected me—which is good enough; all you can ask for at work—and his face underwent a transformation as I stood there, like Dr. Jekyll molting into Mr. Hyde. He arched his shoulders within the well-tailored suit, then gave me the assignment with uncharacteristic, edgy snappishness; as if, hemmed in by circumstance to demand results, he now reflexively blamed me for it before I could blame him.

I said, "I can't possibly get all that mail up and out today."

Delwood's no-nonsense facade faltered and he frowned, knowing that Benny Cadwaller rarely authorized help on a route assigned to a substitute. Nevertheless, he replied, "I'll get you help … two hours' worth …"

I shook my head, said, "It's still not possible."

"And as much overtime as you need," he added.

He was kneading his hands now, averting his glance, reverting back to his usual, uncomfortable self. I'd met touchy people before, and I always identified with those trying to do the right thing, so I wanted to make it easier for him. But my own version of the Golden Rule, "Do unto others as you'd have them do unto you," included the caveat: "And make sure they do unto you as you'd do unto them."

So I said, "I have a hard and fast personal rule, Delwood—I don't work more than ten hours a day, and even if I did, there's at least eight trays of mail under the case. There's no way I can clean it all up today."

He looked up at me and our eyes locked, a couple of pawns confronting each other. But on this game board, I had a worker's moral authority, and Delwood only had authority. He knew it, and his disinclination to pull rank forced him to back down. He sighed, looked away, said, "I know it's a rotten assignment ..."

Meanwhile, across the station floor, Benny Cadwaller turned away from a conversation with one of the other supervisors and peered in our direction.

Delwood was saying, almost plaintively, "You'll just have to do your best ... Maybe I can stretch it to two days and get you more help tomorrow," since we both knew that Wayne Hooper would take off sick the next day too, and by then Benny Cadwaller had clicked across the polished floor and come to a tapping halt behind me.

"What's going on here, Mr. Ray?" he said in a loud voice. "This carrier giving you trouble?"

Delwood seemed to contract within his stiff shirt collar like a turtle, unable to face me now that his role and the distance between us had been so severely defined. "No, no, everything's fine," he mumbled.

Cadwaller glared at me. "You have your assignment?" he demanded.

I glared back at him, spun around and walked silently away.

Behind me, I heard, "Be firm, Mr. Ray. Don't reason with them—command!"

Not for the first time, I cased the mail in anger, which built into a furious haze as I imagined Benny Cadwaller clicking up the aisle, stopping behind me, talking down to me, awaiting a military, subservient response as I launched my body around into an awesome cartoon punch, coming up under his jaw with a rocket-launch fist and sending him skyward, up and away in a twenty-foot arc, then down in a parabola and into a tub of mail. Or, with marginally more realism, my cartoon self sneaked down to the garage, heaved a brick through the windshield of his emerald green Cadillac, and disappeared before anyone knew I was there. Once, on a Check Day that overlapped with

Columbus Day advertising brochures that had to be delivered, and a sirocco blowing out of the Southwest, making everyone irritable, I'd asked Cadwaller for help and he refused, and I spent the entire morning seriously wondering where I could find a cinder block.

But Delwood Ray was made of better stuff, and soon enough he came quietly down the aisle and stopped at my assigned case; Hooper's putative route. "I've been thinking about this situation," he said as I continued to case. "Why don't you pull down today's mail when you finish casing, and I'll get other carriers to take it out. Then, you see, you can stay in the station all day and case the rest. You should be able to clean it all up then, don't you think?"

I eyed the clutter around me, spilling out beneath the case, teetering like a decaying ziggurat on the ledge above it, and said, "I guess so ..."

"That way, the route will be cleaned up after tomorrow's mail goes out." It was a statement, but made with the lilt of a question.

I nodded and grunted, since remaining in the station all day was hardly agreeable; the best part of the job was getting out on the street, away from the tediousness of casing and the scrutiny of supervisors. But it was a good solution to the problem; surprising as well, because I'd only had sympathy for Delwood Ray before, but no particular reason to believe he might be a competent administrator.

I pulled down with the other carriers, bundled Route 629 into five sections to be delivered by substitutes, took a coffee break as everyone else punched out and quit the station, then began casing again. By noon half the trays were cleaned up, mostly bills, magazines, and a few personal letters that were a quaint reminder of why a postal service had been established.

Meanwhile, I discovered that the supervisors had little or nothing to do when the carriers were gone. They ate lunch, took card-playing breaks in the swing room, and loitered up front with the window clerks, bored and perhaps embarrassed by their own idleness. I noticed, however, that Delwood Ray didn't mingle with the others or try to look officious. At lunchtime he left the station, alone, returning to the front desk to read a book and answer the telephone when it occasionally rang.

There were only two trays left to case when I came upon the first welfare check. I assumed it was a mark-up that Hooper had put aside, intending to get to it later and then forgotten—a state of mind I'd experienced myself while working amidst a maelstrom of undelivered mail. Though I'd spent much of the day mentally attacking him for being infuriatingly scattered and stupidly potheaded, it never occurred to me that Hooper was too walloped to even meet his own minimal standards of avoiding trouble, until I waded into the last tray.

There were dozens of welfare checks—rumpled, folded, mutilated—hidden within the rest of the undelivered mail.

How could it be that all the poor people they represented hadn't complained? Or maybe they had, and were dismissed as fakers, as poor people often are ... until someone with clout heard the complaints, which might have been why Benny Cadwaller ordered that the route be cleaned up.

But these questions and possibilities only occurred to me in passing. More immediately, I was outraged.

Delwood Ray stared at the green and brown windowed envelopes I'd dumped on the supervisor's desk. The affinity I felt toward him, based upon his discomfort at giving orders, led me to expect that his reaction would be identical to mine. But instead he was at a loss, his pupils flitting from envelope to envelope, which left me stranded in vengefulness toward Wayne Hooper, and what's more, feeling like an informer.

I said, to dispel this latter, undeserving thought, "The son of a bitch doesn't deserve any sympathy!"

Delwood looked at me without comprehension.

"Look at those postmarks!" I half shouted. "Those people must be desperate!" Your people, I thought, surprising myself.

He picked up a handful and read, "March ... April ... May ..."

"It's outrageous!"

Still he didn't react, except to thumb through the checks, as though he might find some sort of answer there.

What's wrong with this guy? I wondered. What was there to think about?

Finally, he said, "I'll take care of it," and turned away.

The checks went out the next morning; I know, because I delivered them.

I assumed something was said, the transgression reported. But a few days later Wayne Hooper, whom I thought had been fired, was back at work ... and Delwood Ray was gone.

I asked one of the more human supervisors where he'd been transferred, and was told he'd been fired. "Something about checks ..."

It didn't seem to bother Benny Cadwaller that his protégé was gone. He strutted around the station as pompously as ever. Why was that? Could he have used Delwood Ray to get himself off the hook for the chronically late checks? Was Benny cleverer than anyone realized, knowing that his naive apprentice would merely have them delivered and not tell anyone about it?

Or was the answer simpler?

That recognizing how sincerely he was disliked by the young man he'd attempted to befriend, Benny was glad to see him gone—had in fact engineered it—because Delwood Ray made him as uncomfortable as he made everyone else.

Spiritual Valley

Gary once told me there were special geomagnetic properties to east-west valleys, which were rare on the planet. I didn't like the notion that some places were more spiritually more propitious than others, but I had that in mind as I inhaled the luscious scent of flowers and glimpsed a mountain knob through a gap in the trees when I got out of the car; it arced like a Hokusai wave against the sky.

The antiegalitarian notion of a unique spiritual place lingered, appropriated my feeling of well-being when Gary met us at the door and welcomed us into the small house, though it flickered with doubt as he led us into a dimly lit room in sharp contrast to the salubrious scene outside. Slats of light filtered through blinds on the windows, the walls bare, the room containing only a sofa, a wing chair, and a long fabric-draped table. Then, when Noreen and I sat down on the couch and Gary took a cross-legged position on the floor, instead of taking the remaining chair, I knew something was out of whack. With the two of us looking down at him, it seemed we were supplicants to a guru.

Which was disturbing because I'd never seen him take on spiritual airs, or imagine that he would not have noticed the sense of imbalance in the room as he launched into talk.

His garrulousness was at least familiar as he launched into talk, telling us about Krishnamurti, who was in Ojai, staying in his house in the upper valley. For years he'd come there every spring, the same cottage with the tree in back, beneath which he'd had his well-known epiphany after his brother Nitya died, and afterward renounced the title of world teacher bestowed upon him by the Theosophical Society. In fact, Gary said, he'd met Krishnaji—as he called him—at a meeting to discuss the school people anticipated would eventually be established in Ojai, following similar principles to the Krishnamurti-inspired school in Brockwood Park, England.

While he spoke, a seam in the fabric draped over the table stirred and I caught a glimpse of a forehead and tiny hands, as his daughter, whom I'd never met, peered out at us.

Gary noticed too. Pausing, he turned toward the draped table and in a soft voice said, "These are the friends I told you about, honey … You can come out and meet them when you're ready," then turned back to explain that it was important to respect his daughter's independence, that he didn't want to unduly influence her, sentiments I recognized from the Krishnamurti dialogues I'd read and lectures he'd given.

The fabric fell back into place, then the seam opened again, wider this time, his curious daughter watching as her father went on to explain that he was hoping to enroll her in the Krishnamurti school when it was eventually established, and pay for her tuition by working as a carpenter or handyman.

The somber room, the one-sided conversation—a discourse, actually—with Gary cross-legged on the floor and the little girl watching us … It was hard to concentrate. After a while I broke in, saying, "You don't have much here, do you?" gesturing at the bare walls.

It seemed then that I'd been insulting. But Gary didn't take umbrage, hardly hesitated before replying, "Jill wanted to put up pictures here, as she has in her room, but I didn't want paintings, or television, or even a radio or record player, to be a distraction."

A spiritual decision. Our apartment in Berkeley was lush, compared to this one, with Noreen's paintings and photographs on the walls. But what was wrong with that? Was it a spiritual necessity that everyday life should be unameliorated by art?

Offering to show us Jillian's room, Gary led us down a short hallway, where he opened a door and moved aside as we peered in.

Framed reproductions of Renaissance paintings were on the walls; a cello propped in a corner, next to a music stand and sheet music. Madras fabric covered the mattress on the floor, and on a plank table next to it, a candle, an incense burner, and several paperback books; the teachings and lectures of Rajneesh, Maharishi, Chinmoy, Krishnamurti, and Vimala Thakar, which surprised me, since I didn't know that Jillian was interested in self-study or meditation.

When she showed up a few minutes later, I was relieved to see her, though we'd never gotten along, because her arrival drew us into the sun-bright kitchen. She set a bag of groceries on the counter before embracing Noreen, then cordially, if coolly, welcoming me.

I didn't actually set eyes on Gary's daughter until the four of us were sitting at the kitchen table, drinking tea, Jillian telling Noreen about the town, the mountains, the fresh air. The girl appeared in the doorway, eyeing us shyly. Jillian faltered, then fell silent as she moved into the room, to her father's side, and leaned against him, regarding us with wide eyes, a wave of flowing sandy hair on either side of her upturned face.

He gently cupped the back of her head with a hand, said, "This is Noreen, honey, and this is Peter …"

"And what's your name?" Noreen asked, leaning forward.

She'd stuck her thumb in her mouth and talked around it: "Grace."

Though she still clung to her father, she didn't appear frightened by strangers, continued to stare at us without flinching. Jillian, on the other hand, withdrew, her shoulders slumping, the exuberance that had characterized her only moments before gone.

It was unnerving. Looking away, out the window, at a slice of sky and the mountain knob visible above the café curtains, I said, "Why don't we take a walk while it's still light outside?"

"Oh yes!" Jillian exclaimed, perking up as quickly as she'd deflated. "Bring your camera, Norry. It's one of the most beautiful places you can imagine …"

As we left the house, she linked her arm with Noreen's, old friends catching up; Noreen tall, lithe; Jillian shorter, wiry; Gary's daughter running ahead of them, not shy at all now, ducking into bushes along the sidewalk, leaping out as the women approached and laughing at their feigned surprise. Gary and I ambled farther back, more relaxed now as he filled me in on what had happened to him since we'd seen each other last, in Berkeley.

That night, sitting on the brick steps, he'd said to me, "I'm not what you think. All this time you've known me, I've been living in pretense … supposedly on a quest for spiritual truth." He said this last disparagingly, mocking himself. "Far from being open to the world, and truthful to myself, I was a fraud, *avoiding* the truth, denying who I was."

It was an odd way to put it; as if he'd discovered he was his own worst enemy. "Who you are?" I said questioningly, and because listening to the confessions of others makes me nervous, I added, "And what do you mean, a fraud? That doesn't sound like you at all."

"What would you call a father who abandons his child and denies it?" he replied.

He went on to tell me that when he and his wife agreed to separate and he left Alaska, he'd felt liberated, with hardly a thought about Grace, who he left behind. She stayed with Suzanne, which they'd agreed upon—still further proof of how self-centered he was, how irresponsible his notion of freedom … until now, when he realized he couldn't truly be free if he didn't go back and retrieve his daughter.

"You think your wife is … what? Abusing her?" I'd asked as we sat on the steps.

"No, no, not at all," he said quickly, "at least not in the way people use that word. Most would consider Suzanne a good mother, because she plays with Grace, dresses her in ribbons and bows … but it made me cringe to see Grace dressed up like a little doll, posing in the mirror … Or I'd walk in after being out on the boat all day and see her staring at the television screen because Suzanne was tired and planted her in front of the set.

"That's where she was when I left, sitting on the floor, staring at the screen …" His voice turned sarcastic. "… while I set forth to pursue enlightenment."

He headed for Alaska the next day, to rescue her, and now as we walked down the street in Ojai, the women up ahead and Grace darting out of bushes, pretending she was a lion, he told me what happened when he went back.

His wife was glad to give Grace up. She told him she was tired of being a mother, didn't want to worry about a child … wanted to go out at night, to have some fun for a change. So he took Grace without an argument, hitchhiked south with her, taking his time, camping out along the way, getting to know her better, and she to know him as well.

"There are times," he told me now, with concern, "when Grace craves an audience."

I said, "I'm not a dramatic type myself, but there are people like that—who enjoy acting. Maybe Grace is one of them."

"That's what Jill says," he replied. "But I don't want Grace to think she always has to play a part. I told Jill how Suzanne dressed her up—because it amused her—and then one day I walked in when Grace was playing what she calls 'dress-up,' and I told Jill afterward not to encourage her to play make-believe games."

Jillian and Noreen rounded a corner up ahead and disappeared. Grace hung back and ducked into a store at the end of the block. It was a small health food supermarket, and when we entered, looking for her, she beckoned at us from the grain and cereal bins.

"Look, Papa!" she said. "*Granola!* The kind we like, with nuts and raisins!"

"We have some at home, honey," he told her.

"But not enough for so many persons!" she declared, regarding him out of wide, credulous eyes. "We need more, Papa!"

"Okay," he told her. "We'll get it on the way back."

And then we were walking again, Grace running ahead, turning the corner onto the main street, the picturesque town sheltered by mountains that imbued the scene with dimension.

*   *   *

The mood in the house was unsettled whenever the four of us were together. Only Grace seemed unaffected, drawing pictures, playing with her toys. Noreen and I slept in Gary's small bedroom, with only a rug and a mattress on the floor, but the vibes permeated there as well. He slept in the living room, his daughter in a sleeping bag under her table, Jillian in her own room. In the morning, after breakfast, Noreen and I would quickly leave.

Now, soon before we'd have to return to Berkeley, we came back to the house and walked in on Jillian at the kitchen table, reading a book. She splayed it on the tabletop, to keep her place, looked up and asked where we'd been as Noreen sat down to rewind the film she'd shot that afternoon. Without looking up, Noreen told her we'd gone to Santa Barbara, tersely answered a few more questions, and having stored her film in a canister, labeled it, loaded a new roll, and abruptly stood up.

"I have to catch the fading light," she said, and left me there, with this woman who didn't like me at all.

I like to travel, to see new places, and it seemed I should have enjoyed the university town on the coast, permeated by warm sunlight. Instead, the yellow haze was oppressive and I felt alienated as we walked the ghostlike streets of posh stores. Driving back through the hills, Noreen had been more talkative than usual, and that put me off too, as she went on about Jillian, how she hadn't changed at all; that when men tired of her, she gave them money, supported them, kept them captive, as if Gary, by implication, was her latest prisoner.

Now, in the kitchen after Noreen brusquely left, I felt sympathetic toward her old friend as she picked up the splayed book; ostensibly to continue reading, but more likely to put distance between us.

Breaking the silence, I asked her, "Where's Gary anyway?"

Jillian looked up, and as usual not at me, said, "He's with Grace," then eased her chair away from the table, as if to escape.

"Where do they go?" I asked.

She hesitated, settled back into the chair, but didn't respond for several seconds, until I thought she might not. "He takes her into the hills ..."

It was difficult to talk to Jillian, as tightly wound as she was. "You never go with them?" I finally managed.

She lifted one shoulder in a shrug. "He prefers to be alone with her."

I was still trying to ... do something. I wasn't sure what. Cheer her up? But what could I say that without touching upon the reality that things weren't right between them? "Yeah," I eventually said. "I've noticed ..."

In response, she stood up and moved out of the kitchen as abruptly as Noreen had.

I heard the door to her room close down the hall and imagined her in there, on the mattress covered with Indian fabric, Renaissance pictures on the wall, cello in a corner, alone in her sanctuary.

A while later I was in the living room, reading, when Gary returned with Grace. He glanced at Jillian's door, then said, "Here, honey," handing his daughter a fistful of rocks she'd gathered on their outing. She took them carefully in cupped hands beneath her fabric table house, where I heard her arranging them on the floor.

He sat down on the couch, propped an arm along the backrest, said, "Where did you two go today?"

"To Santa Barbara," I told him, "and on the way back, to that nature preserve you told me about, in the hills."

We'd parked the car alongside the road and hiked into the arid preserve. According to the map, it wasn't far from town, but it felt like wilderness. A hot breeze rustled through chaparral, sharpening my senses, accentuating an underlying silence as startling as Krishnamurti's discourse in the park that morning.

I mentioned the sense of profound emptiness I felt there, and Gary said, "I know that feeling … I take Grace there once a week, as a kind of cleansing—for both of us. To escape civilization."

"A sabbath of sorts."

He considered that a moment. "I never thought of it that way, but yes, I guess it's like that … or serves the same purpose."

I said, "The discourse in the park this morning affected me all day."

He nodded. "It did that for me too …"

At the smattering of applause as Krishnamurti walked onto the stage of the small amphitheater, he gestured in alarm, flapping a hand to dispel it. He was thin, wore gray pants and a plain white shirt, sat down in a straight-back chair and began as if picking up an ongoing conversation. Though he was an old man and appeared frail, he spoke with a clear, strong voice, in an English accent inflected with his native Indian dialect. And as he spoke, he stared straight ahead, body erect, hands flat on his thighs.

I'd heard him speak before, yet fell into an attentive trance as he reiterated his teaching: that we are what we think and feel; that to observe thought, and the emotions that bring thought to the surface and arise in response them, liberates the thinker from the thought, through awareness.

"It reminded me of what's important, again," I said. "Weeks or months go by, and I'm enveloped by … all kinds of crap. I get lost in the details, y'know, without being aware of it, living in a dream of sorts … and then, finally, I wake up, as I did this morning—from an extended interim of taking things for granted—as if from sleep, and sleepwalking, trite as that sounds."

"Not at all," Gary replied. "We fall into habit. It's hard not to … and we need a crisis of some kind, which throws everything into question and wakes us up."

"Funny you should mention that. There's a character in the book I've been working on who actually sought out crises for that reason—to stay alert. But I'd like to believe we can do that without the crises …"

"I'd like to believe it too," Gary said, "but everything significant I ever learned involved suffering."

*   *   *

The four of us ate dinner in the usual tense mood whenever Gary and Jillian were together. Through the open doorway, Grace lolled on the floor in the living room, flipping the pages of an art book Jillian had given her, talking to herself, making up stories about the reproductions. She'd eaten quickly and left the table, but returned to the kitchen every few minutes for something else; a vegetable stalk, a slice of tomato, a sip of juice from her glass, which sat on the edge of the table.

We were eating dessert when she came back again, for a bowl of fruit salad, and Jillian, suddenly ebullient, said to her, "Wouldn't it be great if we all went to visit the Thornhills?"

"Oh, yes!" the girl shouted.

"It will be such fun!"

"Yes yes yes!" Grace shouted. "Let's go visit them! Can we, Papa? Can we?"

Gary frowned, leaned back in his chair and crossed his arms on his chest. "Well, I don't know, honey—"

"Can we can we can we?"

"Well, all right," he agreed, and glanced at Jillian, who looked away.

She'd trapped him, and used his child to do it. I could imagine nothing worse. And yet, I felt sorry for Jillian, as I had that afternoon; the belief that the four of us going someplace together would make them an actual couple, instead of just two people sharing a house.

The Thornhills, an older couple in their seventies, were among the coterie of Krishnamurti followers who had moved to Ojai to be close to him during the weeks he resided there, and who followed him to his yearly discourses in London, New York, Madras, and Switzerland. They must have had money, yet lived simply, in an A-frame house that consisted of a large room with a kitchen alcove and a sleeping loft.

Plants were suspended from wooden beams, Navajo rugs covered portions of the wood-plank floor, and instead of chairs, Turkish pillows and cushions were arrayed around a glass-topped cocktail table set on a massive tree stump.

Gary reclined on the floor far enough from the rest of us to remove him from the conversation around the stump table, a spot from where he watched Grace crawl around the room, pretending to be a lion.

I envied him, since I had a hard time paying attention to the overly polite, soporific conversation. The tepid cautiousness of near whispered speech, the attitude of giving no offense—as if achieving innocuousness were a spiritual accomplishment—the pleasantries that parodied a supposedly enlightened state of mind … it reminded me of Jeremy, our backyard guru in Berkeley. I thought less of the old couple because of their harmlessness, a mean-spirited assessment that made me even more uncomfortable.

Turning away, I watched Grace playing her make-believe games. She'd been a lion, then spotting a dish towel in the kitchen alcove, decided to be a dog instead, on all fours, the towel in her mouth, shaking her head from side to side so it thrashed as she growled.

Leaning back, Gary had linked his hands behind his head and closed his eyes when a throw rug caught his daughter's attention. Dropping the towel, she retrieved the rug and swaddled herself in it like a full-length dress, then sashayed across the room, loudly announcing, "Look at me, everyone! I'm a *lady*!"

Behind me, the adults said encouraging things as Gary abruptly sat up. He watched her prance toward us, in her make-believe gown, and as she sashayed away, he launched himself at her, crawling on hands and knees, growling like the lion she'd been earlier. And then he was wrestling her to the floor as she giggled, and seconds later began crying.

Conversation abruptly ended as Gary pulled back from his daughter, as startled as everyone else. Then he knelt over her, gathered her into his arms and cradled her as she cried.

Ina Thornhill was the first to snap out of the startled silence. Snatching an orange from the fruit bowl on the low table, she crossed the room and offered it to Gary, to distract Grace with it. Stroking her cheek now, as she whimpered, he took the orange but didn't give it to Grace, held it in his hand as he lulled her with his voice until she fell asleep in his arms.

He stood up then, in the bristling silence, which felt like a condemnation, and still cradling his daughter, announced, "It's time we left," not loud enough to wake her, but forcefully, with barely restrained anger.

The house was perched on a bare hillside in the contours of the surrounding mountains, with no trees or foliage in sight. It seemed we were on the roof of the world, brilliant star clusters in the black sky as the Thornhills accompanied us down the gravel drive to Jillian's two-door sedan. We all stood back while Gary leaned into the backseat and carefully set his daughter down. Well-meant parting words said by the older couple were swallowed by the infinite sky above, and then we were in the car and Gary was lurching off, tires spitting gravel as he accelerated down the long driveway.

He drove in a fury, swooping into curves, headlight beams panning desert vegetation that loomed up suddenly and was gone as quickly. He drove even faster as we dropped down again, in the trough of a roller coaster, jouncing on rills and patches of pavement, the landscape a blur of shapes, pinpoint lights in the valley below winking in the opening between trees then rushing toward us as we straightened for a final run down to local streets, where we squealed and braked to a jarring halt.

When he turned the ignition off, the abrupt silence of the quiet street rushed in, which was no more than a grace note before he clambered out and waited impatiently for the rest of us. We scattered outside and backed away, as when he'd set Grace in the backseat up in hills. Still asleep, he lifted and carried her toward the house. Jillian opened the door and moved aside as he carried her inside. He walked through the kitchen to the living room, where he knelt down and gently placed her on the sleeping bag beneath the playhouse table.

Moments later when he strode into the kitchen, Noreen and Jillian were at the counter, preparing tea, staying out of his way, and I was at the table, trapped in one of those awful interludes when everything feels wrong and there's nothing you can do but wait it out.

Gary sat down at the table too, and after a long moment, Jillian broke the implacable silence, saying to Noreen, "Aren't the Thornhills nice people?" as if we'd just returned from an unremarkable outing.

"Nice?" Gary erupted. "Right now those 'nice' people are probably talking about you—about us—cutting us into little pieces! I've seen them do it!"

Who was he angry at? The old couple? Himself? Jillian?

The water in the teakettle began hissing, and Noreen took it off the burner.

Leaning against the counter, facing Gary, Jillian ducked her head and averted her eyes beneath his onslaught. In a near whisper she said, "I only meant they're nice to Grace … That's why she likes to visit them."

To my surprise, Gary's angry glare crumbled and he appeared confused.

"They *are* nice to her, don't you think?" Jillian said in a firmer tone.

"They give her things," he replied, "so she likes them. She's a little girl. She doesn't know better yet."

"What's wrong with giving her things?" Jillian asked, adamant now. "It's natural to give things to people you like, and it's natural for them to appreciate it."

I'd lost sight of the context, didn't know what she was referring to, thought about what Noreen had said about Jillian—that she purchased the attention of men.

Noreen set teacups on the table, Jillian retrieving tea bags from a cupboard, while everyone waited for Gary to respond to what seemed a challenge.

Oddly, now that his stoic detachment had been shattered, I felt better about him. He'd been aloof during most of our stay; not merely self-assured, but self-righteous. And having embarrassed himself at the Thornhills', then trying to outrace his behavior with the mad car dash down to the valley, he'd become a more human, more sympathetic.

"Generosity is natural," he finally said, in a reasonable voice, "but giving presents can be a habit, or worse. Ina Thornhill wanted to give Grace an orange to quiet her—"

"Or to make her feel good," Jillian interjected.

"It comes to the same thing," he said, "and I don't want Grace to think that crying will bring her a reward ..."

"It wasn't a 'reward,'" Jillian countered, angry now, which also made her more human. Usually, when something bothered her, she merely frowned, her lips tightening into a thin line as her disagreement simmered palpably.

"Then what do you call it," he asked, "if it's not a reward?"

"Why find motives where there aren't any?" she replied. "It was a gift, freely given."

Reconsiderations

The familiar hulk of Rocco Granelli filled the swivel chair when I made my way to the supervisors' desk up front. He leaned back with a creak, glanced up at me and said, "How you doin', kid? Glad to have you back."

Rocco was one of the few supervisors at Civic Center who seemed to genuinely like people; the only one who would have recognized my name on the duty roster and known I'd been gone for a week. Leaning against the flap-back chair, he ran a blunt finger down the array of assignment sheets spread on the surface of the massive desk until he found me there.

"Weissman, right?" He peered halfway over a shoulder, looked at me with half his face. "You're from New York, right?"

"Brooklyn," I said.

"Me, I grew up in Yonkers. Been out here twenty-five years."

"Since the war?"

"Right. I was stationed here and liked it so much I decided to stay."

"I've been out here about two years," I told him.

Rocco nodded, but his curly black-haired head was elsewhere now, back to business, leaning forward with another squeak of his chair, studying the columns of names and numbers illuminated by a fluorescent lamp at the gloomy command post separated by a wide, square column from the bustling mail room and its rows of metal cases. He read: "Route 722 ... lotsa hills. You'll need a jeep." And the conversation was over.

I'd been dismissed. A nice guy, but as detached as everyone else.

This is what the post office is like, I told myself, staring at the back of his thick neck for several seconds. My first day at work after a vacation whose affects lingered, the details and particularities of the place more apparent than when I'd left.

The Big Clock on another wide, square column, overlooking the cavernous room, was a pushy reminder of imminent deadlines: mail up by 8:15, second dispatch by 8:30, pick up accountable mail and pull down by 8:45, out on the route at nine. The schedule's demands were enough to instantly oppress me.

But to my surprise, the fact that everyone was in uniform, which always brought to mind the military regimen that permeated the place, didn't recur. It merely identified us as mailmen; to housewives who might otherwise be hesitant to open the door, to welfare recipients on the lookout for checks, to muggers likely to be dissuaded from messing with the U.S. government.

Then, at my assigned case, amidst the shuffle of letters and accompanying banter, the uniforms themselves were forgotten and the characters who wore them emerged like old memories. This one robust and loud, that one brusque and resentful, others joking, insulting, doddering toward retirement, or skittish as a young substitute working unfamiliar terrain, eyes skimming the case as if learning to read for the first time. And for a change another unexpected perception: I was calm, even as the deadlines invisibly approached; divorced from the movement of my own hands reacting to addresses, thinking for themselves, casing thirty letters or so per minute into five dozen cubbyholes whose numbers had become a nearly unnecessary reminder. It was a mechanical task I hated but that today only left me bored as the letters automatically flew here and there.

But it bothered me too, to feel so useless while engaged, and before I even left the station, I had a notion that would stay with me all day; like a tune some wise guy might whistle while casing, paradoxically sending a dozen carriers enhanced by a mechanical state of mind out into the world with an infernal melody dogging their footsteps.

The recurring notion was that if I wanted more out of life than this, I could quit.

Dull work divorced from any meaning beyond the utilitarian. A person can occupy a life that way, in order to collect a paycheck. And few would question it or think it odd. It's earning a living, after all; as if that's the point of life. The job itself: having one.

A prop, Colin Shay would have called it. He'd used the term in his drug poems as a synonym for blind habit, employing it over a range of things he considered addiction. And after loading the jeep and punching out, finding myself on the route, moving into the first loop, the reasons for doing a mindless job seemed props as well: not so much the money—though too much is made of that emblem for security—but the ethos that defined working as a necessity, without regard for what the job happened to be, how it influenced your mental state.

Hillside houses were nestled in well-pruned shrubbery, the thwarted trees resembling giant bonsai, as though this whole route neighborhood had been landscaped by expert Japanese gardeners. Residential streets curved and sloped, ran into each other at various oblique angles pleasing to the eye. The slate and shingle rooftops, balconies and bay windows, shapes, textures, and colors, afforded momentary respite to my trudging progress from box to box, the right hand opening metal flaps, the left one dropping letters in.

Later in the day, in the less aesthetically pleasing flatlands, watching my thoughts form and then dissipate in the crucible of observation—attuned since listening to Krishnamurti in Ojai—I walked from house to house, disbursing letters down one side of a street and up the other. It seemed I coasted over the ground, my feet ushering me from box to box, the air an ether of connectivity, the intense particularity of everything all at once flooding the senses. When people spoke to me, I answered directly and with a minimum of words; when growling dogs appeared, I'd long since sensed their presence and made adjustments. I felt as free as I'd ever been, but paradoxically, at the same time an automaton fulfilling his responsibilities.

But awareness is not automatic, not a permanent condition, and soon enough associative thought undid this ethereal perfection, positing questions that supposed a greater perfection: as in how I might earn a living some other way, so I could float without being tethered to mechanical labor-as if disinterested observation and work were opposites, one keeping me from the other, though I was in fact involved in both at the same time.

As a student—not of life, but of discrete academic subjects—I'd often felt the same way, that classes and homework kept me from other, more significant things. Expectation as subtext: the constant state of preparation for what would come next, when I graduated. This, before psychedelic drugs, accentuation of the senses, and an instantaneous existential state that for a while finessed the future by thrusting me into the moment.

And here I was again, years later, back in the grind, looking to the future for fulfillment. Except I was not quite the same person now. I knew for instance, that education had not contented me with the rewards society had to offer, with its steep price to pay to earn a so-called living. I was more serious now. I knew the stakes.

Why not quit? I asked myself. Why not live in a state of enlightenment and dispense altogether with the mechanical, which seemed a devil's deal struck in order to attain an illusory sense of security. I could be free, I thought, if I had more unfettered time. And so what if I didn't have a job? Whatever would happen, would happen anyway. If I'd understood nothing else after a year of losing myself in drugs, and in the aftermath of examining that dissolution, I'd at least learned that much.

I'd lost some acuity by then, out on the route, rampant cogitation exacting a toll. I was sleepwalking now, thinking about what I'd formerly seen, while believing my conclusions derived from direct observation.

I *would* quit, I asserted, and held onto that resolution, revisiting it as a mantra—an even rougher estimate of my former awareness; in fact not the same thing at all—meanwhile moving amidst the jeeps and trucks on the loading ramp in the lot behind the station, punching in with the others. It had been one of the lightest, easiest days in memory, but that didn't matter. The workload, the weather, the difficulty of the route, the variations that made a day more or less tolerable were beside the point.

Casing the afternoon dispatch for the following day's delivery, the hands again obeyed the rote brain with metronome efficiency, snapping each letter into its proper slot. That was the point: mechanical work as the enemy of absolute freedom; an old political construct.

Slinging the empty satchel over my shoulder, I punched out, but instead of leaving the station, walked toward the supervisors' desk, coming up behind the human boulder that was Rocco Granelli.

"Rocco," I said. "I quit."

I felt easy, relaxed, beyond all fear of consequence.

Had it been any other supervisor—Benny Cadwaller, for instance—I would have been told to toss the satchel into one of the canvas hampers and hand in my badge. Instead, the big galoot swiveled toward me and half shouted, "You can't do that!"

I took a startled step back, for a fleeting moment wondering if in fact I couldn't, then said, "Sure I can." It was my life, after all.

Rocco had risen half out of his squeaky chair at my pronouncement, and now his great bulk sank back down as he continued to look up at me in bewilderment. "Kid," he said, "you sure you know what you're doin'?"

"I've made up my mind," I replied, adamant.

He said, "You might be making a big mistake."

"I don't think so," I replied, but in the face of his certainty, less sure of myself.

"You got something else lined up?"

"You mean another job?"

He frowned at the question. Of course. Given the context, what else could he have meant?

"No," I said.

He didn't say anything for a moment, then asked, "So what're you gonna do?" with genuine concern.

I shrugged. "I don't know. I'll see."

Rocco stared at me for several seconds, his broad forehead lined as he tried to comprehend how a down-to-earth guy from New York had suddenly become a lunatic. "Listen," he finally said. "Whyn't you go home, take some time, think about it."

"I don't have to think about it," I told him. "I've made up my mind. I don't want to do this anymore."

"Tell you what," he said, leaning back, creaking in the chair. "Go home and sleep on it—" He held up a large hand to forestall interruption. "Go home and sleep on it—that's all I ask. If you still feel the same way tomorrow morning, I'll take your badge and satchel, do the paperwork, call downtown and tell 'em."

"I won't change my mind."

"Well okay, but do that for me, willya? Go home and sleep on it."

"Okay," I said.

Rocco was such a well-meaning guy, how could I refuse?

*   *   *

"Colin should be back soon," Maggie said as I sat down at the kitchen table. "Would you like tea?"

"Yeah, that would be good."

With feline grace she moved to the sink, ran water into the kettle, lit the stove, glanced over her shoulder to say, "I like the tea ceremony, don't you?"

"Sometimes after an acid trip," I replied, "I used to do it as a way to touch down, if you know what I mean."

"Yes, I do. And now?" she asked.

"Now, I guess I move too fast to take the time."

"But that's just it, Peter," she said, placing saucers and cups on the table. "The ceremony is intended to slow us down ... Lemon? Milk?"

"Uh ... lemon. And sugar."

She moved back to the counter, cut into a lemon, returned to put a slice on my saucer and one on hers, then sat down, her wide, kohl-rimmed eyes settling on me. "I see you're in uniform," she said. "Still a mailman."

Were it Colin saying "mailman," it would have been in a tone that attempted to hide and thus revealed his feelings. It was why I'd come after work to tell him decision—knowing he'd agree that it was the right thing to do. But Maggie said "mailman," with dramatic emphasis, as if it was a fascinating thing to be.

"I'm thinking of quitting," I told her.

She sat back, blinked surprise. "Why would you do that?"

"Well, mainly because the work's so mechanical, so deadening ..."

She nodded. "That's always the problem with a job, isn't it?"

"Yeah, and with this job in particular."

She said, "Did you know I'm waitressing four nights a week now?"

With her alabaster skin and fine features, Maggie appeared so fragile, it was hard to imagine her hefting trays. "Where?" I asked.

"A coffeehouse in North Beach ..."

"I like it over there."

She lifted one shoulder in a slight shrug. "It's almost exclusively tourists now. The bohemians are long gone."

"Oh ... that's too bad."

The kettle whistled, and she glided from the chair to the stove, bustled there awhile with the hot water, tea, and teapot, then brought the pot to the table and set it down for the tea to steep. Sitting again, she said, "So you've made up your mind?"

"I'm seriously thinking about it."

"Is Noreen working now?"

"No ..."

She regarded me for a long moment, then diverted her attention to the tea. She poured two cups, added milk to hers and stirred with a tiny teaspoon. "So what will you do to support yourselves?"

I spooned sugar in and whirled the liquid around. "I don't know yet."

"The ... mailpersons I see on the street—I believe that's the right term—they stop to chat every now and then, and they appear reasonably content, or at least as much as one might expect while at work ..."

"There're times it's all right," I said, "out on the route, sensing different realities. But in the station in the morning—"

"'Sensing different realities'?"

"Yeah. On the route, the world sometimes seems a place you're visiting ... the West Oakland flatlands, with its dilapidated houses and picket fences, with no sidewalks and unpaved streets that turn to mud after it rains ... or the white neighborhoods in the hills, with their gingerbread houses and neat landscaping. The industrial routes too, the warehouses down by the water, the vacant lots full of rubble, discarded tires, rusted appliances and the like ... for some reason that appeals to me-maybe the sense of ... desuetude I find there."

"You do occasionally encounter people, don't you?" she asked sardonically.

"Well, yeah, of course ... all kinds. The merchants on business strips, usually looking dour—solid citizens, or petty fascists, depending on my mood. And the simple people who've got nothing better to do than hang around, waiting to say hello, or on check days to pester me ... or those just looking for trouble, though for the most part they're just posturing ..."

Hearing myself, the job didn't sound so bad, which undercut my rationale for quitting. Shifting gears, I said, "But usually it's just drudgery, or I'm running around like a chicken without a head, trying to keep up with the deadlines. And then there's all the time I spend in the station every morning, casing mail, day in and day out, and worst of all after a long weekend, which is a choke point, because the flow of mail never ends, it just keeps coming."

"But you're off in the afternoon, aren't you?"

"Well, yeah, but—"

"So you have time to recover, and do other things."

"You'd think so, but with the demands of the job, when I get off, I'm beat."

I picked up my teacup and sipped gingerly. Maggie sipped too, returning her cup to its saucer with a civilized click, her movements delicate, precise. But for all that, a tough cookie. She had me on the ropes and had hardly thrown a punch. "By 'do other things,'" she said, "I assume you mean your writing."

"Well yeah," I said, "that's just it," though in fact I hadn't given writing much thought while ruminating about quitting, and only considered bringing it up when I decided to visit Colin, whose opinion on the subject I already knew. "When I get home, like I said, I'm exhausted. I don't have the energy to do anything."

"Oh, come on, Peter. You're wearing your mailman clothes now, so you must have worked today."

"Yeah …"

"And you seem energetic enough, even if you aren't making much sense."

"What'd you mean?"

"I don't understand why you can't do both—work *and* write? Of course, I don't work full-time like you, but I'm often tired too, and I wouldn't dream of giving up poetry. I couldn't even if I wanted to. So I create a space, go off by myself—"

"Maggie, when I first started at the post office, I'd get home and sit down every day after work and try to work on my book, and I never got anywhere, because I was too tired or my brain was too wired—maybe too stimulated after delivering mail all day, even though I was physically wiped out. I'd sit there with pen and paper and try to go back and remember how it was—the drug days, y'know, the book I'm working on—and I just couldn't get to a place where I could evoke the people, the sense of place, the—"

"Then why not put it aside for now and write about being a mailman? You won't be a mailman forever, right? You can get back to your drug days another time ... Why not describe the different realities, the landscaped neighborhoods and unpaved streets, the industrial scenes, the tediousness of the morning routine, the afternoon exhaustion ..."

Her suggestion made sense, actually gave me hope. But I said, anyway, "That still doesn't solve the problem of how enervated I feel after work, to the point where I can't do anything on my day off but lay around." My voice, I noticed, had a plaintive edge, like a child aware of losing an argument and grasping for sympathy.

She arched a thin eyebrow. "Peter, you're the most energetic person I know. Cole describes you—not without reason—as 'buoyant.'"

"Really?"

"Yes, really. You're a fire sign, aren't you?"

I grinned. "Yeah, and after a day of casing and delivering mail, I'm burned out."

"Oh, come on. If you truly wanted to write—like today, for instance—you could do it, couldn't you?"

"Yeah, I guess so," I replied grudgingly.

"Then why do you have to quit?"

"Well ... you're saying I'm not disciplined enough."

"That's not the kind of thing I would ever say, to anyone."

"But it's what you mean."

She lifted a shoulder in another gentle shrug. "We all have our own obstacles to deal with."

"Well, yeah ... of course that's true."

"I'm sure," she said, "that you'll do what makes sense for you ..."

When I left, Colin still hadn't shown up.

Racetrack Meditation

On Check Day, after delivering the ghetto routes, I'd drive the half-ton truck away from those streets, looking for a deserted spot where I wouldn't be bothered while eating lunch. Beneath a leafy tree would have been nice, but finding one in the flatlands wasn't easy, so I'd usually settle for a slant of shade cast by a warehouse near the docks, eat my sandwich in the truck, and peruse the bulk mail left in the tray, mainly the distinctive fund-raising appeals from Reverend Ike and his ilk: "Sleep with this piece of prayer shawl and cure hives, blisters, warts, and otherwise blemished skin." From Reverend Broom, Palace of the Swept Clean, Odessa, Texas; and Pastor Love, Oklahoma City Chapel of Hope; and Giddings Birdsong, Locator, Healer, Fortune Teller: "Place this piece of blessed cloth under your pillow, sleep on your faith, and your loved one will surely stop drinking, whoring, philandering, stealing … Bind this bracelet to your wrist and ward off arthritis, rheumatism, and impure thoughts …"

With well-planned precision, these inducements to God always arrived on the same day as the checks: "Don't waste that money on drugs and demon liquor; send it here!" And having purposely put those bundles aside, I would later sneak them into my car, take them home, and, no matter how hot it was, burn them in the fireplace, which otherwise went unused. It hardly made the job tolerable, but at least, once a month, I felt socially redeemed.

Yet I had something in common with the flock I rescued from charlatan appeals, for I was looking for answers too. It had gotten to the point that I'd become my own holy roller, believing that horses, of all things, might rescue me from the job I hated. Like many of my carrier colleagues, I'd rush to the track to catch the last three races after work—admission free, courtesy of the racetrack management—the blue-gray uniforms entitling us to special respect. Only this was my day off, and here I was again, bent on outwitting the hoi polloi, the other pie-in-the-sky plungers (whose checks I might have saved from Reverend Ike), to turn gambling into a sure thing, make a bundle, and not have to work like a draft horse anymore.

In truth, my detour to the track only made my life less profitable. After losing a modest sum—for in truth I was more cautious than the typical full-fledged gambler—I'd finger the anonymous bills left in my pocket when I got home, loath to take them out and look at the revealing denominations. Knowing I'd lost, again, I wanted to believe I'd done no worse than breaking even. And when I eventually did take out the singles and fives, which had been tens and twenties when I left work, I'd crumple the bills beyond easy recognition while tossing them on the dresser, then quickly turn away to do more significant things, the specifics of which eluded me in retrospect.

Thus, out of desire and self-delusion, did my racetrack meditations begin.

That, and the benign astrological aspect of planets that happened to bring me a downtown route one day and a bookstore bin where I came upon an esoteric work, a primer titled *How to Win at the Track.* Curious, I purchased it, and that night encountered the following in the very first chapter:

Count your money before you get to the track and again when you leave. Don't shove those crinkled bills into a drawer. Spread them out on the bureau and take a good look. Face facts.

Imagine my amazement. A spiritual guide written, published, and discarded in a bin—three for a buck—with me in mind. It seemed divine intervention.

Following its counsel, I faced up to what I'd secretly known all along, and thus attracted further truths I'd avoided: that I wasn't superior to the racetrack bunglers I'd thought to outwit. My losses, clearly seen, told me I was as benighted as everyone else.

Thus humbled, I found myself capable of picking an occasional winner.

I don't recall the name of that first winning horse, perhaps because it instantly became the vehicle to a greater reward, having kept me alive in the daily double. But I recall the second winner, *Bold Venture,* thundering down the homestretch, fairly flying like Pegasus over the dirt track, leaving the field farther behind with each enormous stride, crossing the finish line a good five lengths in front, securing a $67.60 double.

If before I'd been lost, wandering the track after work, ineffectual, overwhelmed by the certainties of bettors I overheard citing pedigree and weight, jockey and distance; unable to locate an internal logic of my own, betting wildly with the odds or against them, resorting to astrology and omen, at one point finding myself scouring the cement infield for impossible, discarded winning tickets, like the lowest of the low in the racetrack pecking order, now that I actually calculated the results when I got home, I held a valid claim to win. And even when I lost, felt bigger, if not better.

Having thus done the prep work of accepting monetary reality for what is was, I embarked on a deeper, meditative path: to observe myself while handicapping the horses; in order to make money, of course, while at the same time achieving spiritual transcendence.

If you find equating gambling with self-knowledge sacrilegious, what can I say? God is everywhere; in location, method, and revelation. On a picturesque ocean shoreline, in the recesses of a pristine forest, even in a traffic jam on the freeway. (Pastor Love used a version of this line of thinking before trotting out his list of miraculous cures.) You can stare at a spot on a wall to lose your identity; visualize a topaz sky overlooking pastoral green meadows to affect a mood, while breathing deeply; chant a Sanskrit phrase until your head swims in similitude of what some consider transcendence. Or meld your mind with appearance, situation, and circumstance, and abstract the numerical properties of an animal in confronting the Golgotha that is the fifth race.

Why the fifth? Because puffy clouds mass in the pale sky over the Berkeley Hills in the distance, and it seems that a palpable penates of the track hovers nearby, perhaps in response to my modest success so far. Which is to say that at the moment, I'm breaking even, coasting on the ebb and flow of things, feeling optimistic but not euphoric. I'm in balance.

And why not the fifth? One race is pretty much like any other, when you get right down to it.

Ten horses are listed: one out of competition too long, two slated to run an unfamiliar distance, three hopelessly beaten their last few times out, four that can conceivably win today. I've come to this conclusion after studying past performances in the *Racing Form,* applying certain mathematical principles from *How to Win at the Track,* and weighing these facts, figures, and a set of assumptions with the arbiter of common sense, which bears careful scrutiny, lest it mislead with extraneous influences.

A few grandstand seats away, a disheveled character seemingly roughed up by fate sits with a pink tout sheet in hand. Seeing me glance at him, he grins, revealing discolored teeth, and says, "The four horse is the class of this race, right?" while gesturing at the dirt oval.

A question hidden in an assertion. A wishful statement seeking confirmation.

The usual crushing feeling of inadequacy in proximity to craven neediness courses through me. What can I say to alleviate his suffering? I don't know which horse will win this race … though I now suspect that the four horse won't.

I look at my *Racing Form,* notice that it's among my four possibilities, and boldly delete it.

Which leaves three horses. Two are front-runners, and one prefers to storm from well off the pace with the kind of finishing kick that brings the crowd—and me—to its feet in a screaming pitch.

And therein lies what seems my greatest meditative obstacle in this race: the clash between cool, unsentimental analysis, which doesn't bog down in style configurations; and personal inclination, which does.

It's difficult to see the indiscriminate nature of our personal affections. Books, movies, and music that make an impression; familiar language and mannerism; particular people, places, and recollected ambience that render certain moments memorable, and then influential; habits, predilections, convictions, opinions. Were I as indifferent to the past as the unlikely buddha who'd come to a racetrack on his day off to parlay enlightenment with a modest bet, I would have no such attachments. Indeed, I try to be this blank slate, and at times even succeed. But more often nostalgia and sentiment color my thoughts, and all I can do to prevent them from attaching me to a Rorschach horse is observe the cloying influences, in order to set them firmly aside.

So now I study my three possible winners, and focusing first on the one I know I'd like to see win, disclaim personal interest in *Attachment,* the horse who comes from behind. Is this ostentatious disclaimer a trick of the mind, a pirouette around the long held belief that my intelligence and abilities were for so long misunderstood? And is the rejection thus as much of an attachment as embracing the animal would be? That is, has it led me to oppose a horse out of the same biases that attract me to it? Have I actually disengaged, seen this horse (and myself) for what it is, or through overcompensation short-shrifted the animal?

I'm not sure …

Stick to facts, I tell myself, while noting the colt's unimpressive pedigree—its mother an honest slogger, its father a hardworking claimer—and trying not to commiserate with its prodigal history: it won its first race eight months ago, after dropping into low claiming company following several dismal performances (not unlike me in junior high school), then showed flashes of brilliance, hit the board in a couple of races and climbed into somewhat respectable company, where it finds itself today.

This *Attachment* intrigues me; I can't deny it. But I also know that were I to bet it over a more likely winner, and were he to lose, my choice would taunt me afterward, and might even prove they were right to drop me into my own lowly company in the middle school cauldron of assessment.

It's a roundelay of attraction and repulsion that leads nowhere ... and squanders energy. Yes, it helps to remember that. We are what we eat—a hot dog at the track always leaves me dull, with a nitrate hangover, and not thinking clearly—but we're also the disbursement of our thoughts, which, overdone, can induce dullness as well. And from this realization—about the need to husband my energy—comes the sword-stroke question that cuts through subjective confusion: Can this *Attachment* kick hard enough in the final furlong to pass the front-runners and win the race? That's the point here, after all, since I'm looking to make a few bucks.

I stare at the mass of notations I've made on the newsprint page. The answer is as obvious as it ever gets: No.

Well, I think, probably not, and decide to more closely examine the other two before reconsidering this one I am all but certain will not win.

The pace-setting horses are a toss-up, so far as I can see. One likes to lead the field, the other to stalk the leader, and there's nothing significant to separate them ... until, looking up at the animals that have been led onto the oval by their jockeys, I see the stalker prance on its toes, head high, ears perked ... and looking directly at me, which triggers a primitive connection. With the harmonic fluidity of elements I like to think are parts of a whole, his name jumps off the page when I glance down: *Imtheone.*

Undoubtedly. With sudden, absolute assurance, I cross off the other front-runner, *Candoo*; no, not today you can't. I have my horse.

(Note, however, that I have not yet boldly slashed the come-from-behind *Attachment* from the page with similar certainty.)

Out of habit, I continue to handicap for a while, calculating, making notes, factoring in the imponderables of track condition and jockey; double-checking. And meanwhile another factor enters, which shouldn't matter now that I have my choice, but in fact does: Time. There is always too much or too little of it.

I first came upon this inexorable reality after the initial charm of the track dissipated, in concurrence with my losses. It was a period during which I could find nothing attractive about the place, and wondered how I ever had. Between the high rollers who arrived at the clubhouse entrance in limousines, and the more obviously depraved losers who rooted about the littered infield after the last race, looking for redeemable tickets; between such equally meaningless extremes and the dungeon innards of the grandstand, where feverish last minute calculation and unwarranted hopefulness fermented before each race— it seemed something spiritual had to be at play. For God was supposed to be everywhere, even a place as awful as this.

I realized then, as I pondered the figures in the *Racing Form*, the track condition, jockeys, trainers, odds, and all the rest, that it was impossible to gather every last, conclusive bit of information before making a choice. There wasn't enough *time*. A corollary presented itself, a back door to the spirituality I was seeking: to grasp the essentials in time to act, all distraction in the twenty or so minutes between each race had to be eliminated, or at least ignored. One had to suspend time as long as possible, had to be in the moment, every moment; a paradoxical eternity, existing in Time as if timeless, before sidling up to the betting window to cash in, so to speak, on the fruits of this meditation.

And now this invisible colossus was there with me as I stood on line beneath the grandstand, waiting to place my bet. Time. It was silent at the moment, but right there, beside me. Keep it in mind.

A tote board suspended from the high ceiling is visible from every spot in the concrete interior. There are totes, in fact, throughout the track, winking and flirting with the would-be-wise bettor; every bet relayed to a central computer and fed back to the crowd; a state-of-the-art polling operation, never more than two minutes out of sync, reflecting the perfect democracy, making this one 5–2, that one 8–1, as bettors vote with their money. Exact opinion results on every horse; yet one is prone to believe more, because we live in essential uncertainty, and when enough people express an opinion, the average, totemic, all-too-human individual posits a false god of cumulative prediction. That's why Kierkegaard railed against public opinion, believing we'd all be better off not knowing what everyone thinks they believe. Yet, as one among the all-too-human, I was capable of being influenced by the tote as well, even now, with my carefully chosen fifth-race horse.

There's too much time, you see. I should have eschewed my habitual double-checking after reaching a conclusion and gone to the betting window right away.

Beneath the grandstand, waiting on line, bills clutched in my hand, I peruse the odds on one of the ubiquitous tote boards … and see that *Imtheone* is 4–1, a respectable price, and *Attachment* 7–1, a longer shot—as it should be, I remind myself. Curious (while killing time), I check the *Form* again, review my scrawled calculations, stare fixedly at the stats for *Imtheone* in order to recapture that moment of absolute clarity in which I'd made my choice. Of course no bells ring this time. They only ring once; after that you're on your own.

Time is beginning to undo me. Things are not as clear as they once were.

Someone in the next line over says to someone else: "The price is kinda high on this one that comes off the pace. He gets a good start, maybe he can do it …"

A detail I've long since considered, reconsidered, and rejected. The come-from-behind horse *never* gets a good start; that's why he has to come from behind. But now, as the line creeps toward the window, too slowly, I wonder if perhaps this time he might finally get a decent start, and whether I might not have rejected the come-from-behind horse too quickly. Did I underestimate him by overreacting to my innate bias in his favor? The thought had occurred to me earlier …

Again I check the *Form,* with prissy care (which is not like me at all), as if nothing I concluded before can be trusted. But in truth I'm being *less* careful now, inhibiting the usual, discursive way I operate in order to examine minutiae with the concentration of a scholar, which I never was, even when I wanted to be. And a bad scholar at that, seeking his preconceptions in the text. And *still* I can't find the pilpul in my talmudic analysis to justify switching from my rational choice to my sentimental one.

Close to the window now, I notice through the smoky gloom that *Imtheone* is down to 3–1, *Attachment* up to 8–1, a set of figures I can't shrug off in my time-weakened state. I'm losing it; no question.

To hold back the chaos of Doubt, and the seduction of his cousin, Expectation, my old hippie self falls back on magical thinking; legacy of the dark days when I was consumed by wishfulness. In present circumstances it takes the form of gematria, the kabbalistic numerology of the Middle Ages, which I've read a bit about, which inform me that a winning ten-dollar bet on my rational choice, *Imtheone,* at 3–1, will put me forty bucks ahead, and, with four races left in the day, guarantee that I'll break even.

On the other hand, a win on *Attachment,* at 8–1, will put me up ninety bucks and guarantee that I'll leave the track with at least fifty dollars in my pocket, no matter what happens in the remaining races.

Yet even as the greater payoff entices me, my recent calculations that a bet guaranteeing break-even accord with the proper tao for this midpoint race: that the race upon which my karmic day hinges should have no gain-loss result better than, more perfect than, zero.

This hippie gibberish comforts me somewhat, ameliorates me to a choice I made for a much better reason long ago. With one bettor now between me and the window, I've managed to steel myself against the come-from-behind prodigal colt, the novelist who begins writing late in life and breaks through nonetheless, the artist who works as a bank teller and becomes Gauguin. I've gotten myself to the point of making the right bet; to pick the actual, present-day winner. Once more I'm sure of it.

And then I'm at the window, staring at a clerk behind scuffed plexiglass. His nose is bulbous and red; no doubt from ruptured, alcoholic capillaries. I know guys like him in the post office—they develop deadline ulcers, drink too much, too often get heart attacks. This clerk's face is fleshy, gray, stubbled, with tired eyes. The unlit stump of a cigar protrudes from the side of his mouth, the continual demands of the job keeping his hands too busy to relight it.

In an instant every obstacle I've encountered up till now was nothing compared to this guy's sorry, overworked puss. And from far away I hear a hopeful voice intoning the logic of the long shot. It's the voice of a congregant of the Reverend Broom, who would sweep us clean; of a time-clock worker who hates his job.

It's my voice, and it's saying: "Ten to win on *Attachment*."

Entrepreneur

It was hard to keep track with the people in the brown-shingled house on Benvenue and the renovated garage in back. Noreen and I had hardly been there a year and already were among the oldest tenants. Coming home from work one afternoon, I came upon a new neighbor by the mail trough outside. He was short and muscular, like a weight-lifter, with close-cropped dark hair and a toothy smile.

"Buddy," he said affably, thrusting a hand at me.

"Peter," I replied, and held on as he pumped.

Cued by my uniform, Buddy asked how I felt about working at the post office, and as if he'd opened a spigot, my grievances, always close to the surface, poured out: stumbling out of bed before dawn, the drudgery of casing the mail, the daily abuse from foremen and supervisors—and the so-called patrons too, on Check Day, waiting on street corners for me to show up, late, as usual. My usual litany of complaints. But Buddy was a good listener, nodded along without comment as I went on and on. When I finally paused and he invited me to his pad for a beer, his receptivity had put me in his debt; I could hardly refuse.

It was a studio apartment on the ground floor, overlooking the concrete backyard ending at the former garage, now a two-room pad with tie-dyed curtains in the solitary window. His room was no less spare than the view, with a mattress on the floor, which Buddy gestured me to take, as if I were an honored guest. He pried two cans of beer from a six-pack in an otherwise empty minifridge beneath a counter and handed me one before seating himself cross-legged on the floor, a few feet away.

I noticed a telephone on the bare kitchen counter, a pen and pad, and on one wall, a poster of skiers shushing down an alpine slope, the only decorative touch in the studio. It was a warm day, in a place where it never snowed, and Buddy wore Bermuda shorts, a bodybuilder T-shirt, and flip-flops, the winter scene incongruent. All of which made it difficult to concentrate while this stranger spoke to me like we'd known each other forever.

I made listening noises at appropriate moments, when his voice dropped or slowed, and then he paused and looked at me with tilted head, expecting a response of some kind. Retrieving the last thing he said, I replied, "Yes ... people who value their independence ... I agree."

He stared at me a moment, as though digesting my response, then nodded and went on: "Just what I was saying. Your own business, that's the way to go. Working for yourself. What could be better?"

"That makes sense," I said, though the idea of owning a business was alien to me. What was I talking about? What was I doing here?

"In fact, I've been looking into a promising opportunity ..."

Finally, I recognized the cadence of a sales pitch, which threw me as much as the alpine poster. Not that people hadn't tried to sell me ideas before, but usually they were notions I'd pretty much sold myself in advance. This was different; Buddy was trying to sell me something that had never occurred to me ... though now that I retraced what he'd said, I saw the connection to my blurted post office grievances out by the mail trough; he assumed I was a disgruntled worker, which was indeed the case.

"What kind of business do you have in mind?" I asked him.

Buddy sat up straighter and wagged his beer can at me, his way of asking if I wanted another one. I'd only taken a sip from my can, and told him no, but took another sip, to demonstrate there was more left. He nodded, sat back and went on to describe what he had in mind: a pizzeria on Telegraph, a few blocks from the campus, and how his notion had come about.

"It would be a gold mine," he concluded.

I might have been tired, and more prone than usual to latch onto whatever entered my head. That was known to happen to me after a long day at work. Now, listening to him talk about a restaurant, my mind wandered back to Brooklyn, sitting in a chair overlooking the brownstone street, rain coming down in thin sheets as I read *Sexus,* or maybe it was *Nexus,* or *Plexus.* And breaking in, I told him about the restaurant Henry and his girlfriend opened in Manhattan.

This associative tangent brought Buddy up short. He'd been describing the layout, the pizza ovens, the tables, when I interrupted. He smiled apologetically, said, "I don't read much …"

"Well, it was a hole-in-the-wall. They invited all their friends to come, and told them to bring *their* friends. They only served one or two dishes a night, but always something special—lobster or paella—and hors d'oeuvres—caviar, pâté—expensive stuff for rich people, friends-of-the-arts types, who showed up in limousines and essentially paid the rent—and champagne, of course … and after a while everyone knew everyone else, because they ate together at long tables, family style, and had heavy philosophical conversations that went on and on and lasted until dawn …"

Buddy, propped on an elbow, set his beer can on the floor. "A place like that," he said in a serious tone, "without much turnover, wouldn't make it here."

Well, of course not. Still, I felt deflated, having all but convinced myself to open a restaurant just like the one in the book. "Well, maybe a coffeehouse, then," I said, still thinking about Miller's hole-in-the-wall.

"You mean cappuccino, espresso, like that?"

"Yeah. Something bohemian."

He shook his head. "You'd never make enough to cover the overhead. A pizzeria is a high turnover business. People sitting at tables, lingering over coffee and pastries—there's no profit in that."

Abruptly, he got up, went to the fridge, tore another can from the six-pack receptacle, brought it back to his spot and popped the tab.

Abashed, I said, "Of course, I don't have your experience running a business," taken by his casual use of *turnover* and *overhead.* "Or any experience, actually. The truth is, I've never even met anyone who ran a business."

Buddy took a swig from his can, set it on the floor and looked at me for several seconds. "Tell me something, Pete …"

Except for my mother, no one had called me that since I'd been in college. It left me feeling younger, and as naive as I'd once been. "Okay," I replied.

"You like Sicilian pizza … the kind with thick crust?"

"You know how to make them?" I asked, impressed.

"Or my name isn't Buddy Cappallano!" he replied with a grin.

"You're Italian?"

"Sure, what else?"

"Where're you from?"

"San Diego," he replied.

San Diego? I didn't know they had Italians in San Diego.

"Believe me," he went on, "you can't get that kind of pizza on Telegraph Avenue. The college kids'll love it! And the smart businessmen who tap into that market will make a killing. High volume, quick turnover—we'd break even in two months, three at the most. After that, it'd be nothing but profit."

Suddenly it seemed I'd gone too far, that I'd led him on. "Well, I don't know, Buddy, I've gotta tell you, I wasn't really thinking about opening a pizzeria—"

"You hate your job, don't you?"

"Well, yeah …"

"That's why I brought the subject up in the first place."

"Well, yeah, I see that."

"So why not at least consider it? It would get you out of a bad situation and into something much better, where you'd be your own boss."

"Well, there's something else, of course … I'm not sure I can afford it."

He finished the beer, plunked his can back on the floor, regarded me questioningly. "How much you think you could scrape up?"

I had some savings, money I'd put aside while working for the post office, but it seemed too small a sum to even mention.

"We might need less than you think," he said, as if following my thoughts, then got up, retrieved the pen and pad on the kitchen counter, next to the phone, sat back down and began to make notations as he jotted, saying, "First, rent, probably three months in advance … Then utilities, water and electric—a fair amount, what with the big oven— that'd be equipment … And then there's supplies, of course, dough, tomato sauce, cheese … and syrup for the soda machine." He looked up. "Did you know it costs about a penny—one cent, maybe less—to make one glass of soda pop? We charge fifty cents. That's five thousand percent profit!"

He looked back down at the pad, tapped the pen against his chin. "Okay, what else? … Advertising," he said, and wrote that down too, then did some calculations and looked up again. "I'd say five grand to open the doors, and another grand for odds and ends."

"That much, huh?"

"Three thousand each."

Three thousand? Where could I possibly come up with three thousand dollars?

It hit me then. The same name that always surfaced whenever anyone talked about big money. My rich uncle Jack. I said, "I don't know, I might be able to do it, but I'd have to write a letter first …"

Without a word, Buddy went to the fridge, pried two of the three aluminum cans left in the plastic receptacle, popped them open and brought one to me. He held his up, and with a nod urged me to lift mine. "To our new venture!" he said with a smile, and we clinked cans.

Not that I took it seriously. I planned to wait a while, then tell

Buddy I couldn't raise the bread.

That night as we ate, I told Noreen about it, in the way I always told her stories—things that happened during the day that I found interesting—like the bundles of mail I'd locked in the truck earlier that week, when I had to call the station to bring a spare key, which was why I'd finished the route in the dark. To my surprise, she was taken with Buddy's idea: a pizzeria on Telegraph Avenue.

More than I'd realized, in fact, for the next day when I came home from work, Buddy was in the living room, lounging in the soft chair. Noreen had invited him over for coffee and cake.

I tried not to stare at the huge peace amulet that rested on his hairy chest in the vee of his half-unbuttoned Hawaiian shirt as he recited some of the details he'd laid on me the day before and Noreen listened attentively. Then, like me, inappropriately influenced by something I'd once read, she began to talk about photographs that could be displayed on the walls, different ones every month, a changing gallery of her work.

From where he lounged in the soft chair, Buddy faced her latest exhibit of prints pinned to the long wall. As soon as she finished talking, he said, "I see you have a good eye. We could use that. For starters, we need to design a catchy sign," and he looked at me, as if to confirm it. "Something that'll attract attention, draw people inside …"

It seemed an odd thing to focus on, what with everything else involved, but again Noreen appeared pleased. "I'll work up some sketches," she said.

"Remember, it has to be big …" He held his arms wide apart. "Our name in lights … and you should go with her, Pete, to keep track of the costs."

So after work a few days later, we went to a warehouse next to the freeway, a nondescript place except for its thirty-foot billboard, ACME SIGN COMPANY, and were led into a conference room where a similar unprepossessing man whose name I immediately forgot talked to us about signs. But first he placed plastic cups of tepid coffee before us on the laminated tabletop, along with a jar of powdered cream and packets of sweetener. I added all of it to the thin liquid, as if on holiday in dreary postwar England, took a sip and put it down forever as the bland salesman said cheerily, "So, what can I do for you folks?"

Fluorescent lights hummed an annoying soundtrack, topping off the deadening ambience. Unnerved, I blurted a long and mainly irrelevant description of our imaginary store, as though describing something of transcendent importance but hardly listening to myself, as the neutral salesman toyed idly with a pencil. When I stopped, however, he came alive, pupils sharp, smooth-shaven face creased with guile around the semblance of a fixed smile as he leaned toward me, barely restraining his eagerness to get at easy prey.

But before he could pick at the pieces of myself I'd carelessly strewn about, Noreen said, "Let me show you the sketches I drew up," and passed a sheaf of pages across the laminated tabletop.

Instantly, the Acme man forgot about me; the woman, he concluded, would make the decisions. Relieved, I sat back and watched as he looked at her sketches, nodding and saying complimentary things—not much different in word and tone than what Buddy had said to Noreen, as a matter of fact—then moved to a cabinet and returned with a looseleaf notebook of glossy specimens.

Like buying a car, each sign had a base price, and the various accessories were extra. Noreen skimmed through the samples and passed the book to me, an interaction with the smattering of a connection that had become increasingly rare between us in recent months, a bond of familiarity that momentarily rendered us a team, a dynamic duo. Since she could barely add, I toted the costs of the two, three, and four color signs, some with heat-blinking lights, others with timed pulsations, the two of us exchanging knowing glances, she doing her visual thing while I did the mental scrambling toward lower ground as the price rose. Finally, we settled on a simple pie circumference with a few words within: NEW YORK STYLE PIZZA. Which, the now complaisant salesman informed us, would cost fifteen hundred dollars;

about one-fourth of our entire six-month budget for everything.

That evening at our apartment, Buddy, solicitous, said, "Don't worry about it," flicking away the pricey news with a nonchalance that told me the sign hadn't meant much to him anyway. "Location is what counts. We'll put up neon lights, something simple, and the customers will come ... because—good news—there's a store that'll be available next month, corner of Telegraph and Bancroft, windows facing two busy streets, lots of car and foot traffic ..."

The rent was due the first of the month. "You should call Jack right away," Noreen said when he left.

Jack, the family success story, who got into computers when they were made out of vacuum tubes. Ever since he struck it rich, however—through mergers, takeovers, stock options, and whatnot—Jack had become just another businessman. He'd changed in other ways too, and not to my liking; nor, unsuccessful as I was, did he feel about me as he once had.

"I'd rather send him a letter," I told Noreen.

"But Buddy says he'll need the money before the end of the month."

"To tell you the truth," I said, "I have to think about it some more."

Her face fell. "But you hate the post office!"

"Yeah, but I also don't like asking Jack for money."

She misunderstood, said, "Tell him about Buddy, that he knows what he's doing. Jack's a businessman. If he knows about Buddy, he'll feel better about it."

At such moments, when Noreen underestimated me, I'd glimpse more about her—and my own assumptions—than I cared to acknowledge. And then, for a change, I'd get angry, as I did now, saying, "It's not your place to tell me I should borrow money from him. He's my relative, after all, not yours, and right now, like I said, I want to think about it some more." I could have added that as long as we'd been together, she'd never had a job, that I'd always been the worker, or the one collecting unemployment checks. So it behooved her to stay out of it.

Not that the idea of doing something different wasn't attractive. The scrutiny of the supervisor, being told what to do all the time … and now Noreen as part of the mix, with an attitude that said she thought less of me for working an ordinary job … and Buddy, who'd walk in the door after I got home from work in the afternoon and tossed my satchel in a corner, adding his own deadline pressure by bringing up the oven, that had to be in place, the formica counters, cash register, tables and chairs, not to mention lining up gas, water, electricity, license fees, insurance. He'd bang away at it even before I took off my shoes. Time was collapsing around us. We needed money. Had my uncle gotten back to me yet?

"No, not yet," I said, without mentioning that I hadn't contacted him, adding, "These wealthy people, they're not like you and me—they can't be rushed."

*   *   *

One night Noreen and I had dinner at Carole's pottery studio, and afterward sat around smoking dope, which I hadn't done in a while. It took my thoughts in an unexpected direction.

What did I know about running a pizzeria?

Nothing.

In fact, I only knew what a fifteen-hundred-degree oven and all the rest of it would cost because Buddy said so.

And what did I know about Buddy?

Nothing, really.

His apartment occurred to me then, in an associative pothead way-that there was nothing distinctive there: oversize pillows, a stereo, a new poster on the wall, of a Hawaiian waterfall. The place always felt so bare.

And where were the accouterments and ingredients of Italian cooking? While looking for a can opener the last time I was there, I'd come across no oregano or basil, no garlic press or olive oil. What kind of Italian was Buddy Cappallano anyway?

Was he even Italian at all, as he'd claimed?

And how did I know his name was actually Cappallano? I hadn't seen it written anywhere, and there was never loose mail in the trough. Buddy Whatever, from San Diego, whose swarthiness might have been suntan, rather than Sicilian pigment.

Thoughts that had me quaking with paranoia.

I couldn't fall asleep that night. The circumstantial evidence was overwhelming. He was planning to rip me off! To con me out of my money!

The next day, when I got home from work, I went to Buddy's apartment right away, to get it over with, and told him I'd changed my mind.

He tried to hide his disappointment, shrugging in a way that indeed seemed Italian. "Better now than later, Pete," he finally said, "when we were under way."

Abruptly, I felt bad, for having thought the worst of him, said, "I'm sorry I put you through all this, Buddy …"

He gestured the apology away. "No sweat. Don't worry about it."

"I mean, you did all the legwork, made all the contacts, looked into all the details—"

"It wasn't much. Just the preliminaries."

"Maybe so," I said, "but I should've told you right off that I wasn't interested."

Again he shrugged. "No harm done …"

And that was that.

He moved out at the end of the month, and I assumed I'd never see him again. But I spotted him on Telegraph a few weeks later, wearing a three-piece suit, which momentarily resurrected my paranoia. Who was he anyway? Clearly a master of disguise. And what had he had in mind for me?

Before I could duck out of his sight line, he spotted me and strode up the block, smiling broadly, hand outstretched as he approached. "Pete, how're you doing? Long time no see."

"Buddy … " I didn't know what to say.

He stepped back and fingered the lapels of the well-cut suit, as though modeling it. "What'd you think?"

"Seems like you're doing all right …"

"I work there," he said, gesturing with a thumb at the Jaguar-Porsche showroom across the street. "Lot of moolah in selling those babies …"

I felt foolish. Buddy was what he was. A guy who belonged in his habitat as much as I belonged in mine.

He pointed up the block, to the corner where our store was supposed to be. "Someday," he said, "someone's gonna open a pizzeria there and make a killing."

Cuckold

Out on the route I'd ruminate on all kinds of things. Noreen was among them, as I pictured her at school, or in her darkroom behind the house, or perhaps at the racetrack, capturing horses in stride, jockeys weighing in after a race, and the infield crowd. But I rarely reflected on the unspoken difficulties between us; my emotive censor firmly kept that door locked.

And then one day I came home and she dropped a bomb on me, and I was still grappling to decipher it as she added, "I didn't want it to happen," sounding rattled. "He listened to me, and I found myself telling him how unhappy I am …"

Overwhelmed by a flux of emotion, I took the chair opposite her. She sat on the couch, arms pressed to her sides, calves parallel, feet flat on the floor. A posture that usually announced that she wanted something. It took me a moment to realize that this time she didn't, that she was confessing, and at the same time seemingly asking for forgiveness.

Which thrust me back to the close quarters of mailmen casing in the morning, snickering about randy housewives, cuckolded husbands, bored housewives waiting in open doorways, wearing negligees. Or rumors about Jeanie Moss, who parceled out huge sections of her route that I delivered while wondering which house she might be in, engaging in the rumored tryst.

Coarse stuff, which I could nevertheless not dismiss and apparently were waiting to appear in vulnerable moments, like now, when I'd so suddenly become one of those absent husbands, the butt of cruel jokes.

My wife was fucking another man!

Outrage almost obscured the fact that for a long time our relationship had been a nearly sexless affair, without passion; more routine than platonic now. When we coupled at all, we did it in the shower, which Noreen preferred to the mattress, as if it was a dirty business to be washed away while in the act; water gushing over us as she leaned forward with her hands propped against the tile wall and I sputtered for air while ramming it in.

A ludicrous image, but one that added fodder to my humiliation as I sat there, the object of my own ridicule.

As if reading my mind, Noreen quickly added, "Nothing happened."

I found that hard to believe, but I wanted to believe it, and so took some solace from her assertion, and then was instantly revisited by the ridiculous man, cuckold, personification of that tremulous moment in which he discovers the truth about his wife …

"Who was it?" I asked grimly.

"It doesn't matter," she said, brushing the question off, and at the same time gathering strength from the gesture, as if it relieved her of responsibility.

"It doesn't matter?" I repeated, incredulous.

But then: Why would it? How would knowing change anything?

And in the next instant, in high dudgeon, with outraged principle on my side, the innocent party.

I had a right to know!

But instead I said, "What happened?" straining for a reasonable tone.

She welled up, and trying not to cry, said, "This afternoon, I was in back, coming out of the darkroom, and David—he used to stay in the cottage with Jeremy, when Jeremy lived there, and he still comes around sometimes—"

"Him?" I blurted, recalling a short, thin boy—he looked so young, I didn't think of him as a man—with a wispy mustache.

"I know it seems unlikely. It did to me too. I never would have thought I'd find someone like him attractive …"

"He's a student at the university," I said, remembering, "studying psychology … " A glib tongue, and he'd preyed on my gullible wife, stirring up her insecurities, then comforting her when she fell apart.

"Yes."

"Did he hypnotize you?" I asked sarcastically.

"You can make fun if you want to," she said, sounding hurt. "All I know is—"

"Excuse me," I interrupted, "but I've been too busy working my ass off all day, every day, to be sympathetic while you're here at home, doing what you want to do, having these tender liaisons."

She came back at me, with some fire, but banked enough not to enrage me—Noreen knew my moods as well as I knew hers—telling me how alone and unhappy she felt.

Another time, I might have appreciated the irony, since loneliness had been the psychological nexus of our relationship: Noreen seeking me out, then moving in; me, longing to escape a solitary existence, welcoming her.

Though rarely talkative, she couldn't curb herself now. She wanted me to know how she felt. Was it as hard for her to locate her feelings as it was for me? Or were her feelings closer to the surface and merely tamped down? It was not something I'd ever explored.

Details about young David poured out, more than I wanted to know, though I'd been the one to ask. He was from Flushing, Queens, of all places, grew up next to the park she'd discovered shortly after moving into my studio apartment …

I imagined her meeting him in Kissena Park, with its rolling paths and faux gaslight lamps; transported the two of them from the present to the past, as if her infidelity had begun then and only resumed now. Jealousy conjured that absurdity, a rush of adrenaline roiling my emotions as I gyrated from insecurity to self-righteousness, which in turn plunged me into sudden abject misery again.

" … I didn't want to feel attracted to him," she was saying, looking into her lap, where she absently kneaded her hands. "But it's been hard. It seems I'm always alone, both when I'm here and when I'm at school—"

"Not long ago you sat here telling me you'd lost interest in painting and wanted to do something else. And now—"

"Since Alan and Mary went back to New York, I don't know anyone at school—not really—which is why I spend so much time in the darkroom in back—"

"Or at the track."

She looked at me oddly, at my accusatory tone. Indeed, it made no sense. I'd been the one to take her there one day, to introduce her, and she fell in love with the photographic possibilities. "Well, yes, of course, there too."

"Here's my point," I went on, to put that bit of irrationality behind me. "You wanted to switch to photography, so I bought you all that equipment, helped you build the darkroom, took you to the track—where you go more than I do now, to shoot who knows how many hundreds of rolls"—I gestured at the plasterboard covering a living room wall, a gallery of black and white photos or horses and jockeys—"and while you're there, or developing and printing in back, pursuing what you consider your vocation, I'm at work at a job I hate—the only one I could find out here—so you can buy lenses, film, paper, a new printer ..."

"But most of the time I'm here alone—"

"Doing what you choose to do."

"Yes, but sometimes I need more ... to hear a friendly voice, to speak to someone. And David listened to me, and spoke to me ... the way you used to ..."

That struck a nerve. He was a sensitive man; I wasn't. An indictment.

The times had changed, and it seemed I'd been caught in the lurch, a bystander now, not a participant. There was feminism in the air, and I was not immune to it. At the Laskers' it conflated with Anais Nin,

Henry and June, as literature. In the poets and writers group there were women who approached everything in terms of gender. I was not unsympathetic, though I was put off by the anger ...

I recalled, then, running into David when he was staying with Jeremy. He'd been friendly at first, then abruptly cool, as if I'd done something to offend his sensibilities. And now Noreen's confession, corroborating that impression: her unhappiness had been the source of his hostility.

But what, exactly, had I done? Other than earn a living?

Though in truth, I knew that when I came at home after work, I hid behind a newspaper, and in the evening, after dinner, glazed out before the television set, watching sitcoms, like the rest of America—*All in the Family, Sanford and Son, Maude,* all reiterated while casing in the station the next morning—as Noreen lay next to me on the mattress ... before getting up and going out back to her darkroom. Even when we went out to eat, which we did often, and faced each other across a small table, I'd discourse on news and current events, talking to myself as much as to her, self-absorbed.

"... He told me I could change my life if I wanted to," she was saying, "that I didn't have to be unhappy ..." She pressed her elbows to her body and interlocked her fingers in a tight grip. "But I thought of you, and what we've been through together ... and though I wanted to go to bed with him, I couldn't."

Every few months, waking suddenly out of deep sleep late at night, I'd find myself in a bleak, existential world, in an apartment whose familiarity mocked me. And now, as if jolted awake to one of those episodes, it struck me that despite our history, the life Noreen and I shared, the things we'd done together, we were on our own; that everyone is always on their own.

I'd heard married couples who separated say that in the end, familiarity was all they had in common. A long end, in which months might pass before one or the other, or both, eventually accepted the reality of their situation. That they remained together until circumstances got so bad, the facts of their lives could no longer be denied.

Now, in the living room, the walls receded, and I was mourning the illusion of permanence, as if our marriage were already over.

I looked at Noreen as at a stranger, her cheeks wet with tears, which she wiped with the back of a hand, first one cheek, then the other. Lifting her chin, she looked back at me, her blue-gray eyes pleading for understanding …

And I recalled the first time we met, when she sat in a paint-splotched convertible, staring at me as if I were everything. The object of her dreams.

I felt empty all of a sudden and wanted to dispel that feeling, to be reassured. It pushed everything else aside … that need to be part of the world, not alone.

I leaned over the low table between us and took her hands in mine. "Okay," I said. "Let's be attentive to each other again."

She tried to smile, but her lips trembled and she began to cry again, soft little sobs. I moved next to her on the couch and stretched an arm around her shoulders, her head falling to my shoulder, her chest heaving. She brushed her flaxen hair aside with another of her economical gestures. Then she stopped crying and a stillness came over the room, with its photographs and abstract canvases; light streaming in above the café curtains on the bay window; my desk in the corner, beneath the window with leaded panes.

But something still nagged at me despite this homecoming. In response to it, I moved back to the armchair across from her, and when she looked at me questioningly, I said, "I want you to make lunch for me again."

The shift from her concerns to mine surprised her.

"We should be attentive to each *other*," I said. "I've had a hard time of it too …"

"I know I haven't gotten up to make lunch for a few days," she replied, "but—"

"It's been a few weeks."

Of getting up as she lay beside me on the mattress, hardly stirring when I staggered into the bathroom to throw cold water on my face. No coffee brewing in the kitchen, wafting into the bedroom as I got dressed. No Mozart either, the lovely sound track that once ameliorated the dark beginning to still another day. The simple pleasures I'd come to appreciate, and to expect.

Again she seemed surprised, perhaps at the precision with which I'd measured the time, or that it had gone on as long as it had. Two possible mind-sets, one detached, the other engaged. Unable to make up my own mind, I was wary, unsure which version was her.

I'd never told Noreen what I expected of her. In truth, I had a hard time expecting anything of anyone. Emotionally, I was a child, accompanied only by himself, eventually grateful for any attention at all. And of course I'd brought that to our marriage. It was difficult for me to ask her to do anything for me, and I accepted what she voluntarily offered as more than I deserved.

Now, aware of that grateful reflex, I pushed it aside. Was it unreasonable to expect her to make my life easier?

I said, "When I finally get a chance to eat, I drive around looking for a restaurant, and more often than not I can't find any ..."

Softly, she replied, "I didn't know it mattered to you," as if she hadn't grasped what I'd said, glided over the context and only heard that I wanted to eat lunch from a box, a personal preference unique to me. "When I asked about it a while ago and offered to make it, you said you'd just get something on the route ..."

Which was true. I didn't like asking people to do things for me.

"I shouldn't have to ask," I said. "You should get up, as you used to, and just do it."

"If it bothers you," she replied, "then of course I'll get up and make you lunch."

"Of course it bothers me. I'm working for both of us."

"I'm sorry," she said, lowering her head, averting her eyes. "I didn't realize …"

I didn't realize.

But by then attrition had set in. We both wanted resolution … for things to go back to where they were when we hadn't been on edge; to a different time.

I'd fought myself—the urge to accept whatever was given, and ask for nothing more—and now, to say more, I'd have to fight the atmosphere as well, and reopen a wound still open and raw.

I didn't realize.

I knew what was missing. The caring that diminished details, rendered them less significant than the underlying reality. But it would take two of us to care. Without that, it would just be another stem in an argument.

I bowed to the determining mood then, as I had ever since adopting that particular tao, and perhaps for longer than that, and chose to ignore what I wanted in favor of what the atmosphere was telling me.

She'd said she was sorry, after all …

And so, closeting the knowledge that we hadn't reached a satisfactory conclusion, we kissed and, as they say, made up.

Contrary Advice

I punched in at 6:15, late as usual, and was assigned Route 715. The supervisor said it as casually as any other number: 601, 625, 704, 715. Little did I know …

I found the case at the far end of an aisle whose routes had never been kind to me, the carriers at work in the vicinity unfamiliar and quite old. Despite the generation gap I'd been on the younger side of a few years ago, it was my inclination to ascribe mellow indifference to the aged—I liked to believe people transcended pettiness as they get older—but the two graybeards in proximity to the case assigned to me were bitterly arguing over which building was the tallest in the world. One held that it was in Kuala Lumpur, and the other touted the Eiffel Tower, until a vociferous assertion that it wasn't a building but a radio tower forced him to back off in disgust and to opt instead for the Transamerica Tower across the bay.

After a while the old man working next to me—Eiffel Tower guy—noticing my halting efforts at casing the mail, leaned over and offered to street my letters, for which I thanked him profusely; I was having the damnedest time figuring out the scheme. A minute later his nemesis swooped in from across the aisle, grabbed a handful of letters, and began to street them too. Then, before I had time to roll a cigarette, the two old-timers were at each other again.

Eiffel Tower guy said: "Don't you have something else to do, Ford?"

Norwegian Ford, I would realize, after spotting the name plate pasted to his case, brusquely replied: "Nothing that can't sit."

"You don't know this route like I do!"

"And when was the last time you carried it?"

Eiffel Tower guy considered the question, rubbed his chin, scratched his flaky gray head, dislodging scaly flakes, and finally replied, "Nineteen fifty-six," as if it had only been yesterday.

Ford snickered. "Everything's changed since then, don't you know."

"Not you," Tower guy said. "You still don't know your way around the bus."

The bus? What bus? What were these guys talking about?

"Don't fight over me, fellas," I said in an attempt at humor, a New York reflex that had never gone over well in the irony-challenged confines of Civic Center Station. Indeed, they both glared at me as if just noticing my presence and resenting it.

Tower guy turned back to his peer. "As a matter of fact, Ford, I don't even want to help him. I'm only doing it because he's obviously short some teeth."

"Well I don't want to help him neither," Ford retorted. "I'm only doing it 'cause I was assigned." And plunking his handful of mail on my case table, he returned to his own route.

Not to be outdone, Tower guy plunked his stack down too and also went back to his case.

It had occurred to me by then that it would be a difficult day. Like Zen punches, the omens were working me over. But Ford had been ordered to get me out of the station at a reasonable hour, and obedience was the first and last virtue in the postal service, so after a time he returned, routed my flats—while lecturing me on the advantages of good old-fashioned string compared to rubber bands, ancient wisdom I'd heard before—then said so long and punched out.

Only then did Tower guy step back in with some helpful advice of his own: "Out on this route, son, don't turn your back."

I didn't know what that meant, but it certainly wasn't good news. Eyeing my canvas hamper brimming with bundled letters and flats, I innocently remarked, "Seems like a lot of mail."

"Nothing to it," he replied, and handed me a crudely drawn map he'd been working on earlier.

"Gee, thanks."

"Just keep moving and you'll eventually come out the other end."

Weird old guy, I thought, loading the half-ton truck. But without his map I would never have found the intersection of Fourteenth and Nineteenth Avenues, which I would later discover was referred to in the station as the Void.

The sun was shining in that pocket valley, and as I ate my lunch—as always, after finally leaving the station—I glimpsed a crumbling tower at the top of a distant hill, resembling the ruins of a medieval fortress; an asylum, I'd been told, which added to my unease. Dusting off the sandwich crumbs, I stepped out of the truck, hoisted the heavy satchel to my shoulder, and with a can of dog repellent clipped to each hip began to walk.

Only something wasn't quite right out there. It was a subtle thing, streets intersecting at disturbing angles, houses leaning somewhat off plumb, birds squawking as if undergoing some sort of torture and then abruptly, all at once, falling silent. I paused, surveying the empty boulevard, hoping to locate it in my déjà vu file, but nothing I'd encountered before came to mind.

Taking a deep breath, I moved to the first house, had trouble locating the address, finally found it scrawled on a rusty box hanging lopsided from a railing, and shoving the mail in, felt the lid snap down hard on my fingers, leaving a tetanus imprint as a dangerous growl emerged from beneath the porch.

I scurried away, turned around and backed warily toward the next house, keeping my eye on the bogeyman darkness I was leaving behind. Walking backward, stinging hand hovering over a can of repellent, prepared to quick-draw, I tripped over a baseball bat, got slowly to my feet and was scared witless by a piercing shriek.

I saw nothing while limping away as fast as I could, bypassing half a dozen houses, adrenaline pounding my plexus, pumping smoke into my eyes, the air turning soupy with fog.

What happened from that point on is but approximation.

Dimly, I recall descending a steep hill, the atmosphere ponderous, the sound of baying dogs reaching me from a great distance until a bloodcurdling yelp inches away sent me fleeing again. When I finally slowed down, turned back and looked around, there was, again, nothing there. Not even a fence a beast could hide behind.

Pushing through the smoke tendrils of fear, I methodically delivered mail left and right down a narrow alley, finding courage in the steady rhythm, moving toward the final address in the first loop, where (thank God!) the truck would await me. But when the mail ran out, I found myself instead at a dead end, staring with dismay at a whitewashed six-foot fence—where two humongous Saint Bernards, rising in unison, suddenly appeared, flopping their giant paws on the top, to bark down at me with a guttural fury I hadn't thought possible in that supposedly gentle breed.

The fence clearly no obstacle if they decided to push it down, I ran back up the hillside alley, passing unseen dogs that had been silent on the way down and now raised a cacophony while throwing their bodies against wooden and cyclone fences to get at me. Reaching the truck, I fell inside like Buster Keaton, the sliding door slamming shut behind me as I collapsed on the steering wheel.

Eventually I opened my eyes and scanned the mail trays, hoping to see less than I knew was there. I drank what was left of a thermos of lukewarm coffee, and putting off the inevitable, glanced through one of the day's magazines, then stuffed the satchel again, picturing myself bravely setting forth on a well-defined mission, which implied that it would soon be over. But the truck door slammed shut of its own volition, an exclamation that disabused courageous pretense.

A hot sun now speared shards of light off car windshields, stabbing at my eyes. And instead of the din of dogs, there was an eerie silence, people walking from house to car and car to house without footfalls. In the presence of these phantoms, I almost missed the dogs.

And then, as though in answer to a wish, two of them appeared. I backed up several steps, drew both repellent cans, spread my legs like a gunslinger and stood staring at them. They stopped a few feet away, a three-legged collie and a white German shepherd, regarding me with curious, tilted heads. I took a wide circuit around them and set off again, peripherally aware of them following me, one ambling, the other limping, and then moving to either side, keeping up. I realized then that they were my friends and breathed easier.

They accompanied me several blocks as I gently dispersed the mail, feeling safe, protected. What Olympian myth was this? I wondered, and a moment later, when my guardians disappeared, understood, not for the first time, that I'd dispelled a magic moment by seeking to explain it.

I knew then I was in for it.

The Void now stretched like elastic from hill to hill as unseen dogs growled at me. And then they were closer, though still invisible, until a rottweiler attached to a chain leaped at me out of nowhere and nearly strangled itself, gurgling in its own phlegm. Then a giant, malevolent thing rose up behind a porch facade, resting its elbows on the ledge, its biceps lean and muscular and all too human, its snout enormous, its bared teeth glistening. This *was* the stuff of dreams. No way such a monster could be real otherwise.

Keeping a fearful distance, I counted down the letters in the remaining bundle as I delivered them, and with a sense of relief cut across a lawn to deliver the last one to the final house, when surreptitious teeth clamped around my ankle from behind.

I nearly collapsed with cumulative anticipation, fell into a swoon as the scroungy mongrel, the smallest beast I'd seen all day, slunk away.

As it did, I backed off in the opposite direction, shirt sticking to skin, sun swirling in the sky the way van Gogh portrayed it while in the St. Remy asylum as a siren dopplered off in the distance, on its way to nowhere.

*   *   *

Colin looked up when he finished reading, smiled modestly, shook his head with what I took to be approval. "A lot of over-the-top images here," he said, then went back to the typewritten pages on the kitchen table, flipping them over and slowly scanning each one. "'Filbert Thomas, blissed-out sergeant-at-arms of the American Postal Workers Union, who broke his leg kicking a sack of special delivery potatoes' ... 'Jeanie Moss, supercarrier of the Treeless Forest District, who claimed she needed help, and gave me a Tuolomne Meadow of boulders to deliver ...'"

He looked up again. "And this bit about the Void and Eiffel Tower guy, 'Virgil of the Underworld' ... it's different than anything of yours I've seen before. Reminds me, in a way, of Burroughs ..."

Though I'd never been able to read William Burroughs, or any other so-called stream of consciousness, it was a name to be reckoned with. Colin had known him once upon a time. So I took it as praise, forgetting that he had built me up with outlandish comparisons before, even to Shakespeare once, before lowering the boom on me for operating beneath my capabilities.

"Very different than Patrick Malone," he said, "and his commitment to creative suffering ... or Tom the alchemist, experimenting on himself in order to observe the results ..."

It took a moment before I saw where he was going. "So you're saying you don't like it."

"No, no ... just that it's not quite the same."

"Well, yeah. It's altogether different ..."

He straightened the pages and leaned back. "That's all I'm saying."

I said, "One thing the drug stories lack is humor, and this gives me the opportunity to get into it ... I keep a journal and make entries when I get home from work in the afternoon, with an eye toward expanding some of the sketches and maybe using them later as material for short stories, maybe put together a collection."

"Like William Carlos Williams in *The Doctor Stories.*"

"I thought he was a poet."

"Yes, but he was a doctor too. He went out on calls and wrote a short story collection about his visits …"

"Sounds good."

"Like you do here, commenting on the things you see on the job, only Williams writes about the patients he sees—not just the ailments, but who they are … He explores their lives, gets under their skin."

"And you're saying I don't."

"What's missing here," he said, not disagreeing, "is the insight that animates the stories in your novel … the deeper workings of your mind. That's what intrigues me, Peter. How you see yourself in the world."

"I think that's in there too," I replied, nodding toward the pages. But I knew what he meant. The deeper me. The one plumbing for meaning, not just relating discomfort.

"Well, yes, it is in here, but like you said—they're sketches."

Sketches. I'd called them that myself, but now cringed at the word. It implied something insubstantial. "Well, yeah, but it's not as if I'm not trying to convey a state of mind …"

He nodded. "And you do … and with humor, as you pointed out. But don't sell yourself short, Peter. There's humor in your novel too, a subtle irony, and this …" He tapped the top page with a finger. "… it has a slapstick feel."

I frowned, reluctant to defend myself, to identify with the writing as if it were me. But I said, anyway, "*Everything* at the post office is extreme, Colin. It lends itself to slapstick."

"Okay," he replied, nodding. "It could be I'm wrong."

"Maybe I was straining too hard to make it humorous."

"Well … maybe. But then, I know you can portray humor and seriousness at the same time. You've *done* it, in the novel. In fact, it amazes me that in it. in the most dire situations, or the most poignant, there's also something to smile about."

I was flattered by his praise, but still upset by his criticism. "Maybe I should tone down the description," I offered, "convey the deadline pressures more realistically, the impervious supervisors, the exhaustion …"

"The thing I don't understand," he said, "is why you put it aside."

"The drug book, you mean?"

"The novel, yes."

I thought about telling him what I'd told Maggie: how tired I was after work, how difficult it was to write then. But that would have sounded like an excuse. Had I been more confident—and known more about life—I might have pointed out that not everything is deep, that there's something to be said for capturing the surface of things when it's of the moment and the deeper things are elusive.

"Don't let yourself be led astray, Peter," Colin said encouragingly. "What you have to say about the sixties is too important."

It sounded grandiose, but his compliment had the usual effect. Yes, I did have something to tell the world. An era I wanted to capture …

"It seems to me that what you have here," he went on, in a gentler voice, resting a hand on the pages, "is material for another novel. But first, why not finish the one you started?"

Yes. The post office would be my *next* novel. The workingclass novel I wanted to write. But before that I'd write the one I couldn't get out of my head.

A week or so later, however, after several unsuccessful attempts at picking up where I'd left off, I put the novel aside, and then stopped writing altogether.

Honkytown

I assumed I'd been bumped to an unfamiliar station because I called in sick the week before, for the umpteenth time. I'd done it so often that I was now required to produce a doctor's note the next day. As a result I frequently visited the hospital complex, waited at the Kaiser clinic to collect my permission slip, then faked the relevant symptoms. And now it seemed my errant behavior had been duly noted, though of course a clerical error or bureaucratic inanity, rather than a purposeful decision, might have accounted for my precipitous transfer to Honkytown Station. Not that it mattered; the new assignment was no less a punishment either way.

I had a hard time finding the place, and though I woke up even earlier than usual, arrived, as always, fifteen minutes late. Right away it was clear I'd been consigned to my own particular sociological hell. Not merely alienated from my surroundings—a state of mind I'd grown accustomed to—but in downright hostile territory.

The back room in the old station was silent when I walked in, except for the shuffle of mail being cased, which was akin to breathing on the job. A grim-faced supervisor with a quarter-inch crew cut stood waiting near the time clock, legs spread, arms crossed on his chest. He greeted me with a brusque thumb thrust at the only vacant case in the adjoining aisle.

"Get to work, Weissman," he said, pronouncing it *Wise*-man. "You're late."

The other carriers barely glanced at me as I parked myself at the case and picked up a stack of unsorted mail from the desktop tray. They swallowed my appearance without expression, though overgrown hair and a disheveled uniform clashed with the local cultural norm, visible in their straitlaced, well-creased uniformity. The attitude of a stoic generation of men—there were no women present at Honkytown— pale-skinned with crew-shaven heads, casing with the silent discipline of Marines.

Paradoxically, or maybe paranoically, I took their lack of reaction as an announcement, something like, "Fire in the hole!" and responded accordingly, facing forward, dealing with the mail to the exclusion of all else. And yet, after a while I had to admit that they elicited a certain grudging admiration. No matter how dehumanizing the situation, these guys would never complain, or admit to unmanly discomfort with boredom by engaging in talk to ameliorate the mechanical sameness of the chore.

This platoon, as I thought of them, were all of a certain age. They'd been in the Big One, and the daily regimen of the post office was their umbilical to simpler times. Beatniks, hippies, and the like, who didn't wear a cap out on the route or bother about dry cleaning their uniforms to keep the creases crisp; civil rights protests, antiwar demonstrations, young people burning draft cards—affronts to the American way of life; and now a gas shortage, of all things, because of the Arabs, with lines two and three hours long to get to the pump … the world had gone to hell. But at least the ball-busting job was familiar, the rules of engagement clear.

After an hour or so in this military setting, during which I wrestled with a route I'd never seen before, I heard some murmurs here and there, which told me I was indeed among human beings. As benighted as these guys might be, they were still human and couldn't help but vent relief once the heavy lifting was done; private conversations, in their context, unlike the free for all at Temescal, which was a different, more socially integrated community. In confluence, the guy casing next to me began to mutter; to himself or me, I wasn't sure.

Not wanting to insult him, in case he was in fact trying to tell me

something, I said, "I can't hear you over the racket of those birds …
Those *are* birds up there, right?"

It startled him out of his mumbled discourse. He stared at me a full
five seconds before replying:

"To feed to the boa constrictor."

"The boa constrictor?" I stepped back and checked the floor beneath
the case.

"In the pet store, up the street," he explained, and falling silent,
went back to flipping his remaining letters into cubbyholes.

I went back too, to my abstruse puzzle, and half an hour or so later,
when the pet store guy began muttering again, I looked over and saw
him routing his flats.

He took my glance as an unspoken question. "Keno," he replied.

"Keno?" I asked.

"It's big in Reno," he explained.

Keno. Reno. Who would have thought he was a poet?

"I play the slots too."

"Oh, yeah … I see. *Reno*."

My comprehension affected a change in him, and as if starved for
attention, he took a step toward me and launched into talk.

He'd moved out in 'forty-seven, he said; after the Big One. He'd
been stationed at Treasure Island and then was shipped back there. The
weather was so fine, and the Bay area so easygoing, he fell in love with
it. When he was discharged a few months later, he and the missus
packed up, left Iowa, and went west.

"Been here ever since."

I thought about my father, who'd also shipped out from Treasure
Island—for the Solomon Islands, and Guadalcanal—and looked at the
pet guy more carefully. He was thin, but with a beer belly paunch, and
balding, his receding hair flecked with gray. Finished casing now, he
was drawing down letters, fastening them in bundles with string, the
way the older carriers did. I gazed around the room, saw that they were
all pulling down and bundling with string, and looked back at my case,

which was only half done.

He moved closer, to bundle his flats, speaking again, this time about the changes that had occurred to what was once a paradise.

Back then, everyone knew your name, and when you walked down Main Street, the sidewalks weren't crowded and there was hardly any traffic on the street. Now, you saw people everywhere, most of them strangers, and everyone always in a hurry.

As if he and I and everyone else in the room, working under deadline pressure, weren't.

There'd been eucalyptus trees in the hills, up on Foothill Avenue; cut down to make way for a shopping center. The same with Skyline Drive, for a housing development when the real estate people carved up the land. And it was even worse down in the flatlands, where his kids used to play ball on vacant fields, before they built the project and the dark meat moved in.

Dark meat?

He didn't notice, but a wall went up between us, erected by my repulsion.

In fact, I'd been on the verge of commiserating when he brought me up short and threw me back to Canarsie, the row houses, the sense of dread that came over me, transported from the past, before I trumped that visceral reaction with boyish recollections, which did not wholly dispel my initial unease: the sense of uncertainty while walking to school, the Quonset hut with the army camp behind it, trucks rumbling by schoolhouse windows, tank treads stirring up dust … the radar installation tracking the sky for approaching enemy planes as I dove under a desk, kneeling with the other kids, hands clamped to heads to protect ourselves from falling bombs.

Life is never a paradise. What we actually remember with longing is how it felt to be young.

A few years later, another project, this one built of brick. Flimsy saplings planted in rectangles of lawn between sidewalk and street. A more orderly, seemingly better place, but with its own, no less opaque frisson of fear. One day, the newspapers and newsletters in the back of a closet, behind the fall of hanging coats, disappeared.

"We cleaned a few things out," my mother explained, long before I was told they'd been communists.

Another day, I came home to school to find her ironing in the living room, watching the Army-McCarthy hearings on the black and white TV. It was on again the following day, and every day that week. It seemed to me an odd preoccupation …

Or maybe boa constrictor guy did sense the wall I'd reflexively erected, because he fell silent, kept his antediluvian thoughts to himself. And then he was gone, and everyone else too, as I finished up the job, bundled the mail, punched out a jeep, and left the station.

From a distance, ranch-style houses adorned the hills like a necklace; a newer version of America than the one I recalled; someone else's promised land. Up close, the houses were more ordinary, the manicured landscape blasted by sun as I parked, hoisted the satchel to my shoulder and began to trudge the streets without sidewalks or even curbs. No trees here, an aesthetic choice made by whoever designed this automotive age paradise. Yet this was not a so-called mounted route, since there were no mailboxes at the foot of each driveway, only slots in front doors, requiring me to perambulate.

I delivered a curve or two—the streets blended into each other like a Möbius strip—before a woman opened a door as I hiked up the walk, waving letters she wanted me to take back to the station. But then she held me there, with a postal question, and after I answered it, had another question about something else, another an excuse to keep me, to speak to an actual person as soap opera voices wafted out an open door with the fluorescent television glow of a living room. Her neediness hit me like a blast of sad air. I fidgeted as she went on, then excused myself and couldn't get away fast enough.

There were more after her, but by then I'd cottoned to the lay of the land and fallen back on the credo of delivering ghetto routes on Check Day: "Always keep moving." With that guiding principle, I completed nearly two-thirds of the route with only sporadic interruption.

By which time I was ravenous, having eaten nothing since gobbling the remaining half of my sandwich, which was supposed to be my lunch, while driving to the route. So now I retraced my drive down to the business district and parked the jeep, intending to find a restaurant.

Boa constrictor guy was right—it was a busy street. I paused at the pet store window, where an exhibit of cute puppies frolicked over sawdust, and scanned the aisle of tropical fish tanks, looking for the hungry snake, then continued up the block, past a hardware store, a shoe store, a bridal shop, the five and dime, an appliance store, to the corner and a bank that appeared more serious than the rest, with its faux marble facade, arched entrance, and revolving glass door. On the next block, another shoe store, this one for women, a dress shop, lawyer's office, real estate agent, stationery and bookstore, then the post office, wrapped around another corner.

Finally, I came upon the restaurant I'd been looking for. Through plate-glass misted from the cooking and the breathing bodies inside, I saw a counter, stools, a roomful of tables three-quarters full. A quintessential gathering spot where ordinary people gather to eat, the kind of place I always sought with curious optimism and then inevitable disappointment, after I encountered the food and overheard the derivative, uninspired conversations.

But as I peered in on this day, something else was at work, and it abruptly undercut my usual enthusiasm: that everyone in the place was white. That had never bothered me before. Instead of entering, I crossed the street and kept walking … to a fast food hut on the next block, it turned out, flanked by a wraparound parking lot.

I hadn't eaten meat in six months, yet blindly ordered a platter of hot sliced beef and fried potato sticks at the sliding window, sat down at a plastic table outside and ate anonymously. I chased it with a milk shake so thick I had to punch holes in it with a straw to find some liquid at the bottom. And then, bloated, I returned to the jeep, checked the handwritten map I'd been given, and drove off to deliver the last third of the route.

The red brick project appeared suddenly in the flatlands, beyond an old railroad track. It covered several blocks, scrawny grass between each row house unit, clotheslines in back—I recognized the nondescript landscape—gang boxes set in front, half the compartments off their hinges, hanging open.

It threw me back again, to Canarsie, which was never far away. The former GIs working during the week to build up a stake to move their families to the sturdier housing projects being erected in the promised land of Queens ... and, as our number moved out, black and Puerto Rican families moved in.

I'd met Henry then, during my last few weeks at the Quonset hut school. He lived in a row house apartment with his uncle and aunt, three sisters and two brothers, and his grandmother. Though I was curious how so many people could live in one place, I never asked him about it, and he never invited me inside. Instead, I'd stand in front and wait for him to come out; Henry always seemed to know I was out there, and within minutes would join me.

I didn't know what it meant to have a friend then. There were other kids around, of course, and I did things with them, but didn't think about them afterward. And then one day, on the two-wheeler I'd just learned to ride, I saw this kid I'd noticed in school. He had a hot dog he'd just bought from a vendor who set up a cart in front of the supermarket. I braked and asked him for a bite. Instead, he broke the frankfurter into two parts, sauerkraut and all, and gave me half. It was astonishing. I'd never expected or encountered such generosity.

We hung out after that, and once, Henry ate at our apartment; no one else I knew from school ever had. My father and mother sat on one side of the table, Henry and I on the other. He was quiet and ill at ease, said, "Yes'm," to my mother when she complimented him on his manners, and, "Thank you." And I knew I was making it more difficult for him by acting rambunctious, but I couldn't help myself; it was an unusual situation for me too, to have a friend.

The day we moved out, my mother suggested that I say goodbye to Henry. We stopped in front of his row house unit and I got out of the Studebaker. As always, I waited outside, and within a minute he appeared. Then, after we'd said our awkward goodbyes, he waved as we drove away, his grandmother standing behind, at the door, watching us ...

I thought about Henry while delivering the gang boxes, wondered where he was, what he was doing, and returned to the station in a somber mood, to punch out.

The supervisor was waiting for me when I walked in. "You have a new assignment, Weissman," he said, thrusting his thumb at a tray full of mail on another desktop. The regular carrier had gone home sick. "You're authorized for all the O.T. you'll need."

A sudden fury came over me—for being dumped on by a supervisor, I thought, instead of another carrier, which I'd gotten used to. But it wasn't that ...

I loaded the jeep, drove to a quiet street on the route, parked beneath a tree, out of sight line of the houses, removed the thick rubber band from a stack of flats and read *Time* magazine, from front to back ... and then, in succession, *Newsweek, The Sporting News,* and the *Christian Science Monitor.* And when I was through reading, I returned to the station with the entire load; I hadn't delivered a single piece of mail, hadn't even gotten out of the jeep.

I set the untouched tray on the casing table, dwelling within an anger that pushed all else aside, an anger that somehow elevated me and within which I felt almost serene.

The other carriers were all back by then, working on markups or lolling about. One of them came over to stare at the tray of letters and magazines.

"Hey, what's this?" he said, dumbfounded.

Another approached, looked at the mail, and regarded me with equal amazement. "Are you crazy?" he asked. "Why'd you bring this back?"

Indeed, no one there could have understood it. I barely understood it myself.

"It's the mail," I replied. "There was too much of it."

Then I punched out and went home.

Up in Mendocino

The insect sound built gradually from a hum to a screaming crescendo—then abruptly stopped, plunging the sun-blasted clearing into silence ... before beginning again and slowly ascending toward another air-vibrating scream. And in the sudden silence I heard smaller sounds, things rustling, crawling, the slither of snakes in the woodpile next to the ramshackle house.

What a wild place this was!

The country.

A generational idyll, a utopian ideal, as the sixties fell into discord and chaos: to escape from the America we knew to a paradisiacal getaway. Transcendence through geography. A pristine place devoid of the frustrations and annoyances of ordinary life.

Not that I actually knew anything about rural settings, having only sampled it as a boy, in summer camp and on family vacations. Otherwise, I'd lived in urban settings my entire life, took buses and subways to school, and then to colleges situated in a dense residential communities, the sprawl of streets and houses broken only occasionally by a park, an exhibit of trees and grass. The proximity of people, of newspapers and radio stations—that was my world, in which each was always connected to all. The startling absence of that now, the sense of isolation in this new configuration, made me edgy.

Noreen was with me, but that made no difference. We sat on a blanket spread unevenly over wild grass, in sight of the splintered wooden house where we'd put our things. Having lolled on the hilltop clearing for half an hour, maybe less, the noises and silences, the vertiginous sense of dimension, were already freaking me out.

To counter the illimitable, to assert control by adding boundaries, I'd begun work on the scene, reducing it to its components: the trees marking the end of the clearing, their jagged spires set against a pale sky; the weather-beaten house, with the woodpile to one side; and behind me, a fallen tree, its bramble of branches and leaves rising above the chaotic strokes of yellow grass.

And having somewhat tamed the landscape by cataloguing it, I went on to alter it; a newly arrived pioneer, rather than a naturalist. I added a new, more solid door to the house, to replace the splintering one; a bay window to the flat plank facade. I imagined a supply of running water from the ravine, pumped up from a flowing creek, though the one we'd crossed to climb to the hilltop house was drought dry. Knowing nothing about water tables or underground streams, I went with a simpler, more godly solution to replenish the creek: I posited rain. And since a full creek would be an obstacle to cross, an aerial tram, suspended over the creek and steep forest slope, would convey us up without ever touching ground, from the dirt road where I'd left the car, almost to the front door of the now renovated house.

Meanwhile, the guilt of a pioneer looking back from an overdeveloped future slipped into my thoughts, commenting on a civilizing agenda that entailed chopping down trees, building cabins, taming the land after chasing the Indians off, or eliminating them.

I assumed, from Noreen's silence, that she'd coped with the unnerving dimension by sketching the scene, and she well might have, for a while, but then slapped the pad down on the blanket and said, "Let's go somewhere. Let's *do* something!" as if the insect racket and sudden plunging silences had rattled her too.

So we crossed the clearing, plunged into the cool shade of pine trees and down the ravine, walking and sliding on needled soil. Conical shafts of sunlight slanted through the high canopy, dazzles of light amidst the dense brown forest floor. At the foot of the hill, we crossed the dry creek bed, hiked up a smaller hill to the dirt road where I'd left the car, and headed toward the shack forty feet beyond.

The door creaked open halfway before getting stuck, and we sidled in; one room, filled with clutter. Noreen moved carefully through the detritus to a crumbling wall of cardboard boxes and began to delve for curiosities. I angled toward crates and boxes against another wall and looked for books.

She found a pair of old boots, fashioned to be worn on either foot, and a misshapen frontier bottle, held them up and asked, "Do you think they'll mind if I take these?"

The Laskers, Phil and Doris, owned the property, along with Julian, Doris's brother. It was Phil who told us we could stay there.

"Bring it back and show it to them," I replied, "but I don't see why not," and went back to the broken footlocker I'd been examining.

It contained decaying copies of *Life* magazine, moldy hardcover books, and a smattering of paperbacks. I'd both hoped and expected to come across something valuable. Old, out-of-the-way stuff, ordained by curiosity to be something special. When I did find what I'd been looking for, however, I didn't know it: a paperback book with a comically lurid cover; *Lady in the Lake*, by Raymond Chandler. I'd never heard of him, but took it back to the hilltop house, where I spent the rest of the day reading.

We'd bought produce at a roadside stand on the trip up, and in late afternoon began to prepare dinner. It took a while, in the rudimentary kitchen, with a propane stove and no electricity, but that seemed right. What else was there to do? The insects were subdued now, the sky and trees out the window a still life portrait.

Eventually we ate, and though that should have transpired slowly too, since there was no reason to hurry, habit took over as we sat at the table, compelling us to get the eating over with in order to move on to the next thing … which was twilight.

Outside, bats fluttered out of the woods in erratic flight. The sky, brighter than the clearing rimmed by trees, brought Magritte to mind; supposedly surreal paintings that realistically conveyed the earthly mysteriousness of dusk.

And then, abruptly, it was dark, and after a moment of absolute silence, the insects started up again; another type, or maybe the same ones sounding different. Noreen curled up in a quilt to go to sleep and I lit the oil lamp and picked up *Lady in the Lake* where I'd left off, as moths fluttered around the oil lantern.

The rhythm of a place is irresistible; it seeps into you. But I was surprised how quickly it happened. Drinking coffee in the morning, my thoughts drifted out the window to the clearing and the insect symphony building from nothing to its shrill conclusion. The urge to read a newspaper, to see what was happening in the world, pushed at me like an addiction. And I wondered: Could I be in this place without falling back on abstraction? Look out the window without feeling the need to explain what I saw?

The morning sky was more white than blue; later, in the afternoon, eggshell blue; and as evening approached the great dome seemed to recede, nearer things taking precedence, the air shifting from blue-gray to smoky dusk in subtle gradations. A bird heralded the darkness, and then silence, as on the day before, with not even the distant whoosh of a car to contrast and accentuate it, only a high-pitched whisper in my ears, pulsing to the beat of my heart.

And then full night, the sky prominent again, a pitch-black field for those twinkling stars the Egyptians believed told of an illuminated world beyond, peaking through the holes in a dark canopy. Catching myself trying to locate the Big Dipper, I wondered: Could I take in the nighttime sky without looking for constellations?

The post office had suspended me for a week, for what was called insubordination. It was intended as a punishment, but I welcomed it. When I woke up at four-thirty in the morning, before realizing where I was, my body told me to crawl out of bed and get dressed. And realizing, not for the first time, that my life didn't have to be determined by those working habits, I rolled over and went back to sleep.

*   *   *

Julian showed up in the afternoon with a woman he'd been seeing. Noreen and I were sitting on a blanket in the clearing when they emerged from the forest ravine. They veered over, he introduced us to her, we talked awhile, then the two of them went into the house with their knapsacks and returned a few minutes later, naked. While ruminating about the difference between this place and what I thought of as civilization, it never occurred to me to shed my clothes. But why not? Who would see us?

Later, as Marne and Noreen prepared dinner in the house, Julian and I walked down to the dirt road, where we sat across from an overgrown meadow and talked about living in the country. I told him about going to the general store a few miles away. He knew the place: the gasoline pump in front; the junked cars, car parts, and tires in a dirt lot alongside; a picture of everyday life, atrophying, rusting, falling apart.

Teenagers hung out on a wooden porch when I'd pulled up and got out. They stopped talking and scrutinized me. Naively, I'd expected something else; that we were of the same generation and thus shared something essential. But in fact they were no less suspicious of me than the wizened proprietor inside, who warily eyed me as I moved among the three aisles, browsing the sparse shelves. When I placed my purchases on the counter, he wordlessly toted them up with a grease pencil on a paper bag, took my money, and doled out change.

Julian said, "I felt the same way when I first came up here … like an outsider, like I didn't belong."

"So, at the general store, they're friendly to you now?"

He laughed. "Not exactly, but they're getting used to me. They don't stare the way they used to, and the old guy nods when I walk in."

He and Marne had come up a few months before and stayed for two weeks, to see what it would be like to live there. "I missed the usual conveniences," he told me. "But you get over that quickly. You realize you don't need a lot of the things you think you do. Not that I wouldn't want to make some changes when we move up here …"

"Really?" I said. "You're going to do it?"

"I'm seriously thinking about it," he replied. "If we do—Marne and I and some other people who've expressed interest—we'd need to build two, maybe three small houses, to accommodate everyone—nothing elaborate, one- or two-room structures—and we'd redo the house on the hill, with plumbing, so there would be an indoor bathroom and a modern communal kitchen … a small generator for electricity … a common room, with a library, a sound system …

"But before I even cut down a single tree or plant a garden, I want to be here awhile, feel part of it, understand it … which means to observing it over time … where the sunlight hits in spring and summer, and what it's like in winter, when it rains—if it ever rains again."

It was a relief to have company. Noreen and I had gotten tired of just being with each other and manufacturing things to do.

Marne and Julian left after dinner, to stay in a tree house built between limbs, overlooking the ravine, perched above the dry creek bed. In the morning they returned to the hilltop house and we ate breakfast together and then they took off, to hike.

*   *   *

Too soon, it was Saturday, the day before we had to return to Berkeley, since my suspension ended on Monday.

"Why don't we all go to town?" Julian suggested.

"Comptche?" I said.

"No, not the general store … Mendocino."

So we piled into his old VW bug and, feeling adventurous, headed for the coast.

The town of Mendocino sat across the coast highway, on a bulge of land protruding into the ocean. Emerging from a road closely flanked by trees, rounding a bend, the sudden vista of open sea and sky turned us giddy, and we headed down to the klatch of buildings perched on the peninsula as if on a rollicking joyride, a crew in an R. Crumb comic panel.

We rolled past the two-story wooden facades, and before we knew it were beyond them, chugging along in the beat-up car toward the sea and the distant horizon amidst curiously incongruous houses, seemingly built for small people; tidy structures on plots of land separated by picket fences and trimmed hedges, streets without sidewalks. The fences, the notion of private property, seemed a joke, against the panorama of sky and ocean. The street—a road, actually—ended abruptly at a boulder-strewn shoreline splashed by rough surf. We turned around and headed back.

We passed a red-brick school not unlike schools anyplace else, but smaller. Then more hobbitlike houses on property defined by those incongruous fences, then the mercantile town again; a library, post office, hardware store, grocery; a one-of-a-kind town with all you might need or want, in moderation.

The simplicity of it was intriguing, but then we got out of the car, and entering the real world, encountered hostility, which broke the goofy spell. Just like that, we were outsiders, viewed with distrust.

Like a guide, Julian took over, producing a list of food and supplies he and Marne had drawn up. A passport, of sorts, to give our presence meaning.

The grocer was friendly enough, but then we crossed the street to the small health food store, with its barrels of flour and nuts, and the hippies who ran the place regarded us warily. As with the teenagers at the general store, I expected they'd be pleased to see us, allies, cousins in the same generational family. But we made them nervous, reminding them of their own status as newcomers; and more, that welcoming us would undermine their tenuous acceptance, based on the anonymity they'd nurtured.

Still, it didn't prepare us for the elderly librarian's reaction; an unprepossessing, middle-aged woman who looked up from her desk, eager to be of service, and seeing us, ducked back down to the drawer of file cards she'd been examining. Looking up again as Julian asked about applying for a card, she feigned the helpfulness she'd been about to offer freely, passing him a form to fill out, officially checking a piece of mail with his address on it, projecting discomfort as she went about her duties.

We split up then, wandered about the small town, and when we met again, Julian was upset.

"What's the matter?" I asked him.

He nodded toward a hippie-looking character up the street who was staring at us; long hair tied in a ponytail, a hoop in one ear. "I just came out of the hardware store," Julian said, "and out of nowhere, he accused of me of being a narc."

"What'd you mean, a narc?"

"You know, a narc, a narc," he snapped uncharacteristically. And then pulling himself together: "I didn't know what to say. I was dumbfounded. I told him he was wrong, that he had to be confusing me with someone else, but he said no, he knew who I was, and then he held up two fingers and pointed them at my eyes, as if leveling a curse ..."

He frowned, shook his head. "I swear, I never saw him before ..."

At the Friday night gatherings in Berkeley, listening to Julian argue politics with his brother-in-law, I'd come to respect his fierce sense of morality. He'd clashed with me a few times too, but I'd never seen him lose his bearings before.

"Why would he say a thing like that to me?" he asked, questioning himself more than me.

I said, "Y'know, I've noticed that the people our age up here seem sort of unhinged, like strangers in a strange land ..."

He looked at me questioningly.

"I mean, they don't fit in, except among their own kind ... Maybe they turn paranoid because of the isolation."

In one of the buildings down by the bay, the teenage waitress in the town's only restaurant, a local girl, couldn't handle our order. She would've had an easier time of it had she written it down, but for some reason, perhaps flustered by us, she didn't. Then she brought back the wrong sandwich, the wrong soup, forgot the drinks, and when she finally got it straightened out, disappeared into the kitchen and didn't return.

Julian was still upset when we got back in the car. Again, as we drove off, he brought up the backwoods hippie who'd confronted him, as if the accusation had undermined his confidence, called into question the community he'd envisioned, up there in the woods. "I never saw him before," he repeated.

Then Marne, in the backseat, told us about a job she had when she and Julian came up a few months before. A quiet woman, she'd hardly said anything all day, but now spoke without hesitation, as if ignited by Julian's encounter.

She'd read the help wanted ads in the Fort Bragg newspaper, and the only place with any work was twelve miles up the coast; a part-time job in a doughnut factory. For two dollars an hour, not including lunch, which she ate on her own time, she dunked dough into vats of hot oil.

"I couldn't take it," she concluded. "I had to quit. The heat, the spattering oil …"

We drove in silence then, around the long bend that led away from the coast, the little town once more small and tidy in the distance, a pretty picture, as the twilight forest of pines closed in, hinting at unseen things.

Uncle Jack

My uncle Jack was tall and thin as a teenager, with a head that seemed small for his body. In an old photo, he stands next to the stoop of a tenement building long since demolished, wearing one of those long winter overcoats that appear formal today and was commonplace then. Jack seems intent on looking older than he is, like other young men and women back then, cloaked in the premature seriousness of the Great Depression. But he's smiling shyly, as if embarrassed to be the focus of attention, still more boy than man.

He was sixteen then, the year I was born. My father, whom I wouldn't see until I was three, was with the Marines in the Pacific. There was Jack, my mother, my grandparents, and me; in Brownsville, a Brooklyn ghetto then and one now too, though its complexion has changed. The only son, he was the family hope, and I was the bright face of the future.

In real time, where babies mimic those around them and then become toddlers, Jack of course had his own aspirations and ambitions: mainly, to play the piano well enough to someday be in a band, like those he heard on the radio. My father introduced him to Benny Goodman, and afterward Jack found his own influences. He knew, however, that the serious business of life lay elsewhere. He had a living to earn, after all, a family that needed a bread winner. Jazz would have to wait.

He must have had jobs when he wasn't in school, since I rarely saw him. My mother worked too, so during the day I lived in a cocoon of sorts with my immigrant grandparents. There were no other children

around, no toys to play with or books to look at. I could have been
Adam, had God decided to make him younger at creation.

My grandfather told me stories before I fell asleep and took me for
neighborhood walks in the afternoon, the streets and tenement facades a
diorama of dimension, in contrast to the gray confines of the apartment.
He would stop when I glanced here or there with curiosity and let me
take it in: the ice house across the street, the corner candy store up the
block, the high, red brick walls of the reformatory at the top of the hill,
where I'd tugged him toward the redolent smell of baking bread from
unseen Italian bakeries.

I called him Pa, as his grown-up children still did. Perhaps when he
was younger, Pa had been a different kind of father to them. With me,
he was a good-natured but distant presence; patient, acceptant, but with
other things on his mind. Finding work, no doubt, and the dissipation of
his alcoholic brother who lived a few streets away.

My grandmother was tougher, a thin, hunchbacked woman too busy
cooking and shopping to do more than make sure I was clean, dressed,
and fed. She took care of the family necessities, was a fact of life for
me, but distant as well. Much later I would discover that she spoke five
languages.

When Jack was home, he was the only one who knelt down and
talked to me, making an impression on me as deep as the one he felt
himself. I saw as much in his pride in later years, when he'd tell stories
about me, which were also stories about him.

Like going to the Catskills one summer to work as a waiter, and
upon returning, standing by my crib, where I gesticulated and shouted
at him for half an hour. "Like Mussolini," he'd always conclude, before
explaining that though my words were gibberish, he was sure I was
berating him for being gone so long.

There was an upright piano in the drab room with a faux fireplace, a
table, and some soft chairs. Jack sat me down next to him on the bench
one day, plunked the keys and showed me the foot pedals, which I
couldn't reach unless I knelt on the floor and depressed them with my

hands. Shiny black and yellow-white keys … When he was gone, I'd climb up on the bench and plunk them myself.

I recalled, too, the afternoon he burst into the apartment eager to show me something. A gift, he said, and from behind his back produced a child-size sheepskin jacket. He spread the arms out, held it toward me to put on. There was no cat in the apartment, yet the fur lining inside nevertheless frightened me, hinted at something alive and with claws, and I ran away. He caught me, spoke softly, somehow knew why I was spooked, persuaded me to touch the fur, to prove it was safe; reassured, I put it on.

Jack must have been in college then, part-time, because at some point he moved out, to a dorm at City College. He took me there one day, to a room with two cots and a window crisscrossed with cyclone mesh, and gestured at the concrete courtyard below as if it were something to see; but to me, another drab scene, with even less to stir the imagination than the tenement air shaft out the kitchen window, with a clothesline suspended between ledges.

These recollections came to mind when I was a boy, a teenager, a young man, whenever I saw Jack. Always, he'd greet me with delight, blurting "Peter!" with an intonation that seemed to emerge from someplace deep within him. But after a while that welcome greeting took on a different meaning for me, reflected and echoed a disconnection between us, because I was no longer an innocent child, but someone he didn't know at all.

Back then the city colleges were free. He studied engineering, graduated in the early fifties, and must have had a few jobs before the Horatio Alger tale that would become the family template for success reached its penultimate chapter: in a warehouse in New Jersey that stored a machine Jack and two other guys had built; a mammoth thing consisting of wires and tubes connected to a typewriter. A primitive computer.

I was in grade school at the time, living with my parents and brother in a garden apartment complex in Queens. Jack invited my father to see

the setup, and he brought me along. I typed a problem, the longest
string of numbers that could fit on the page, to be added, subtracted,
and multiplied. But Jack and his friends were not involved in
mathematics so much as a way to typeset pages by machine; to move
the art of printing beyond Gutenberg, beyond the need for actual
printers who worked in shops and at newspapers. A revolutionary
machine that eventually attracted the interest of a corporation.

Overnight, as it's said, he and his partners became rich.

In retrospect it seems that one day Jack lived in a modest garden
apartment complex, similar to ours, with his wife and baby girl. And the
next, they moved to an exclusive suburb on Long Island.

He still wore thick black-framed glasses after his material
transformation, his hair short, almost a crew cut; the technocratic look
of his warehouse days. But it disconcerted me, watching him cook
steaks on the deck in back, overlooking a thick pile lawn, tall trees and
rich foliage, pointing out how thick the slabs of meat were; his wife in a
balloon dress that might have been the height of fashion for all I knew;
the little girl, my youngest cousin then, squalling for attention. I was a
teenager and knew that something significant had happened; something
good, supposedly. But I distrusted it; people I'd long known were now
acting oddly, didn't seem the same at all.

*   *   *

When my grandmother was hospitalized following a heart attack,
my grandfather was persuaded to move into the maid's room at Jack's
house. Had there ever been a maid there? I didn't know. In college then,
I had little connection with Jack and his family, which included a son
now. The split-level was neat and clean when I drove out there, so there
might have been a cleaning lady, but I couldn't imagine the need for
full-time help. I was there to help out, to pick up the old man and
chauffeur him to his bank in Rockaway so he could deposit a dozen
social security checks.

As always, Jack greeted me with that heartfelt "Peter!" then led me from the foyer to the sun-bright kitchen.

We stood there awhile, talking about one thing or another, catching up since the last time we'd seen each other, then Jack went to work preparing coffee and I sat down at the table. Pa was stubborn, he said— we both still called him that—wouldn't open a new bank account out there, insisted on going out to Rockaway instead. And then Pa appeared, said hello, with that glow he always had when he saw me, and sat down across the table.

Three generations in that room at the same time, and then my new youngest cousin—a boy of five or six—was there too, seemingly representing a new generation. He stopped short in the archway to the kitchen, saw his grandfather at the table and flew into a rage, bolting across the floor, shouting, "It's my chair! It's my chair! Get up! Get up!" grabbing the backrest in his little hands and angrily shaking it back and forth to dislodge the old man.

My grandfather was a gentle man. I'd rarely seen him upset, and then only when he argued politics, getting red in the face. But never at another person. It didn't seem to be in his makeup. And now I could see that there was more to his family portrait than serenity, that he bypassed the stages between anger and resignation.

Without a word about his dispossession, he stood up as his grandson attacked the chair, said to me, "I'll wait for you outside," in his Yiddish accent, and left by the back door, taking the deck stairs down to the driveway.

The boy was gone by then, having made his point, and Jack was still fiddling with the coffee, apparently unaware of what had occurred.

I said to him, "Did you see that?"

He turned from the counter and looked at me without comprehension. "What?" he asked. "What happened?" And then out the window, seeing his father in the driveway, standing by the car: "What's Pa doing down there?"

At the bank in Rockaway, Pa asked me to help him fill out the deposit slip, but hesitated before giving me the checks, saying, "Promise me, Payta." It was as close as he could get to saying my name. "Promise not to tell them how much it is. If they find out, they'll make me and Mama move when she comes out of the hospital."

He had about a thousand dollars of accumulated checks, and another two hundred in the back. To him, it was a lot of money.

Later, when I drove back and we were passing through the suburban town, he spotted a liquor store and asked me to stop. I idled by the curb as he went inside, returning with a pint of whiskey in a paper bag. Except for a glass of Manischewitz now and then, I didn't know he drank.

He was halfway into the car when he stopped and asked, "Do you want I should buy you some too?"

"No, that's okay," I told him after a moment, both touched and nonplussed by the offer.

After we pulled into the driveway, he entered the house through a door to the garage, secreting the paper bag under his coat as he hurried down the ground floor hallway and ducked into the maid's room.

*   *   *

I had no idea that Jack's marriage was disintegrating until I heard he moved out.

Families take sides after a divorce; they rally around their own. It's an understandable reflex. But in acting as Jack's sounding board during his break-up, my parents went further, became part of a wider conspiracy, reciprocating his grievances by airing their own grievances over the course my life had taken. And out of that same loyalty, Jack appropriated their ill will, adopting the same attitude toward me.

I wouldn't see him again until he moved to Manhattan.

I'd finished college by then, moved into the city, spent a year taking drugs, got a job afterward and pulled myself together, got married, moved away, and traveling back to the city from California, had once again sunk below my parents' level of expectation, becoming a mailman, of all things.

Jack no longer wore black-framed spectacles, but silver-rimmed glasses that matched the gray streaks in his longish hair. When Noreen and I entered the foyer of the posh apartment, he blurted "Peter!" with delight, then caught himself, as if realizing I was no longer the boy he'd known, but the disappointing son he'd heard about.

His woman friend, who lived a few blocks away and acted as hostess at his social affairs, was at his side, and when he turned to greet other guests exiting the penthouse elevator, she ushered us in, pointing out the African art set on chrome and glass shelves, the massive abstract paintings on the walls, then the catered buffet, before moving on to others.

Spotting the Steinway piano that had been in the suburban home, I wandered over to it, and a few minutes later Jack was at my side, telling me about a musician he'd met at a club on Fifty-seventh Street who played in this or that ensemble and came to his apartment once a week to give him lessons. He pointed out his record collection on a wall of built-in shelves, and in his enthusiasm, slipped back in time, became younger, the successful businessman in abeyance.

When he held out his hands, to demonstrate how he'd been tutored to hold them over the keyboard—marveling at how little he'd known before—I saw the gnarled look of his slender fingers—like my mother's and her sister's—arthritis, the family disability, and mentioning it, broke the spell, became the dutiful son who'd done the right thing.

"Mary is concerned about you," he said in a somber tone, and went on from there …

There is such a thing as growing up; a notion I'd resisted for years. Of accepting responsibility and doing things you wouldn't choose to do if you had a choice. But disclaim whatever it is that sparks youthful enthusiasm and you lose something essential. I spoke to the teenager that evening, and then the man he'd become, and was relieved when I was able to extricate myself from the grown-up.

I'd gone to college, and then to graduate school. I went to summer school too, and took more courses, to qualify for a teacher's license. Afterward I could have taught in a public school, or become a journalist. But instead I drifted, waiting for life to tell me what I was meant to do. My parents told Jack I was working on a book, and at his apartment he said perfunctory things about that impractical dream: I was nearly thirty now, and married. Wasn't it time I came to my senses?

Yet, after school, except for my drug year, I'd always worked, always had a job. It was a point of pride; I came from an upright workingclass background. He knew that, or should have, and I liked to believe that as someone who had put off his own dreams, he would have understood my aspirations.

Clinging to that interpretation, I sent him a piece I'd written. Jack was a patron of the arts, bankrolling the painter whose canvases adorned the walls like erotic Kandinskys. Maybe he'd help me out. Though had I thought about it, it would have occurred to me that I'd never actually seen him read a book.

In response to the story I sent him, he told me he had a friend whose opinion he valued and that he'd given it to her, to see what she thought—the hostess he called upon for social occasions, and whom he would eventually marry. I'd get the same reaction years later from timid agents who didn't know whether to take a chance on what they'd read. And then he got back to me with this advice: I should write more like Alan Ayckbourne, whom I'd never heard of; a playwright, I would discover, who recently had a hit play on Broadway.

It was the last time, I told myself, that I would ask Jack for anything, or expect anything from him.

But ambition has a way of trumping common sense, so when my parents sent a letter saying he would bankroll me for a year, during which I could work on my novel, I didn't hesitate to accept. How could I turn the opportunity down? A year in which I wouldn't have to worry about money and could instead concentrate on my book.

The provenance of the deal came clear to me later. My parents and Jack had discussed it and together they came up with the idea, which was why Jack stipulated that when the year was over, if I hadn't finished my novel by then, or no one agreed to publish it—for how else could I claim to be a writer if a publisher considered it unworthy?—I'd give it up and get a job in line with my education.

And so, with profound misunderstanding of the workings of karma, I quit my job at the post office, collected my accumulated retirement pay, and booked a flight for Noreen and myself to Amsterdam in December.

What better place to work on my masterpiece than Europe?

Cat and Crab

I was no longer sure what I thought about Colin Shay. Inconsistencies, opinions, and attitudes I either hadn't noticed or chose to overlook left me wondering what was real and what wasn't. Who was he? What made him tick?

His placid exterior and self-effacing manner said one thing, the half smile and raised eyebrow another. Like me, he was attuned to subtleties of the moment; the perception of gesture and inflection, the feel of a setting, which has its own sensibility. Yet I'd come to suspect that the encompassing context eluded him; the wider, generally agreed upon world in which personal preference comments upon self-limitation.

There were moments when the evidence Colin gathered, the crystallization of his senses, set him at odds to my own conclusions, gathered in the same way. Which made it hard for me to understand him; we were alike, yet different. The obstinate mind-set that peeked through his apparent agreeability, for instance, the cold hard look and slate gaze. Reflection of the Colin Shay who'd been a junkie, I assumed, before doubling back to question myself at generalizing from the particular.

Junkie, a category I distrusted, metaphor for the wariness I felt the evening I showed up alone and told him and Maggie that Noreen couldn't make it, that she didn't feel well. It was supposed to be a farewell dinner for the two of us, before we traveled cross-country then took a plane to Amsterdam.

Colin's half smile of commiseration was false, his shuttered look a truer response. Maggie, who was perceptive too, must have recognize

Noreen's awkward discomfort when the four of us got together, yet she appeared genuinely concerned, accepted the transparent excuse I offered and asked if Noreen was all right, saying, "Tell her I hope she'll feel better."

When the three of us sat down at the round kitchen table, she'd been drinking awhile, the bottle of wine only half full. But that never dissuaded her from conversation, and as Colin set the salad bowls on the table, she eyed me for a moment before broaching the subject of poetry readings and asking, again, why I never read my own work; a familiar topic.

"It makes me uncomfortable," I told her, sipping from the delicate wineglass.

"But why, Peter?" she asked. "You're always so self-assured, surely you aren't nervous about speaking before an audience?"

When Maggie used my name, it sounded so personal—speaking directly to me, it seemed—it spurred me to respond in kind. My standard reply, one I trotted out when the subject came up before—about the coffeehouse scene, where everyone came to hear a friend or partner read, and paid only perfunctorily attention to the other readers—came to mind, but I ignored it.

"It's not that I'm afraid of addressing an audience," I told her. "It's not that at all. It's something else …"

"Then what is it?" she asked when I paused.

"Well, okay," I said, "it's like this … Ever since college, where for a while I was the life of the party, an exuberant extravert, I've been wary of performing. You've heard me say that I write not just because it's a way to explain myself, but because as a reader I like it that I can make up my own mind without being influenced by how something sounds, how persuasive a reader is reciting lines. If I have any fear of addressing an audience, the fear is that they'll respond to who I am, or seem to be, instead of what I write … What I mean is, as a writer, I want to convey, not influence."

After a moment she said, "But if you're not published, how else are people going to know what you've written unless they *hear* it?"

"Then I suppose I'll have to wait until I am published."

"But be reasonable, Peter. Who knows when that will happen?" She looked across the table at Colin. "Don't you agree, Cole?"

"I've spoken to him about it, Maggie," he said with annoyance. "I'd print him myself, if I could afford it, and if my press didn't break down every other day."

I knew it was a sensitive subject, that he felt slighted by lack of recognition, craved the repute of poets he knew or had once known. So I wasn't about to complain about the difficulty of getting published.

"But there's something else," I said to Maggie, looking up from the salad. "Something more personal ... It's not that I'm standing on principle when I say I don't want to do readings. I mean, as the life of the party back then, I observed what happened when the performer in me took over ... It brought out the worst in me."

"I have to confess, Peter, I don't believe I've ever seen that in you. I find it hard to believe."

"Well, all I can say is it comes to life inside me ... a giddy feeling of affirmation whenever I sense the approval of others, which calls forth a need for more of it, until I strain to impress, which in turn leads to my monopolizing the atmosphere with talk, blurting whatever comes to mind ... all out of that need for approval."

Maggie dipped her head down to her salad, picked at it as if ruminating, then pushed it aside. I finished my own, then Colin cleared the salad plates.

"I honestly didn't know that about you, Peter," she said then. "You don't at all come across as dependent on others ... quite the contrary."

I laughed. "Yeah, well, there's a lot of things you don't know about me, Maggie."

"But then, even if it's true—"

"It *is* true."

"—don't you think it would be worthwhile to face that aspect of yourself? To face your ... beast and move beyond the need for self-affirmation?"

*   *   *

After we'd eaten, Colin and I moved to the side room to play our ritual game of chess. His play was uninspired, yet after he set the king on its side, he congratulated me as if I'd played well, eliciting the usual sense of discord in me. Surely he knew that wasn't true.

Gesturing at the board, I said, "Not a particularly inspired victory."

"You're too modest," he replied.

"No, it's the truth, Colin. I'm not patient enough. It's not in my nature. Playing as often as we do, I've come to realize I can only concentrate for so long, and then I get restless and make capricious moves, hoping for the best."

"You set a trap," he said, "and I fell for it hook, line, and sinker."

"No, you got me all wrong," I countered. "I'm not a trap setter. I had no idea when you took my knight that it would open up the board." I grinned. "Surely you've noticed that the first chance I get, I sacrifice a knight."

He sat back. "Which is usually the right move."

"Then how come you win most of the time?"

He arched an eyebrow. "Do I?"

"I don't win even half the games we play. It's only that when I *do* win, it's so unorthodox, it's memorable."

"And when I win, it's boring," he said with his own grin. "Is that what you mean?"

It wasn't what I'd meant at all. But I was in a reflective frame of mind, and Colin apparently wasn't. He suggested another game, we set up the pieces, and I quickly pushed a pawn.

That contest ended quickly too, as I kept my knight safe for a change and played my bishops, slicing into his vee formation, lining up my rooks, using the queen to trap him in a corner.

"Two in a row," he said afterward, a wry smile confirming his earlier assessment—that I was the better player.

Maggie was waiting in the kitchen, having cleared the table in preparation for the tarot reading she'd promised to do for Noreen and me. She was flipping cards and looking at them when we walked in, a pint of bourbon on the table, a half full glass at her elbow. She patted a chair next to her, indicating that I should sit there, then began to lay out the cards one at a time on the tabletop.

Colin had headed for the sink and was now washing dishes, keeping his distance, it seemed; like Noreen, when she wanted to avoid contact.

Maggie stopped after laying out a half-dozen colorful medieval depictions and tapped one of them. "This is you," she said, and looked up. "I chose it because it implies strength. And this ... " She stared down at the table, closed her eyes, then opened them again. "I would say this is Noreen," and she turned toward the sink. "Is that right, do you think, Cole?"

Without pausing from his chore or coming over to look, he said over his shoulder, "You're the expert, Maggie."

"At least I think it's Noreen," she said, turning back, looking at the cards in her hand, then flipping another onto the table, then another, until she'd laid them all out in an H pattern.

She studied this for several seconds, in a silence that would have seemed solemn if I hadn't been wondering whether she was having trouble focusing. Then, abruptly excited, she said, "I wish Noreen were here to see this! It's marvelous! This configuration here," her fingers wavering over several cards, "indicates that you'll find, or *discover,* something ... *significant* about each other ... yet it's something you've known for a long time ... " She looked at me, anticipating a response.

And all at once it hit me—not in the cards, which didn't mean anything to me, but the focus I brought to her stray words—that if I'd ever been in love with Noreen, I wasn't now.

The trip to Europe, our plan to live with friends Amsterdam, where I'd work on my novel and she'd take pictures, was an attempt to revive the past, to recreate a former happiness ... the summer we went to

Europe after we were married.

"Does that make sense?" Maggie asked.

Shaken, I said, "Yes, it does."

"I'm so happy for you, Peter! For both of you!" She picked up her glass, sipped the whiskey, then pointed at the table. "You see, this card is the Lovers ... and in this placement, it's the fulfillment of these." She indicated two overlapping cards in the center of the H. "Temperance ... and Strength. But ... an inner strength ... " She took another sip of whiskey. "There's adversity here ... and the strength to overcome it ..."

"What kind of adversity?" I asked.

She leaned forward, close to the tabletop. "Something ... cogent ... material." She frowned at the cards. "That might be a longer time frame, but ... the Tower represents ... let me see ... " She fumbled a book she'd placed on the table, opened it and thumbed through it. "Here it is. 'The Tower' ... 'We draw people and places to us to help formulate our identity ... to construct what we assume is our personality, which is represented by the Tower. Then something shatters our illusions and the Tower crumbles ...'"

I had no idea what she was talking about.

"This is the *only* specific obstacle," she said, picking up a card. "Not a ... *profound* obstacle, but a persistent one."

"Which is?"

"Money," she said, looking up.

I laughed, and Colin laughed too, at the sink, without turning around.

"Well, what else is new?" I said. "Is there any mention of travel?"

She looked down at the cards. "No ... not that I see ..." She tilted her head and studied them some more. "... Though I suppose this might indicate travel," and she reached out and flicked a finger over several cards.

Colin turned off the faucet and began drying the dishes one at a time.

"It's a wonderful reading!" Maggie said, reaching out to squeeze my arm, and with that movement, losing her balance and leaning against me for support. "It's so like you, Peter!"

But instead of feeling good about it, I felt uncertain.

She got unsteadily to her feet. "There's a marvelous poem I'd like to read to you," she said, "by Charles Olson ... one about the Tower ... in the tarot deck." She stood behind the chair, leaning against it for support. "If that's all right with you ..."

"Yeah, sure," I said.

A sense of disquiet hovered in the kitchen as Maggie moved unsteadily out of the room and Colin continued to dry dishes and I was aware that Noreen wasn't there.

She returned with a paperback, sat down and opened it tenderly, took a breath and began reading in a soft, almost husky voice, one line at a time, pausing between each.

> *... in the red tower*
> *in that tower where she also sat*
> *in that particular tower where watching and moving are,*
> *there,*
> *there where what triumph there is, is: there*
> *is all substance, all creature*
> *all there is against the dirty moon, against*
> *number, image, sortilege—*
>
> *alone with cat and crab*
> *and sound is, is, his*
> *conjecture ...*

I didn't know what it meant, but like the tarot cards, it didn't matter. A hollow feeling came over me as she read, one I'd had before, in another kitchen. I was desperate, seeking solace from people I thought I knew, and instead walked in on strangers, a universe where nothing mattered.

Maggie had just put the book down when I blurted, "It's so bleak!"

My outburst took her by surprise, and she looked up, startled. "A lot of people feel that way," she said defensively, as if I'd criticized her.

I don't know what I said then, an emotional outpouring that in my mind conflated Colin and Maggie with Tom and Lila in that other kitchen, Lila standing at the stove, staring blankly at me, as though my existence was an imposition; Tom oblivious, sitting the table, silently eating with head down as I sat opposite him.

Maggie quickly finished what was left in her glass, and then her elbow slipped on the tabletop and she fell away from it in a slow movement toward the floor, her chair toppling with her. Startled, I didn't move to help as she tried to get up, watched her slip on the linoleum and go down again.

"Cole ..." she said, looking across the room to where he stood at the counter.

"Get up, Maggie," he replied tonelessly, drying his hands on a dish towel.

She crawled away from the table toward the open floor.

"Get up," he said again, in the same neutral tone, watching her crawl.

I watched too, dumbstruck, as she crawled past the stove on hands and knees, past the refrigerator, toward the bedroom door on the far side of the room, which was ajar, then toppled into the darkness inside.

... While at the counter, Colin turned away, to scoop coffee grounds into a pot.

Great Escape

Out the window, picture perfect steeples rose above snow-covered rooftops beneath a dour gray sky. A wintry scene in old Europe, a museum landscape to admire. A hotel room in Basel, where the scenery was the stuff I fell back on to keep my spirits up and to attend to Noreen's flagging morale.

Having run out of film back in Amsterdam, she'd nearly filled her sketch pad with poses of me standing by the window, or reading, or sleeping. I'd finished the last book I brought from America, *Don Quixote*, an ironic comment on our trip: me chasing windmills, Noreen an improbable Sancho Panza, trudging alongside. The predicament of an errant knight motivated by youthful enthusiasm, which now found us prisoners in a hotel room while waiting for money to be wired from home.

The innkeeper had begun to regard us suspiciously as our stay approached a week and we'd yet to pay our bill. Like thieves, we darted back to the room after breakfast, dining room rolls secreted in our pockets, hoping he wouldn't spot us; snuck out again in the afternoon, for our daily trip to the American Express office; ducked back inside in the evening, when the coast seemed clear. Half starved, the gnawing in my stomach reminded me of another influential book, *Hunger*, and its crazed protagonist. But where delirium had propelled him through the streets of Oslo, I was in thrall to doubt and uncertainty.

As I stood gazing at the tidy landscape, Noreen began to cry; soft, sobbing sounds. Unusual for her, to break down over the big picture, rather than the particular details of her life, and it freaked me out. And so, imbalanced by hunger, and jumping to the first conclusion that occurred to me, I roused her for a journey outside, to cross the Rhine and ... what? Become part of the postcard scene out the window? Whatever the reason, it moved me—and thus us—out of the room.

It was cold outside, and it turned out the church spires were more distant than they'd appeared from the window. Bundled in our coats— like Dostoievski's St. Petersburg characters; I'd brought *The Idiot* with me too—we boarded a trolley, surrendering the coins we'd been hoarding. There was regret in that, given our dire circumstances, but then we were rolling on smooth wheels, and like prisoners on furlough, gaping at the stone buildings on our ride to nowhere. Twilight came on as we seemed to float down the hilly, cobbled streets, and then bright, fluorescent lights went on inside the trolley, making mirrors of the polished windows. I thought of Kafka then, the world outside opaque, the clean, well-lit compartment, with its inner reflections alienating us from it, the coach stopping periodically to collect and dispense passengers with the regularity of a precise mechanism. Well, why not? This was Switzerland, after all.

At some point we crossed the Rhine. I vaguely glimpsed its expanse as we continued on our predetermined track, stopping and starting, stopping and starting, with never a jolt ... never getting anywhere that I could see, in the moving, mirrored room that threw us back on ourselves, sitting there ... like cows, I thought, as Dostoievski had scornfully described the Swiss during one of his self-exiles ... or cattle—a disquieting thought for a Jew, what with Germany out there, just beyond the city limits.

That thought stuck, and with sudden urgency I said to Noreen: "We gotta get off! We're going too far!"

"Too far?" she replied, confused. We were six thousand miles from home. How much farther could we go, and what difference would it make?

"Yes, yes!" I said as the trolley coasted along in near silence, and half rising from the seat, I frantically yanked the signal cord.

In fact the next stop was the last, passengers dispersing into a klieg-light-illuminated platz. We of course got out too, and with a sense of having been abandoned, I stood there on the brick pavement, blinking at the nondescript scene, Noreen just as discombobulated.

Where were we?

A flash caught my eye then, on the sidewalk—a large silver coin glinting in the klieg-lit scene. But before I could bend down and retrieve it, a blue-uniformed official abruptly appeared out of nowhere, looming before us, a George Grosz figure. I quickly shifted my stance, planting a foot on the coin, hiding it.

The buoyant yet stoic official leaned toward me and spoke in Swiss German, his breath an emission of cartoon vapor in the chill air.

Overly aware of the coin beneath my foot, I stood still, shook my head and shrugged, playing the stupid foreigner.

Switching to English, he said, "You are going *where?*"

"Just … looking around," I replied.

He took a moment to digest this casual response, then said, "You are Americans, yah?"

"Yah … we're from America."

"Ah …" His narrow eyes, set in a ruddy, pudgy face, took us in: my stained and torn sheepskin coat; Noreen's coat, of imitation leather, falling nearly to her ankles. Hippies, did he think? Or something less specific, yet nevertheless posing a nihilist threat to the orderliness of his civilization?

"You are in Messeplatz," he said. "It is a mistake. There is no tourist center here, no place to … 'looking around,' as you say. You must go back."

"Okay," I replied, nodding, foot still firmly on the silver coin. "We'll go back."

His matter-of-fact manner changed then, perhaps because we would indeed be leaving his oblast. He softened, turned helpful. Pointing back the way we'd come, he remarked upon the inexpensive hotels in the district near the railroad station, where we might find a room for the night—and where we were indeed staying—then politely touched the bill of his cap and drifted away.

As soon as he was out of sight I snatched up the coin and showed it to Noreen. She stared at it with as much amazement as I had, and then we began laughing and couldn't stop, standing there in the cold nowhere, laughing hysterically at the best joke we'd ever been part of.

And then we walked back, across the Rhine and up the steep cobbled streets, so we could save the silver coin, and sneaked back into the hotel, looking forward to the stale rolls in our room.

*   *   *

When we got off the plane, customs agents in uniforms that seemed too large for them checked and stamped our passports and gestured us toward a nondescript room where a woman in a glass booth converted our green bills into colorful local money. Otherwise, my first impressions were gray, from the damp mist hanging over the valley where the city of Luxembourg perched on a hill, to the elvish wood and stone houses as the bus brought us to the railroad station, children on bicycles staring with bulging eyes, as if they'd never seen outsiders before. The little duchy, as it was called, had a certain grotesque charm. But not until we were on the train, picking up speed, did the scenery make a more traditionally pleasing impression, wispy fog giving a lyric cast to pastoral fields as Noreen fell asleep, her head on my shoulder.

When my uncle Jack, in collusion with my parents, offered me a stipend that would enable me to work on my novel, I'd quit my job and booked a flight out of New York, for Amsterdam, not necessarily in that order. I might have booked the flight first, the notion of getting away having been extant in me a long while. We'd been corresponding with a Dutch couple we met during a summer vacation two and a half years before, and in every letter they'd urged us to come to Holland and live with them. A pipe dream, it seemed, until my uncle made his offer and I collected a tidy bundle of severance pay—nine hundred twenty-eight dollars, six hundred after paying for the flight—figuring it would last until Jack wired his money in a month or two. And now we were here in Europe. In December.

It was twilight when the train stopped in Brussels to a rush hour bustle of people entering and leaving the car. Noreen woke up as men dressed in suits and overcoats crowded in. It had never occurred to me there were commuters in Europe; my imagination depicted a less mundane place. They found seats, most of them settling behind splayed newspapers. Except for three men who stood by the door and conversed in French while glancing at us and the luggage stacked around our feet.

One of them eventually leaned toward us and politely asked, in English, "You are Canadian?"

"No, monsieur," I replied. "American."

"Ah ..." he said, and smiled. "It is not often we have Americans in winter ... except, of course, at the conference tables."

I said, "You mean the Common Market?"

He was puzzled a moment, then nodded. "Yes. The European Economic Community has headquarters here," and he pointed out the train window at an illuminated building in the distance. "And five minutes away is the residence of our ... how do you say it? Ruling family?"

"You have a queen?" Noreen asked.

One of the others in his group leaned forward from his spot near the door and in simple French I could understand asked what Noreen had said. Our interlocutor answered, which was followed by a burst of more complicated French between the three of them.

When our man turned back, Noreen quickly said, "Excuse me, I didn't mean to offend you."

He laughed, genuinely amused, translated for his companions, and they laughed too. It left me feeling good as well, to be the unusual occurrence that made their ordinary workday suddenly interesting. "Yes, we have a queen," he said to us, "and no, we are not offended."

The number of people in the car dwindled as we made stops in the city, and then more so as moved into the suburbs. Our three commuters were now conversing among themselves, glancing occasionally at us, and then our interlocutor spoke up again, the others listening attentively: "We read about your country in the journals, of course … the antiwar demonstrations. You are the people we read about?"

"Yes," I said, sitting up. "That's us."

I didn't know quite what to expect after blurting that out, or what had come over me to announce that I was a certain kind of American and proud of it. A burst of personal, idiosyncratic patriotism. And I was taken by surprise when he inclined in a bow, and his companions bowed toward us too, with the same show of respect. It seemed he wanted to say something else but couldn't find the words, and then the train was slowing and he turned aside and got off with his companions.

I was sad to see them go, thought about them afterward, returning to homes to eat dinner with families. The thought stayed with me as the train sped on, past towns and villages glimpsed through mirrored windows, past darkened fields and tiny rural stations with names that disappeared almost as soon as you saw them. Then a landscape dotted with lights, followed by apartment house windows facing the now elevated track; a city. Thus did we move through Antwerp, Rotterdam, Delft, Gravenhage, the car nearly empty when the train finally pulled into the Amsterdam station.

A policeman stood within the entrance doors as we struggled to carry our luggage out, hands clasped behind his back, watching a group of teenagers with long hair loitering by a wall of steel gray lockers inside the station. Outside, we maneuvered our stuff to a row of phone booths, but before I could step inside one of them, a young man appeared from nowhere and thrust an index size card in my face.

"Five dollars," he said, pointing to the card, the handwritten address and phone number barely legible. "Cheap." He turned and gestured at the sprawl of emptiness beyond the station, momentarily creeping me out, and I shook my head. In response, he began his pantomime again, his expression even more urgent.

"We have a place to stay," I broke in.

Dejected, he abruptly thrust the card into my hand and took off.

It was cold, and Noreen, bundled in her coat, handed me our little black phone book. I took the receiver off the hook, stared at the printed directions, in Dutch and English, dropped unfamiliar coins into the slot and dialed.

Franz and Maria DeHooch knew we were coming, though not when we'd show up. The idea of surprising them had appealed to me. It seemed a typically American thing to do; optimistic, exuberant. But the phone rang eight, nine, ten times, and no one answered, and suddenly the whole premise of our trip was in doubt. We'd been corresponding for a while but hadn't seen them in over two years, and even then only for a few days.

Noreen huddled by the booth in the chill mist, and I called every few minutes. Across a stretch of cobblestone pavement that ended at distant buildings, a few streetlights were reflected in a canal. The ink-blue water curved under what appeared to be a bridge then disappeared into dark shadow.

Were our Dutch acquaintances out for the evening, or longer?

"Maybe they moved," Noreen said, sounding distraught, which calmed me down. I hate uncertainty, but respond well to outright adversity.

"They'll be there," I assured her. "We just have to be patient."

I hid my own nervous impatience, for Noreen's sake, restraining myself from stepping into the phone booth as often and revealing my disquiet.

Finally, a good while later, someone on the other end picked up.

"Is it really you?" Maria said after I'd spoken, and in an instant everything was all right in our world again.

"Yes, it's really me, Maria. I've been calling all night."

"We just this minute arrived," she said. "Is funny. Franz told me you would come today ... " I could hear him in the background, shouting; Noreen at my shoulder now, leaning close to the receiver.

"Where are you?" Maria asked.

"At the railroad station," I said. "Can you pick us up?"

"… We don't have an automobile anymore."

I paused, hearing that. "You don't?"

"No. We'll tell you about it when you come. You have to take a bus … What bus, Franz?" She paused as he shouted, then explained: "Take the bus that stops on a bridge in front of the station. It will say 'Greuzenfeld' … What, Franz? … Bus fourteen. Franz says the last one is at one-thirty—the last until tomorrow morning. Can you make it?"

"Yeah, I think so. There's one there now."

"Ask the driver to tell you when you get to Frans Halstraat, then walk toward— Wait … Franz says he will be downstairs to meet you. You should hurry now."

We dragged the suitcases across a wide stretch of cobblestone as fast as we could and boarded the empty bus, which then didn't leave for fifteen minutes. Not that it mattered, now that we knew where we'd be sleeping that night. Having been on a plane and then the train, we were exhausted, but out of giddy relief were hopped up now … until, as we sat waiting for the bus to leave, it occurred to me once more that our well-being was entirely in the hands of other people.

Franz DeHooch

Out the bus windows as we drove off, just two of us aboard, we gazed at lights lining an embankment, emanating haloes in the vaporous air and twinkling in the Zuider Zee beyond. The three-story stone and brick buildings hovering over narrow streets, hoist beams protruding from the attic story—shades of Hendrik Hudson and the fur trade—arrayed along canals that opened into wider channels where piers jutted into the water next to ancient warehouses with buttressed facades; here and there, barges and houseboats moored to wooden docks, plants in barrels, bicycles in racks.

The streets undulated, buildings sometimes closer, sometimes farther away, arcades sheltering small shops suddenly appearing, bridges angling in all directions, more bicycles parked in stands, a bric-a-brac scene, an exotic panoply of sights that gave way to boulevards as we left the canals behind for broad sidewalks, modern buildings in newer neighborhoods, then a housing complex or maybe two or three identical complexes set next to each other, which went on and on …

The aesthetic change from historical past to commonplace present was sobering, and then the driver indicated that we should get off. We stumbled outside, stood surrounded by luggage in the shocking glare of mercury lights as the bus pulled away … and like a curtain rising as the performer behind it awaits his entrance, the compact figure of Franz DeHooch materialized, striding across the empty street in our direction, waving, shouting "You are here!" as he approached. And then, closer: "You are here and I am here and we are all togedder!" The Beatles.

"Yes," Noreen said as he threw his arms around her in a bear hug.

"But where are we?"

"This is Greuzenfeld!" he declared, stepping back with a sweeping gesture, as if doffing his chapeau in *The Three Musketeers*. "We hate it. But come!" and he shook my hand vigorously while pulling me into the street, snatching up one of the bags. "Maria is expecting us."

After waiting and sitting for so long, everything was happening fast now. We lugged the bags into one of the matchbox buildings and through a lobby of yellow-tiled walls; gang mailboxes, I noticed. We took one of the two elevators to the fourth floor and followed Franz single file along an open-air balcony that ran the length of the building and overlooked the empty floodlit street.

He stopped at one of the doors, put the bag down and delved through his pockets, saying, to himself and us at the same time, "Where's that blasted key?" He might have been annoyed, but saying it again, played with the phrase, "I know I have that blasted key!" feigning exasperation.

From the balcony I could see water and swampland, railroad tracks on a raised bed of gravel cutting through the netherland, and jokingly said, "If we'd known you lived so far out, Franz, we would've gotten off the train at Haarlem and walked."

"No!" he replied, turning and pointing. "Haarlem is much farther. It is almost at the North Sea."

A jolly fellow, with his own sense of humor.

"Peter!" he shouted, pronouncing it *Pitter*. "Which is correct, farther or further?"

"Either is okay," I replied.

"Ee-ther or eye-ther?" he asked, his mouth open in a silent laugh. It struck me then that his head appeared too large for his short body, his close-cropped hair accentuating a broad forehead; he looked like a gnome.

Behind him, Maria opened the door. "Here you are," she said with a quick smile; tall and thin, with short blond hair and an elongated face. Not unlike Noreen, to whom she said, "You must be tired, yes?"

"We were at the station almost three hours," Noreen replied.

We were in the narrow hallway now, suitcase and bags on the floor.

"Leave them!" Franz shouted. "You get them later. Come now to our living room!" and he was moving again, down the hallway, shouting back at us, "Come, come! Don't just stand there!"

He led us into a simply furnished room with a living area on one side and a small kitchen on the other. In the larger part, horizontal slats covered the length of a window wall, and an el-shaped bench faced two canvas beach chairs across a wooden cocktail table. There were bookshelves, lamps, a few plants, a braided rug on the polished wood-plank floor. On another wall, photographs of Franz in mime whiteface; none of Maria, though I knew she was a performer too.

"What do you think?" he asked as I took in the room.

"I like its simplicity," I replied, and instantly wondered if he'd take it the wrong way. People often took umbrage at the concept of Simple.

"Did you make the bench?" Noreen asked.

"Yes!" he exclaimed, interrupted out of whatever he'd been thinking, a momentary serious look on his face. "It is much too sub-urban here … Don't you think it gives a country feeling—the wood? Wait! Come, I show you something."

We followed him back down the hallway, stopping when he did. He opened a door, stood aside, and we peered inside: at a mattress on the floor, covered with a flowered spread, more flowery fabric tacked to the wall above a dresser, and on an adjoining wall, more black and white photographs of Franz on stage, dressed in a harlequin costume, performing.

"This is where Maria and I sleep," he said grandly, then crossed the narrow hallway to another door. "And the big surprise …" He thrust it open. "… your room!"

It was the size of a large closet.

"We have it prepared since last month." He stepped inside and pulled a cord that raised the metal slats, revealing the balcony in front of the building, the walls of the room suddenly pink-hued from the streetlights below. "You will close these at night."

There was a pallet on the floor next to a heater, with a foot of floor space between it and another pallet. And against another wall, a small desk.

"Of course, you can decorate it as you like," Maria said, standing behind us in the hallway.

"But didn't you use this room?" Noreen asked. "We can always sleep in the living room …"

Maria frowned. "No, no. You must have a room to yourself. This was Franz's study, but he will work at the dining table."

"Yes, but I like that she says this," he said, reaching up to drape an arm over Noreen's shoulders. "She is very … how do you say it, Maria?"

"I don't know what you mean, Franz."

"Considerate?" I asked.

"That's it!" he said, dropping his hand from Noreen and looking at me. "Con-sid-er-ate … Look! Look how she blushes!"

"Cut it out," Noreen said, splaying her fingers over her face as if to hide, which was not like her at all; no doubt she'd been influenced by Franz's theatricality.

"Oh, Peter! I almost forgot the most important! Look!" He moved inside, bowed again, with the musketeer flourish, and pulled open a wooden panel in the small desk.

"A typewriter!" I said, surprised.

"So you are ready to write! It calls for a drink, no?"

"Franz," Maria said patiently. "They must be tired."

"It's true," I said, "but I feel wide-awake, being in a new place—"

"Me too!" Franz shouted. "I am wide-awake!" and he led us back into the living room, where we gathered around the cocktail table and he poured us cups of red wine from a plastic liter bottle. Maria put out a platter of hard cheese and bread, and I reached for it right away, famished.

"Wait!" Franz shouted. "A toast!" He raised his cup and waited for the rest of us to follow his lead. "To a good stay!"

I drank to that, but couldn't help but wonder. I'd expected something else … What? I felt odd there, in the low-ceilinged apartment. That I didn't belong, of course, but more than that …

"Wait!" Franz shouted, jumping up. "You have already received a letter!" And he left the room to get it.

When he was gone, Maria asked, "Do you think it will work out?" leaning forward, cradling her cup of wine in both hands. "I mean, your staying here."

"We'll have to be honest with each other," I replied. "I've been in situations where people share apartments. It can be tricky. We'll have to be truthful and say what's on our minds."

She nodded. "After all these years, I did not think you would actually come. It will be an educate … education, sharing an apartment … You must do this kind of thing all the time in America, but here it is different … I don't know, perhaps we are not so free as you …"

Noreen said, "You must let us pay half the rent."

Maria was surprised. "No. We couldn't think of it."

"But we'll be sharing the space."

"I'll talk to Franz," she said, doubtful.

"Here it is!" He returned with an envelope, holding it up. "I'm sorry we opened it," he said, handing it to me, "but we thought it might be important."

"It's from friends in California," I told him, skim-reading the card inside, written in Colin's calligraphic style. "A couple we know. Poets. They wish us well."

"Ah!"

"Franz, Noreen and Peter have offered to pay half the rent."

"What?" He turned quickly, then again, repeating and embellishing the double take as if pleased with it.

"You're always acting," Maria said, chiding him.

"But of course! I am an actor!" and he bowed.

"About the rent, Franz …"

He sat down in one of the beach chairs and scratched his chin. "I don't think so. You are our guests."

"But we're not just here for a few days," I said. "We'll be living together."

"I could not charge you anyway." He grimaced, "It's terrible here."

"Oh, Franz!"

"But it is. Look at it," and he got up, walked to the window, raised the blinds and gestured out.

Across an expanse of space, there were a few lights on in an identical building across the way. To the north and south, more of the same.

"It's a bloody fucking bore. We couldn't ask you to share the rent for such a place. It's out of the question," he concluded, dismissing the idea with an abrupt gesture. "Actually, we hope not to be here much longer. We will move back to the city soon. We only moved out because we had to."

"We didn't have to, Franz," Maria said softly.

He glared at her. "What do you mean?" he demanded.

"You know what I mean, Franz."

"Explain yourself, Maria!" he shouted.

What was it with him, shouting everything?

She looked at us, said, "You see, we had an apartment in an older building—not the one where you visited us that summer, a different one. It was near the museum and the opera house, on a busy street with many little shops. It was very nice, but we were only there a few months when we had trouble with a neighbor. He lived on top of us—"

"I wouldn't say 'trouble,'" Franz said, back in his chair again. "'Trouble' means something little, and this was something big."

"Okay, how would you say it, Franz?"

"I would say that man was crazy … that he was a maniac."

"No, Franz. That is too much. He was not a maniac."

"What else would you call someone who says he will kill you?"

"He threatened to kill you?" I said.

"I swear it, Peter," Franz replied, holding up a palm in the universal gesture.

"He was difficult," Maria continued, picking up the story. "He would play his records very loud. Too loud. It kept us awake at night, and we had to go to work and school in the morning. So one night Franz went to his door to ask him to lower the sound … He was not what you call a smart man, and Franz yelled at him—"

"He was a maniac!"

"No, Franz. Let me finish. You yelled so loud that everyone heard—"

"It was not like that, Maria!"

"Like right now, Franz," she said. "You see how you lose your temper? That's how it was."

"No, Maria!" he shouted. "It was not like that at all!"

"You did lose your temper, didn't you, Franz?"

"Listen, Peter," he said in a confidential tone, turning toward me. "It was this way: I knocked on his door and asked if he could turn the record player lower, and just like that, he said if he ever saw me again he would kill me."

"No, Franz. You say 'just like that,' but it was not just like that. You were upset—"

"No, Maria, we *had* to move." He looked at me. "Peter, I ask you—"

"We still didn't have to move," Maria said quickly. "We could have talked to the neighbors. We could have called the police—"

"We leave it up to Peter to decide who is right!"

"Franz," she said, annoyed, "this is ridiculous. Why ask Peter? You know how you lose your temper sometimes—"

"Maria!" he said, jumping up and pointing at her, then wagging his finger. "I am your husband!" Then he looked at me with a grin. "Do you like it?"

"Like what?" I asked, bemused.

"My imitation of what Maria is thinking. It's droll, no?" he said, sitting down. "You see, we have that word too, 'droll,' but in Dutch it means 'shit.'"

"Look at Noreen," Maria said, relieved that he'd changed the subject. "She can't keep her eyes open. Let them go to sleep," and leaning over, she stroked his forehead with her long fingers. "You can perform again for us again tomorrow, Franz."

"Maybe now that you're here," he said to me, calmer now, soothed by his wife, "everything will be better."

On Eggshells

For a while my misgivings were trumped by the novelty of the place. The postman peddling up to building B3 on his bicycle, children kicking a soccer ball in a field between the housing blocks, ground floor shops with goods that looked like delicacies, and the peculiar diffuse light of a perpetually overcast sky.

At a marketplace not far away, an arcade opened onto a cobblestone plaza crowded with pushcarts and tents where old ladies bundled against the damp North Sea chill sold vegetables and cheese, and grizzled old men peddled herring out of open lorries, and those not selling anything walked around with paper cones of fried potatoes it was the local custom to eat with mayonnaise. Someone else's idea of ordinary cultural details, which I invested with more significance than warranted.

One evening after we'd come back from that marketplace, with its pickled fish in barrels and wheels of cheese, Franz entered the apartment in a jovial frame of mind, By then I was accustomed to his capricious moods, and seeing contentment, breathed easier. Maria was giving Noreen her daily Dutch lesson, Noreen entering words and phrases in her large, childlike script in the wide-lined notebook she'd bought, while I scribbled in my own notebook, working on my novel.

"Shall we go out tonight," Franz said, his inflection both question and answer. "I met Monique at the school cafeteria today and she tells me of an event at the Stedelijk Museum. A very good group will perform."

"What a good idea, Franz!" Maria replied. "Maybe Peter and

Noreen would like to come."

"That's it!" he declared, nodding vigorously. "That's what I mean!" And turning to me: "Do you like it?"

"Yeah, sure. Sounds like a good idea."

"We will show you something tonight!"

"Monique and her husband Raoul are our dearest friends," Maria said. "We do everything together. We would like you to meet them."

Noreen and I made dinner, vegetables and cheese. Maria set the table with earthenware dishes and cups the size of bowls. And Franz brought in two large amber bottles of beer from the case he stored on the back balcony. We ate, as usual, in the kitchen nook, in a circumference of light cast by a fixture suspended over the table, where Noreen and I mainly listened to Franz discourse on his day. Then we stacked the dishes in the sink and waited downstairs for Monique, who drove up in a battered Citroën; Raoul had decided not to come to the performance, we were told, but he would join us later.

The museum facade was floodlit, cars parked diagonally in the plaza in front, next to a wide boulevard bisected by trolley tracks. Inside, on the second floor, in a dazzling room where the Frans Hals *Banquet of the Officers of the St. George Militia Company* occupied an entire wall, a small audience fell silent as performers dressed in white tights entered to the accompaniment of discordant recorded music, each carrying a geometric shape. Against the tableau of Hals's supernal painting, they walked the shapes around a space cordoned by a rope barrier, carried them from one spot to another, exchanged them, caressed them, jumped on them, and did other mimelike things. When it finally ended, the audience applauding wildly, I wondered what I could possibly say to Franz, who had been so eager to show us this excruciatingly uninteresting exercise.

Afterward, on the way out, he asked my opinion, as I knew he would, and I pleaded ignorance. I was a writer, I told him. What did I know about mime performance?

"But what did you think?" he asked again, when we were in

Monique and Raoul's apartment.

Raoul, thin and nervous and bubbling with good intentions, poured wine into mismatched glasses. There were piles of books scattered across the floor in their old town loft, copies of prints by Matisse and Van Gogh on the cracked walls, a bare lightbulb hanging by a wire from the ceiling. We sat in chairs arranged in a circle, putting our glasses on the floor.

"I'm the wrong person to ask," I replied cautiously. "The truth is, I never cared much for formal presentations."

"You did not like it," Maria said, smiling.

"I did not see it," Raoul said, "but I don't care for it either. It was why I decided not to go."

"It was perhaps too *rarefied*," Franz said, nodding seriously, then eyeing me playfully and grinning. "Only we *artistes* would appreciate the technique."

Monique laughed, tossing her head so her long hair rearranged itself on her shoulders. She was attractive in an insouciant way, affecting a sophistication she considered elegant. In school, she'd told us in the car, she studied French literature, then dropped Camus, Sartre, and Simone de Beauvoir into the conversation.

"Come now," Maria said reproachfully, looking at me. "You saw it. You must have an opinion."

"Let me put it this way," I said with a grin. "I think it's broad-minded of your government to subsidize the arts without passing judgment." Noreen laughed. Monique smiled, and when I looked at her, ducked her head in what seemed a coquettish reflex.

But by the end of the evening the joke would be on me.

"What does it mean, 'broad-minded'?" Franz asked.

"It means, if I am right," Raoul said, "'permission,'" and he looked at me questioningly.

"'Tolerant,'" I replied.

"Yes, tolerant."

"So you mean," Franz said, head tilted in a fighting pose, "the government tells your performers what to do."

"It's more complicated than that," I replied. "There are hardly any subsidies in the United States, so, though people are free to do whatever they like, they're compelled by circumstance to do things that will earn them money—to sell themselves—or else get a job doing something else and do their art—whatever it is—on their own time."

I could see, when I was finished, that no one knew what I was talking about; except Noreen.

Raoul said, "In the United States it is different from here. It is more capitalistic."

"You mean," Maria said to me, "artists in your country are not subsidy ... What is the word? Sub-sid-ized?"

"Rarely. And even then, usually only the most successful—those who need it least."

Raoul nodded, then said to Maria, "It is the capitalistic way. You see, what we have here is not strictly capitalistic ..."

Seconds after Monique had gotten up and drifted to the other side of the studio room, Franz joined her, and now they stood by one of the tall windows, their backs to us, talking in subdued tones.

"So how are you able to write?" Maria asked, drawing my attention back to her.

"I have to work a job and write at the same time," I said, "which is difficult, and often impossible ... or work for a while, get fired, and then write until I have to get a job again ..."

"Fired?" Raoul said. "I think I know what this means ..."

"It means the employer no longer wants you, and I say 'get fired' because if you quit, you can't collect unemployment. Once, I purposely got myself fired so I could collect."

"Unemployment?" Maria asked.

"Yes. Unemployment insurance, for those out of work." I looked at Raoul. "We aren't thoroughly capitalistic either."

The two Netherlanders stared at me, bemused.

"But mostly," I went on, "I have to hustle money where I can, to snatch some writing time. Though, actually, for the past year or so—"

"What does this mean, 'hustle'?" Maria asked.

"It means doing whatever you have to do for whoever is willing to pay you. Right now, for instance, like I was telling you at dinner, I've been promised some money—"

"Yes," she said. "I don't understand that, about your uncle."

"He has a lot and I have only a little—"

"But how can you do it?" Maria asked.

"Do what?"

"Take money that way?"

"Well, like I said, he has a lot and I don't, so I don't feel bad about it."

"Like socialism," Raoul put in. "Redistribution of the wealth."

"You could put it that way," I said, but I was watching Maria, who appeared upset, so I added, "I couldn't pursue my writing if I didn't."

"I can't believe it." She was angry now, but to my relief, not at me—at America. "It is not right that there isn't some way for a creative person to find support. Can't you teach, like Franz?"

"I could, if I were somewhat successful first—some writers do that—but I'm not published yet, except in a small magazine few people know about. Of course, I could teach something else, and in fact I tried that once, briefly, but it took all my energy, and by the time I got around to my writing, on the weekends—"

"But that is ridiculous! How can you be successful if you don't have the chance?"

"I agree."

She was pensive a moment, then said, "Still, to take money from someone … "

"Historically, it used to be done all the time. An artist found a patron … the Church, a wealthy burgher—Franz Hals, Rembrandt— you must know this better than I do. It's European history—"

"But that's different," she said.

"How is it different?"

Too upset to continue, Maria looked at the floor; perhaps to hide her feelings.

"Look," I said, "I'm not advocating anything, I'm just telling you the way it is for people like me and Noreen—musicians, writers, poets, painters ... creative people who have to sell encyclopedias to support themselves. I envy your situation. It's more sensible."

"More human," Raoul said.

"Yes, more human."

"Is terrible, no, that in your country people can't be living better?" Maria said, looking up. "I have seen the cars in Gravenhage when the rich people come to the theater ... big shiny cars, everyone dressed in fancy clothes, wearing jewelry, their noses in the air. They think they are better than everyone else, and there are many Americans there who work for the big companies."

"And Dutch too, don't forget," Raoul put in. "American companies employ half the people in the Netherlands."

"Really?" Noreen said, surprised.

"Yes. I know it."

"Peter," Maria said, leaning forward, "I was asking before ... Why are there so many poor people in the United States?"

"Well," I replied, "there are people who are poorer than anyone I've seen here, but most people in America aren't poor."

"Okay," she said impatiently, "so not poor, but not having enough."

"Most people have enough, though many of them don't think so."

She shook her head. "But from what you say ... I don't understand. We have no poor people, or creative people who sell—what is it ... encyclopedias. Why can't you do what we do? We help each other, so there are no poor, like in your country."

"If you were living in America," I said, "you'd be considered poor. If—"

"We are not poor!" she exclaimed, offended.

Quickly, I said, "No, no, you misunderstand me. I'm not saying you're poor. In fact, it's not really a matter of rich and poor. It's a matter of perception. I mean, most colleges in America aren't free, and for you it is, and Franz actually gets paid while he goes to school … and your rent is subsidized, and you have government health care. But though most Americans don't have any of that, you'd be considered poor because you don't have a television, a car, a washing machine, a dishwasher—"

"We don't need those things!" she said, her pale face flushed, her outburst startling me.

Monique had returned to her chair by then and was looking at me intently, but quickly turned away when I looked back, smoothing her skirt over her legs. Franz had moved closer and now stood leaning against a table, regarding the high ceiling as if there were something fascinating up there.

There were all sorts of undercurrents in the room.

Ironically, it was Raoul, whose simple ideology made me restless, who somewhat defused the tension, saying, "You don't understand, Maria. In a capitalistic society, everything is different. You see, we don't have a strict capitalism …"

"You and your capitalism," she replied fondly. But when I laughed, she darted a distrustful glance in my direction.

Which was a bad thing, because Noreen and I, as acutely wary of Franz as we were, had come to rely on Maria as an ally, to leaven his unpredictable moods.

            *   *   *

Out of that wariness, we contrived to stay away from the apartment until after Franz came home in the evening. Who knew how the vagaries of his day would conflate with the sight of us sketching or writing or, worse, reading a book? But there were only so many places to visit, and the sights soon lost their dazzle, the museums and indoor sites becoming instead a respite from the weather, places to escape the damp chill and the occasional thick wet snowflakes that from a distance charmingly whitened the landscape. Out in Greuzenfeld, a few children were always playing on that snow cover, near narrow canals resembling drainage ditches. But no Hans Brinkers gliding on silver skates. And on city streets, traffic quickly churned it to slush.

Yet even entering the apartment after staying away for hours, we were never sure of our welcome. If we were cheerful, would Franz assume we'd had a good time and resent us for it? If we were subdued, would he wonder why we couldn't appreciate all the free time we had, while he went to school and taught classes? We'd hang on his words as he reiterated his day, affecting empathy when he was sour or irate, appreciation when he was effusive, aware that his mood might shift at any moment, then attach itself to us for living without the constraints his own daily life imposed.

Nor could we expect help from Maria, whose silences now might have reflected indifference instead of unspoken commiseration. Her impassioned reaction in the loft to my description of an artist's plight in America had apparently been an aberration, or else she was still upset with me for seemingly calling her poor. Always, she kept herself in check. And since we did too, because of Franz, who could blame her? Why should she jeopardize her quiet niche in his capricious world for us?

Eventually, I was so nervous over our tenuous situation that I suggested to Noreen that we make ourselves even more scarce, take a trip somewhere, absent ourselves for a chunk of time. Then perhaps we'd be more appreciated when we returned; their life was no great shakes, after all, and we at least were a distraction.

My post office retirement money had dwindled, but I still had a few hundred left, and the check from my uncle would certainly arrive any day now.

We brought Franz and Maria into the planning, because we knew nothing about traveling in Holland, and, thinking strategically, it occurred to me they might be enthused to take part in what we posed as an adventure. In fact they were, told us about a three-day package with government-issued train and bus vouchers to travel anywhere within the country. Franz went even more hyperbolic than usual over a region he declared the most bucolic.

Was it fear of offending him that made it our instant choice?

A few days later we took a train northeast, to Hilversum, Amersfoort, Apeldoorn, Almelo … and then a bus through small and even smaller towns, villages, hamlets, into ever more provincial circumstances.

We finally debarked on the outskirts of a picturesque village where cows idled in lyric mist beneath motionless windmills. A dreamy place, with narrow buildings leaning against each other for support and twisting, cobbled streets ending abruptly at fallow fields bordered with stones and moats that kept the animals penned in. On canvas, it would have been the charming scenes of a van Ruisdael, a van Ostade, and others whom I'd never heard of before spending all those hours in the museum.

But like the wet snow that looked good from a distance, up close the denizens of these scenes were something else. The innkeeper served us vinegar he called wine; the shopkeepers, playing on our language-innocence, assumed we wouldn't notice being short-changed; and everyone in the local pub shriveled up when the teenagers from Germany crossed the border at night to drink beer and swagger around the pool table.

Noreen took dozens of pictures, which she would eventually develop and print: black and white shots of windmills and pastures, duck ponds and footbridges, wooden buildings with crisscross Elizabethan facades. In one, my shoulders were hunched against the chill, hands thrust into the pockets of the beat-up sheepskin coat; a thoughtful pose for the dust jacket of my novel. I'd grown a Vandyke beard, and in the photo looked embarrassingly like a wizened head contemplating his memoir. In another, one of the few I took, Noreen stared at the lens as if searching for an answer: Where do we go from here?

Back in Greuzenfeld, our reunion with the DeHoochs resembled the welcome we'd received when we first arrived. But then, hearing that we'd been cheated on the cost of a room, and other things, Franz went into a long-winded rant about his backward, rural countrymen, well-known for their stupidity and dishonesty, while Maria sat with folded hands, saying nothing, as if she knew her husband well, and where his temper might next lead.

Within an hour the good feelings we'd initially engendered had been dissipated, as though we'd never left at all, and we were walking on eggshells again.

Innocents Abroad

I'm not sure what set Franz off; it could have been anything. He was home that day, and some real or imagined slight had him stomping around the apartment, glaring at us as we tried to get out of his way before we eventually left the apartment.

Later, when I called from the old city to ask if they wanted us to bring something back for dinner, he snapped a curt rejoinder over the phone, "You will come get your things, *if you please*, and move out im-*meed*-jetly," in exaggeratedly accented English; lord of the manor.

Trolleys and buses clattered by and swathed pedestrians trundled past as we waited for the bus back to Greuzenfeld. The facades and shop signs, so pointedly foreign, rendered our displacement alarming as we huddled beneath an overhang against the cold drizzle. In our vulnerability, we were truly innocents abroad, a phrase that recurred to me, momentarily elevating us above our situation. It implied that karma was on our side, since we meant well and had done nothing wrong.

Except ours was not a story about youthful folly. There's dispensation in that, a benevolent god bestowing protection on those who don't know better. And in our case, we'd anticipated this eviction for weeks, knew it was inevitable, though never said as much aloud, as if that would manifest the logical conclusion. Nor had we made no plans to meet this eventuality, and now that it had at last occurred, we had no idea what to do or where to go.

After collecting our things and returning to the old city, we checked the luggage into a locker at the railroad station and aimlessly wandered around the canal streets, bemoaning our fate, reiterating to each other that it hadn't been our fault, which was true but beside the point. What could have been more foolish than putting our fate in the hands of little known acquaintances in a far off place?

Then it was nighttime, and in the curious way life deals its cards, our gloom gave way to giddiness. The tension of our living situation was suddenly, miraculously, gone. We were free!

Admiring the aged facades as if we hadn't taken them in before, we walked along the canals basking in our newfound freedom. In this mood, I concocted a plan as Noreen listened with childlike hope.

We'd find a place to stay till spring, I assured her, and then, with Uncle Jack's money in hand, book a flight to Russia, where I had relatives. In fact, this was the metaphoric allusion that had made Europe so seductive when the idea first came to mind: Dostoievski; *The Idiot,* in particular.

Thanksgiving had fallen on my birthday in November: the Saturn return, a highly significant passage, according to astrologers; and scientists too, who date the complete replenishment of the body's cells to the twenty-eighth year. Ascribing my birthday energy to this transformation, I felt transfused, a new man, a mood I attached my mood to *The Idiot*, the best book I'd ever read. Enthralled, I envisioned nineteenth century St. Petersburg, replete with the same streets and characters in the book, and irrationally expected to encounter all of it when we visited my relatives, the Abromoviches, in Leningrad.

Meanwhile, in our actual, present circumstance, Noreen was no longer the rebellious wife, but had regressed into the uncertain girl who'd written me a letter and moved in with me years ago. In which sense it seemed our European adventure had indeed resuscitated the past. Now, untethered by circumstance and totally reliant on me as we wandered the streets of Amsterdam, she concurred with everything I suggested.

We would head to Basel, because Laurent Fontaine, the artist Jillian had lived with awhile, had a studio there. Since we'd put the two of them up back in Brooklyn, we assumed Laurent would do the same for us. And while there, I'd wire my uncle and tell him to send the money to Switzerland.

The next evening, after dawdling amidst the canals that day, we took a train south. Night came on as we moved alongside the Rhine, my ebullient mood turning bleak. MAINZ, MANNHEIM, KARLSRUHE, FREIBURG … neatly lettered signs in grim-looking stations, canvas mailbags stacked on carts on deserted platforms, the ordinary details of life sobering. What had I expected? Mozart on his way to Salzburg?

In Basel, we checked into a hotel near the station, and having spent nearly all our remaining money on train fare, went to the American Express office first thing in the morning, after breakfast, to wire for funds. Had I known the Buddhist maxim—that to avoid the lows, one has to avoid the highs as well—I conveniently ignored it. Feeling inappropriately carefree, with money no doubt on the way, we walked down the steep main street to the Rhine below, and across it to the renovated school whose rooms had been converted into ateliers for artists.

Again we'd decided to pop in unannounced.

Only this time there was no Franz and Maria merely out for the evening. The handwritten note attached to Laurent's iron door read:

In Prague. Will return in March.

A month away. We'd have to move on, find someplace else to stay.

Fortunately, we'd have money soon, I reminded Noreen, ignoring my own uncertainty, as we returned to the hotel … to spend the next week sneaking in and out, between daily trips to the American Express office and wandering the cold streets in an aimless, hungry daze.

Where was the money from Uncle Jack?

He didn't answer any of my urgent wires, so I called my parents and asked them to contact him. My father replied that Jack would send it when he could, as if Jack were still a tenement boy who worked as a waiter in the Catskills, not a rich man who lived in a Manhattan penthouse.

It infuriated me, hearing that from the former union dissident, a cutter in the garment industry taking on David Dubinsky and the rest of his corrupt crew: that it was impolite to bother Jack because he was such an important man.

Noreen wired her parents too, asking for a loan, and her mother grudgingly agreed to send some, then strung us out awhile, like wealthy people do, having so many important things on their schedules.

Sneaking in and out of the hotel, feeling like a small-time scam artist, I projected a similarly low opinion onto the innkeeper, though only in the past few days had he begun to wait at the foot of the stairs for us to enter or leave.

Finally, he caught us trying to sneak out and said to me, "Sir, your bill is one week due. I would like you to pay it now."

Opting for honesty, I explained that we were waiting for money, due any day now, and felt shammed as he listened to my blurted explanation with more respect than I had so far afforded him.

When I was through, he nodded, chided me for not leveling with him sooner, agreed to wait until the money arrived, and in the same equitable tone, said, "Sir, your passport, please."

"What?"

"Your passport, please."

"Why?"

"Then you will not be able to leave the country without paying the bill."

So of course I gave it to him—where could we go if he kicked us out?—and when he moved aside, we went up to the room for what would turn out to be the next to last time, to sweep the floor for cheese and cracker remains from what we'd snuck up from the dining room earlier.

When money finally arrived, from Noreen's mother, we bolted, if only to get away from a sense of degradation, taking the train northwest this time, toward Paris, through placid countryside patched with snow.

Why didn't we go south, to the Mediterranean and warmer climes? We must have been crazed. When I look back, I can come up with no other explanation.

Not that I had a plan about Paris, which, when we got there, was too expensive to stay for even one night. And after our impoverishment in Basel, it seemed wasteful to splurge on a cup of coffee and a croissant in a café, the requisite for purchasing idle time while drifting in a reverie of philosophy or politics or art. Nor could I reflect upon the inevitable shortfall of human expectations, like Rilke, after schlepping our baggage through the daunting metropolis to get to the Luxembourg Gardens, where he liked to hang out, but not sitting on a bench in the frigid winter. So we never left the Gare St. Lazare, waited amidst the urban bustle for the train to Rouen, where we arrived at twilight, in one of the hues captured by Monet, painting the cathedral, which we lugged our suitcases past, looking for a place to spend the night.

I'm good with maps, and following my sense of direction found the small hotel I'd pinpointed in one of the medieval cul-de-sacs you come across in old French cities. We checked in, dumped our luggage in the room, and immediately headed out again, to a restaurant we'd passed on the narrow street. We hadn't eaten since breakfast in Basle.

The restaurant was a cavernous room with wooden beams, a high vaulted ceiling, and bric-a-brac furniture and tables. A group sat at a long table at one end, conversing over plates of food and bottles of wine, talk abating when we entered, as if we'd intruded on a family gathering. The proprietor, looking sporty in a vest, eyed us with curiosity and ushered us to a table in the center of the room, next to a disused fountain in which a maiden held an amphora on her shoulder. He handed us menus, which we studied as he walked away and the talk at the long table resumed.

When he returned a few minutes later and stood over us, the room fell silent.

"Monsieur," I said, scrambling in my head for high school French, which I'd only barely passed, *"donnez-moi ... pour ma femme, une ...*

ordre de volaille."

"Très bien, monsieur, " he replied, writing it down.

The informal *famille* at the long table held its breath, awaiting my next mangled version of their elegant language, but, I liked to think, cutting me some slack, rooting for me.

"Et pour moi, s'il vous plâit ... le sole meuniere, avec ... des patates."

"Très bien, monsieur," he replied, with an approving nod as the *famille* exhaled, perhaps with appreciative relief.

And as he moved away, *"Et monsieur ... "* turning him back, the room listening again, *" ... une carafe du vin rouge, s'il vous plâit."*

A loud sigh, and then the place erupted in talk, which moments later became muted, as Gallic indifference—an even more rewarding measure of local acceptance—set in, now that the strangers were of no special significance.

A propitious omen, it seemed, as I gazed out the hotel window the following morning at aesthetically pleasing garrets and eaves viewed from the usual salutary distance. And a new plan: we would take a bus to the Norman coast, hunker down for a month or so in a hotel by the Channel in a charming town overlooking a rocky coastline, and with the advent of spring, move on to England. Noreen, in agreement, looked forward to snapping pictures of landscapes the Impressionists had captured, now that she could afford to buy film again. And I would work on my ubiquitous novel.

But in Fécamp, where we'd eaten mussels and drunk a bottle of Sauterne on a pebble beach one summer afternoon long ago before falling asleep in the warm sun, the hotels were all shuttered for the season; and in Étretat too, with its Monet *falaise.* So we took another bus, to Le Havre, a port city big enough to at least have an open hotel, so we could hole up there for the remainder of winter.

But money was still an issue, and we had to settle for a cheap crib of a room up steep, spiral stairs over a raucous bistro; a bordello, for all I knew, what with half-clad women popping in and out, sailors and dockworkers shouting down below. A depressing place we would escape from in the morning, to spend the day bundled up against the chill in a park by the city hall, or on a bench down by the docks where the ferries from England came and went, implying a better future elsewhere.

*   *   *

The travel agent at Piccadilly told us that visitors to the Soviet Union were required to take a package tour. He put it politely, concluding, "Isn't that so?" in the understated British manner. Meaning we were fools to consider traveling when we didn't have the wherewithal of actual tourists; disheveled looking people like us—it was unheard of. But his snobbery brought welcome relief, since the letters I'd sent my uncle were still unanswered, and in addition, my parents were now holding back the Abromoviches' address. The prosaic Englishman, who had no appreciation of what it meant to chase an illusion, took the decision out of our hands. We had no choice but to go home.

Which liberated us, again.

Knowing we'd be leaving soon, we browsed museums and art galleries and the streets of London unencumbered by what might happen next. Noreen snapped roll after roll of film, to be developed and printed when we got back, and I recorded discrete scenes in my notebook with an eye toward rewriting them in longer form, perhaps a travel diary. We stayed in a bedsit near Russell Square, a spartan room where we fed coins into a space heater for warmth; like Orwell in the days of rationing, I thought. And we took the tube from place to place, to the promenade next to the Thames, Trafalgar Square, Bayswater, and St. James's Park, whose flower beds had just begun to bloom.

Without having to worry about what would happen next, the aesthetics of this foreign place supplied the tonic I always looked forward to when traveling: evidence that others had come to different conclusions, had their own unique aesthetic ... before returning to home to the familiar, chastened.

Our final day, we took a bus to Hampstead and walked along the rolling hills, the city spread below us. At Highgate we ogled the ample houses the English call cottages, crossed a cobbled road and entered the sprawling cemetery. Ambling down winding paths, looking for Sigmund Freud's grave, we came instead upon the huge stone head of Karl Marx on a pedestal, overlooking a slope of gravestones.

I thought about my childhood, sitting there, beneath the massive head, the workingclass boarding houses we went to in the summer, the frozen pond in the Catskills in winter, behind the big guest house on a hill. Noreen snapped pictures from all angles, excited about being in the setting where they'd filmed *Morgan!*, her favorite movie.

We stayed there awhile, then slowly made our way back toward the entrance, where a black stretch limousine had pulled up to the wrought-iron gates.

As we approached, half a dozen men got out. They were uniformly thin, austere as priests in identical tan hats, collarless tan jackets, stiff white collars. I recognized the look from newspaper photos; Chinese from the mainland, a rare sight back then. Moving into the cemetery, the group scanned the environs with a dazed tourist expression that characterizes communists no less than anyone else, and then suddenly, all at once, saw us and stared.

We stared back in mutual fascination. Noreen in the fake leather, ankle-length coat she'd worn all winter; me, with hands thrust into the sagging pockets of the battered sheepskin, long hair wild, uncombed, the Vandyke beard I'd had in Holland having been shaved down to a mustache.

They stood out, to us, in their Mao outfits. And we had our uniform look too, just as exotic to them. Maybe they'd seen pictures of hippies in their newspapers.

Then, again as one, as if at a signal only they heard, the group turned away and moved off, into the cemetery, to visit the encephalitic head of the founder of Marxism.

Clark Kent's Secret Identity

The macramé piece hanging in the living room came from one of the colonial outposts where my in-laws vacationed. A room where few ever went, I was both comfortable and alienated there, a fitting sanctuary given my mind-set. I was often there in late afternoon, before the Ainsworth boys came home from school and Noreen and her mother returned from the supermarket to bustle over dinner in the kitchen. The ebony piano no one played, the flowered upholstery, the statuettes and tchotchkes exhibited on polished end tables—it all oozed expensiveness. I speculated that the macramé had been purchased in the lobby of a Hilton Hotel in Burma or Indonesia, and assumed I was the only one who thought about the labor that went into making it.

No doubt it was my mother-in-law who purchased it, just as she was responsible for the fabric on the sofa and chairs, the Oriental rug that covered most of the floor, the massive lamps with German beer hall handles, the landscape oil paintings and Frederic Remington cowboy sculpture prominent in the bay window nook. She liked to think herself a child of the Old West, descended as she was from a Northwest timber baron, whose trust fund provided a perpetual endowment for succeeding generations. For her comfort, her grandfather's company had denuded chunks of western Montana and the panhandle of Idaho.

Eleanor, I called her, which in fact was her name before she acquiesced to "Binky," the sorority appellation assigned to her at Smith College, when she came East from Spokane. I had no idea what she studied, only that she was groomed to become the wife of a successful man; John Ainsworth, it turned out, sojourning in Yale, by way of

Omaha, Nebraska. She lacked for nothing material, and no doubt had the requisite manner and attitude even back then. But she also had a genuine love of the outdoors, reprised in the greenhouse she consigned her husband to have built, an idiosyncratic addition accessed through the kitchen, protruding from the side of the house and onto the patio facing the pool in back.

When Noreen and I lived in Brooklyn, we'd visited her parents' shingle-sided colonial in New Canaan, with its old-fashioned, decorative shutters. This latest house, also in Fairfield County, but on the so-called Gold Coast, was more contemporary; two stories, with plate-glass sliding doors and a mansard roof to add a touch of European class. The front faced a four-car garage plunked onto a sprawl of lawn that ran down to a high wall hiding a country lane and the gardener's cottage where we'd taken up residence. On an equally impressive lawn behind the master house, a double line of thick-trunked trees marched to the coastline.

I had less feeling for John Ainsworth than Eleanor, yet I was more curious about him. A paragon of American industry, he'd been invited to an economic conference at the White House, conveniently leaving his notes on the desk in his den for my prying eyes:

> *Italy no longer viable. Curb investment. No point throwing good money after bad.*

The stiletto letters of his teeny script resembled little daggers. An entire country consigned to irrelevance by the geniuses of American big business.

Like the guest living room, the den was a solitary place. I perused the blunderbuss in a glass case, emblem of the right to bear arms—not for protection against wild Indians, but the specter of urban black rioters on the television news who might someday, somehow, find their way to this wealthiest of suburbs. On the desktop, the steel balls of big business, which I pictured my fidgety father-in-law setting absently in motion; next to them, an erectile gold-plated pen emerging from a marble holder like King Arthur's sword. There were diplomas on the wood-paneled wall, from the Hill School and Yale, and photographs with John Olin—chief shareholder of the chemical company that bore his name, and prolific benefactor to Hobbesian causes—as well as with the president of the United States. And in a corner, the gunmetal-gray safe containing his last will and testament, kept up to date to ensure that his descendants behaved themselves both before he died and then after.

Nearly everything I found in that private room confirmed my opinion of him.

But life is not always as simple as polemics would have it. Ainsworth was also a father and grandfather, There were also framed photos of children—two adopted daughters and two natural born sons, as he and his wife thought of them—and two grandchildren.

Hannah Arendt and the banality of evil came to mind; Ainsworth's pride in the manufacture of napalm. Still, it didn't quite negate the personal touch.

Observing Ainsworth as he sat around the house reading the newspaper, playing board or card games with his favorite son, the younger one—the older one, a guitar player mimicking Jimi Hendrix, was a less appealing rebel—I watched him concentrate on the details at hand—the *Wall Street Journal* or the rummy hand he had to fill—to the exclusion of all else. The rapt attention of his younger boy, who yearned for a pat on the head, eluded him no less than the stoic silence of the older one, except when he was erupting at his favored brother.

Nor, apparently, did Ainsworth notice that he'd been eating too much recently, having become significantly overweight. To which I'd silently, didactically, add that in balancing his firm's books by keeping salaries low, he was affecting other people's eating habits, whether they were union troublemakers or not.

Venturing into his notionally clogged head, I imagined his concentrated vision wavering like a mirage in the heat of his thought processes, abstraction magnifying him as a worthy person in his own eyes, obscuring his shortcomings as a moral man.

A genius, some said, which disgusted me as well. I'd heard that before. About my uncle Jack, for one, whose own self-absorption had stranded us in Europe and was now responsible for our dependence on the Ainsworths.

Like Jack, whose field was technology before he followed the flow of money into the business of investing in computers instead of inventing them, my father-in-law operated on the skim surface of life. We had a few epic clashes on that terrain, after he'd offer a political opinion—to play devil's advocate, he claimed, a glint of superior humor in his eyes. But when I questioned his premises and then proceeded to demolish his arguments, which was easy, since he read only what he agreed with, the glint disappeared, his pupils hardening into beads. On the ropes, he'd employ the tactical silence of an executive who knew how to make underlings squirm. Which indeed unnerved me, since self-expression, both my pride and bête noire, is dependent on the participation of others.

But again, there was the human aspect to this monster, initiating those clashes in order to connect, whether he knew it or not. There were glimpses too of the child he'd once been, ebullient descriptions of flying in the company plane with his vice presidents as they glided over a living map of the earth; the proud popgun hunter, recalling his exploits as I ate dinner with the family, nearly breaking a tooth on the pellets that killed the birds he'd bagged on his most recent foray to the company plantation.

When Noreen and I lived in the tenement flat and then in Brooklyn, we'd meet her parents uptown, on a business trip with Eleanor along, enjoy his largesse at a tablecloth dinner, a Broadway play, a Carnegie Hall box. A charmingly naive historical era in retrospect, before psychological awareness did away with innocence. It seemed another lifetime now, observing the corpulent lord of the manor in his home, playing board games, oblivious to the existential facts of life.

And yet ... her parents had taken us in when we were desperate and needed a place to stay, which complicated matters. How could I sit down to dinner, eat at Ainsworth's table, and indict him as a war criminal?

*   *   *

The town of Westport, perched beside a stream improbably called a river, was an upscale place. Former factories and warehouses had been renovated for entrepreneurial businesses; the Famous Artists Studio, for instance, a mail order outfit that purported to teach amateurs how to draw; a national charitable organization; a host of clean-cut lawyers' officers. The town hall had a colonial facade, reflecting an even earlier past, but it had been rebuilt too; the library a plate-glass and poured concrete structure; the pristine shops on Main Street comforting the wealthy with their elegant displays. A cute town, more nouveau, less Republican, than New Canaan, but no less well-heeled.

Bright young people just out of college, hardly more than teenagers, hesitant to break away and move to the big city they'd heard such dire things about, worked in the bars, bookstores, boutiques, and restaurants … and for the local newspaper that published twice a week, which most considered more an advertiser than a source of newsworthy information.

I walked in one day and introduced myself to the editor, a harried woman unfazed by my ordinary, everyday clothes, reflecting the admirable informality of that underpaid profession, which I'd once gone to college to prepare myself for. She invited me into her cluttered office, where I presented a brushed-up résumé that expanded on the relevant things, finessed the gaps in my life when I'd been unemployed or taking drugs and altogether eliminated swaths of my working life that didn't suit the current purpose.

Seeing that I'd gone to journalism school piqued her interest, though not enough to offer me a job, so I sweetened my presentation with an offer to write a story on the inner workings of the post office, for free. And I threw in my own photographer.

Thus it was that Noreen and I produced a two-part piece replete with photos of mailmen casing in the local station, loading delivery trucks, delivering routes; not an exposé, but a feature to introduce the white collar, commuter town to an aspect of daily life few knew or even thought about. It went over well, and filling several pages in succeeding issues, no doubt pleased the publisher and his advertising department, always eager to camouflage the publication as an essential purchase. Parlaying those pieces into a full-time reporter's job, Noreen benefited too, her photos better than anything anyone had seen before. Within weeks she was put in charge of the darkroom, doling out assignments to a small staff of photographers.

The pay wasn't much, but she and I were living in the gardener's cottage, in exchange for my mowing the lawn and trimming the hedges. And it was a creative outlet for both of us. The kind of thing that would have made a typical TV sitcom: husband and wife team covering stories together, uncovering dirt, having zany adventures with local characters. Though by now we hardly spoke to each other.

It was the first time since we'd been together that Noreen had a job, which changed the dynamic between us, or rather, accentuated a new state of affairs, to my detriment. Being dependent on her father's goodwill for our living situation had already tilted the balance heavily in her direction.

It didn't have to, and it had never occurred to me that it would. But then, while working on my book, immersed in those bygone days that had seen young people together thrown together without regard for the usual barriers—a time when class differences were temporarily forgotten—I'd lost touch with contemporary life. In truth, the old behavioral influences did not disappear in the sixties, but only become dormant. And now, the air of entitlement I'd glimpsed years before, when Noreen moved in with me, described her behavior more glaringly than the old astrological categories could conceal. So far as she was concerned, I was a gardener, working for her father, a seemingly charitable job, something to hold against me and undercut any complaint I might have with her; never mind that all along I'd been supporting her and never copped an attitude because of it.

Other things had lately gone wrong for me too.

I'd broken off relations with my parents for not interceding with Uncle Jack to send me the money he'd promised. And our landlord in Berkeley changed his mind about the apartment we'd sublet while away, informing me in a curt letter that he'd decided to rent it to someone else ... a young man, I'd later discover, with whom he was infatuated. Another thing Noreen could hold against me—as if she'd never wanted to go to Europe but was dragged there against her will. So, with no money and no place to which we could return, there was no going back. Our life in California was over.

"At least we can stay here without paying rent," she pointed out, eliding over the fact that I was manicuring the lawn while working at the paper, and, in response to her mother's wishes, had tilled and planted a vegetable garden on lawn fronting the cottage; hard work. Eleanor wanted to pick peas off the vine, harvest eggplant, lettuce, string beans, and tomatoes, and for an hour or so on Saturday rip up a few weeds from the rows I'd meticulously hoed. To be in touch with the soil, she said.

But at the newspaper it was a different story. I was something there, a journalism school graduate, nearly ten years older than my young colleagues, a former hippie—a living remnant of the glory years they'd heard so much about—a character who'd been places and done things.

With self-assurance, and an appreciation for a job I'd once considered making a career, I churned out copy alongside my admirers; four stories a week. Exploding with long delayed writing energy— discovering anew that I worked best under deadline pressure, when it didn't involve delivering mail for the post office—I wrote pieces no one had ever read in that paper before, giving short shrift to the who what why in order to get to characters and dialogue, using the agendas of school, library, and zoning boards as plot lines. The mundane operations of the town and its previously anonymous commissioners became fodder for my weekly tales of clashing egos and personalities.

As isolated as I was at the cottage, mowing the lawn and trimming the hedges, the newspaper gig was more than just a job. We need to feel wanted, connected to the world. To add something to it, so it's a part of us. I was socially useful, and having a blast.

At first the beleaguered editor was glad to see so many column inches filled. It was hard to keep up with the demand for copy to match the growing demand for ad pages as the little paper expanded, and it redounded to the editor's credit that she could. But then one day she actually read a few of my short stories in newspaper form, wondered what unimaginative people might think of them, and leaving her office, stood over my desk in the close quarters where four of us worked elbow-to-elbow, to carp at me about this and that.

"I'm not going to change that," I told her, and then she argued why I should, squeezing the pages of my story in her red-chapped hands, questioning me as if I'd made up the details.

"All true," I declared. "That's what he said," and produced my notes, done in a pidgin shorthand I'd developed to catch every spoken word, as well as the cadence of each true-to-life character's manner of speech.

Finally realizing I wouldn't budge, and perhaps that I didn't care if she fired me—since my utter lack of control over the rest of my life had rendered me fearless in this part of it—she relented, retreated to her office and closed the door. I never heard from her again.

Which is to say that my diminishment at home with Noreen, or when we ate at what we called the big house—where no one discussed politics, religion, or any of the other issues of the day while chewing food—would have been the most secret of identities to those who looked up to me as Clark Kent, had they suspected there were two of me.

For Noreen, however, it was the opposite.

At the cottage, where I'd helped her convert the garage into a darkroom, and at the big house, where she was cultivating a new, subservient relationship with her father, she was in her element. But at the paper, her relations with the photographers she supervised—young college graduates yet to make their way in the world, like the reporters with whom I worked—deteriorated as she summarily dismissed their work as unacceptable and gave herself the choice assignments.

Thinking about the girl I'd known, the painter who made a comforting cocoon of our railroad flat, I wondered if the shift to photography accounted for the change in her behavior. Once upon a time Noreen had been an agreeable companion, arranging get-togethers, baking cookies, hosting the other art students at our place. And now she couldn't get along with anyone at work, derided people behind their backs, spoke imperviously to editors and salespeople, as if they were beneath her. I toyed with the notion that it had something to do with capturing people on film, where the result more closely resembled actual life than colors and shapes on a canvas. Or was a less subtle egotism at work—in identifying with the images she chose to print out of the numerous possibilities on a contact sheet, which she could then alter with exposure settings and infusions of light or whatever other tricks photographers employ in order to play god with the similitude of life a celluloid picture represented?

Fanciful interpretations, no doubt. I'd always been prone to overthink things.

People change as they get older, assimilate experience in light of numerous factors and in accordance with a kernel of character that eventually flowers into something recognizable: a rose, a lily, and sometimes a weed.

Existential Dog

The dying leaves were a trumpet blare of orange, yellow, and shades in between on country roads, the season too picturesque, too pretty, as my marriage to Noreen devolved toward a conclusion.

We saw each other more in the newspaper office during the week than at the house we shared, and then only in passing. Noreen left the cottage early and came back late. Nor were the weekends much different; she took off to snap shots for feature stories while I did gardening chores on the property.

People get sentimental about gardening. Maybe they're made of different stuff than I am, that somehow they aren't prey to associations that ignite annoyance and anger. It's hard to imagine what magic properties there might be in the soil that trumps the human condition, but I suppose it's possible. The chthonic mint smell of decaying leaves as I raked them into piles brought my employer, father-in-law to mind; resentment, uppermost, at the thankless chore, followed by assertions that I was an honorable person for doing them … and then that by paying our way, I owed Noreen nothing. Other thoughts responded, reminding me that she discounted my labor and instead credited her father for the roof over our heads.

The sixties entered this mélange of rumination; a metaphor for youthful optimism, with its prevalent notion that we would change the world. Then counterthought asserted that the world we'd been so confident about supplanting had in fact swallowed us, that our dreams were all but forgotten.

We, because I'd become the collective whole, reliving those years of imminence while writing about it and contemplating the aftermath, when it actually got better, as we began to pursue callings and vocations, to experiment not just with drugs, but with new possibilities raised by that earlier tumult of self-indulgence.

And now, in this autumn of inescapable conclusion, the assumption that a new world was being born had become untenable.

My novel, for instance, in which I intended to capture the essence of an era, seemed a quixotic undertaking. A foolish exercise. A waste of time. Nobody cared anymore.

I saw it in the local movie theater, where I gone with Noreen and the young reporters and photographers from the newspaper. *Star Wars.* I sat mute amidst the bombardment of special effects as people bounced in their seats and shouted at the screen, delirious. What was wrong with them? I wondered.

And: Was I missing something?

But what else could I do but work on my novel? Not for pleasure, now that I was chronicling the details of what seemed an irrelevant past. But because the book and my job at the newspaper were all I had, trapped as I was within unhappy circumstance.

Then one day Noreen came home—though that didn't feel like the right word for our situation—and said to me, "Let's get a dog."

What could have been less relevant? But then, disco was the rage, and *Star Wars* was a huge hit. What did I know? Old stuff that no one remembered, or if they did, were trying to forget.

So instead of just saying no, I hesitated …

When we met, Noreen was eighteen, and since then had, as they say, matured. Always intuitive, she'd learned to used that gift to become canny, to find opportunity in its blank spaces, and now as we stood outside the cottage, she leveraged my pause by assuring me she'd take care of the dog herself … and then, before I could formulate a reply, pointed out how convenient it would be, now that we lived on a spacious estate. Our dog would have room to roam, and could play with the family dogs up by the big house.

Which was the wrong thing to say.

I might have frowned. More likely it was something subtler; the quality of my silence as I pictured the big house, her parents, the two dogs that ambled across the lawn or slept by the koi pond. After seven years she knew me as well as I knew her. And before my reaction could attach itself to this imaginary, less privileged dog, she jumped in, said, "Please!" imploringly. "You know I've always wanted one!" With the simplicity of the girl she'd been when we met.

Nor was I the same person. At thirty-one, my personal force had been dissipated in obligation; to mow the lawn, trim the hedges, rake, cart, and burn the leaves, which nevertheless could never *earn* the gardener's cottage, not while she regarded her successful father's offer as a handout.

So I said, "All right."

Then an odd thing happened. Because we'd shared a decision for a change, in the desert of immutuality our marriage had become, the dog we found at the pound became for me the aspect of a better future. Enthusiastic, I went to the library in town to research names for a tan and white Siberian husky with one brown eye, one blue. Poets, writers, and rebels I'd formed attachments with over the years suggested themselves. Baudelaire ... Orwell ... Big Bill Haywood ...

But in the library I found a new name, Sorokan: a Siberian poet who satirically declared himself king after the Russian Revolution, wore a mock crown, sat backward on an ass and rode it through the villages of Irkutsk.

"Let's call him Saroki," I said to Noreen.

Pleased by my enthusiasm, she quickly agreed, then resumed her workaholic ways and was once more rarely around.

The frisky puppy, on the other hand, was almost always with me. He romped in piles while I raked, raced circles around the double row of trees that marched behind the main house down to the water, cavorted at the edge of the Long Island Sound as I burned the leaves on the narrow beach.

One day, nosing around the flagstone screened-in patio, he sniffed up to the cat's dish and was examining it when Rose the cat suddenly appeared, arched her back, and as Saroki regarded her with curiosity, bopped him on the nose. The dog bolted, scared, and for a while afterward kept a respectful distance from both cat and dish. Which pleased me, for I'd grown fond of Rose, my companion during solitary evenings in the cottage. I liked it that she could hold her own, and that Soroki understood size wasn't everything.

But then, another day, when Rose wasn't in sight, he approached her bowl again and was sniffing it when she leaped out of the house and onto the patio to bop him as she had before. Only this time Soroki indignantly stepped back and warbled an eerie lament that spooked her. It brought tears to my eyes, seeing her run away. She steered clear of him after that.

This, while I'd been trying to train him.

"He's only a puppy," my mother-in-law said, and gave me one of her dog books. Back at the cottage, I'd skimmed through it, flipped the pages with annoyance at photos of assertive masters bringing dogs to heel, then went about teaching him my own way.

I tried reasoning with him, staring into his mismatched eyes while explaining why he shouldn't burst through the patio screens, which by then were a shambles, hanging from the wooden frames with rents and tears and loose flaps. I spoke to him about important things, like the necessity of standing up to the neighborhood dogs who wandered onto the property, instead of cringing with fear, tucking tail and fleeing in the other direction. How do you teach an animal courage? I had no idea. Or not to work himself up—all things in moderation, the Buddha said— because overexcitement leads to chaos.

And then Soroki began to run away.

I'd scour the grounds, looking for him, then jump in the car and drive up and down the road, looking to one side and the other, calling from the rolled down windows. And then I'd continue the search by turning into nearby estates, hidden by walls or hedgerows, veer over to cottages like the one on the Ainsworth property and speak to a daughter or daughter-in-law, or a son-in-law who wasn't expected to actually garden, before getting back in the car and heading up a similarly long driveway to the big house, which might be a Victorian manse with turrets, a chateau with appendage wings of modern design, a sprawling Mediterranean stucco with a Florentine roof, pass garages, gazebos, and decorative ponds, and knocking on doors in pursuit of the runaway dog, meet dowagers and stockbrokers, bored housewives who wanted to talk and whose husbands were lawyers or corporate managers. And I'd wonder what I was doing there. These were not my people, nor was this even my dog.

It was a rhetorical question. I was there because of Noreen—and myself, of course, tethered to an unrequited marriage that had long since annealed my emotive loyalty … somewhat like an obedient dog. Just as I was a gardener out of a sense of obligation, a character Tolstoy might have appreciated, clipping hedges, mowing the lawn, raking a harvest of dead leaves.

Once in a while, when I was alone and the dog was on its runner between two trees, and the heaviness in my chest precluded trying to write, or even read, I'd take one of the Ainsworth boys' bikes and pedal up the road.

I hadn't been on a bicycle in years, and though anger and regret would come to mind, like when I was gardening, my lungs took in the flowing air, and the scenery flew by—swampland and estuary to my left, a crescent beach in a cove to my right, the sound flowing out to a horizon of sky—and it felt good to be alive, momentarily free. For a while then I could almost forget that soon enough I'd return to my predicament.

Then Soroki had his first epileptic seizure.

He shook in spasms, tongue lolling, eyes rolling up into his skull … like Myshkin the idiot, who not that long ago had a hold on me … like Dostoievski himself, and Noreen, of course, running barefoot down six flights, raking me with sharp nails when I caught up to her, then collapsing to the pavement in an unconscious heap.

An epileptic dog; I thought a lot about it. Another reminder of my diminished state, that I'd dwell upon its condition more than my own. I noticed this displacement with chagrin, having assumed I'd changed so much, grown, as it's said, with age and self-study. But in truth I was only somewhat sturdier than in the final chapters of my unfinished masterpiece.

The medicine knocked Soroki out for a while, but then he became even wilder, uncontrollable. He'd take off as I tried to attach him to the dog run, the ground he restlessly trod now a dusty path bound by the sprawling lawn. Racing toward the bank of hedges on the far side of the driveway, he'd ignore my shouts, or perhaps in his dementia didn't hear me at all. And again I'd jump in the car and go after him, first checking the spots where he'd fled before, then ranging down to the beach as it got dark, standing on the edge of the tidal marsh shouting his name.

One evening in October, after looking for him that afternoon, I got a call at the cottage that he'd been found—the phone number was on his collar—and went to retrieve him.

I had trouble finding the place, and it was dark when I got out of the car. This time it was no gingerbread mansion or Tuscan villa, but a cinder-block and aluminum-sided trailer near the commuter railroad station. The man who opened the door wore an ill-fitting gray suit and held Soroki with the leash tight by his side. Seeing me, the dog tried to leap, and the man yanked the leather tether and drew him back, Saroki squealing.

He invited me while backing up to a counter in the small kitchen, dragging the dog with him. And squinted at me out of a fleshy face, while not relinquishing his hold on the dog, seemingly held me captive with that leash while proceeding to lecture me on the proper treatment of dogs. An animal, he said, needed more than just food and shelter. It required a firm hand and regular discipline …

As he droned on in a gravelly voice in that dim room, I fell into a dreamlike prison in which he was my warden. His harsh little kitchen, a half-eaten TV dinner on a formica table, became mine, encapsulating a sordid loneliness I strained with impatience to escape … and then I lost the reference points, forgot why I was there, his mawkish recitation a relentless punishment as I despaired at my powerlessness.

When he finally stopped talking, I found my voice, though it wasn't mine so much as a sound trying to fill a vacuum of emptiness as I told him things I hadn't meant to reveal; as though my character—that measure of what we value in ourselves—had totally collapsed.

When I mentioned my father-in-law by name, an oleaginous smile creased my captor's thick lips. He told me then that he was a salesman, of some sort, and that I might somehow benefit from … something.

It was unclear what he was getting at, but he took my discomfited grin as tacit agreement to whatever he'd implied, which left me feeling unclean. And then, finally, he surrendered the skittish dog's leash, handing it over as if we'd struck a deal.

Now that he'd finally released me, I yanked the poor dog out the door, with more than reasonable force, and into the car.

I thought about it afterward: what I'd revealed, what the salesman expected of me. And hoped I'd never see him again.

But the following night he showed up at the cottage.

I hadn't given him the address, and that slice of truth put some steel in my spine as he got out of the beat-up car and walked up the macadam drive toward me. Having heard a car drive up, and wondering who it might be, I now stood by the woodpile, my body blocking his path to the patio door.

He didn't seem to notice, or pretended not to. "How's the dog?" he asked, idly scanning the pumpkins and gourds arrayed on ledges and on the table within the battered screens of the patio.

The scene was illuminated by moonlight; the vegetable garden I'd carved out of the landscape, with its stakes and naked vines, the bare tree branches silhouetted against the sky, the expanse of lawn between the cottage and the big house beyond.

I have no idea what I said to him, except that I offered him little, answered questions with no more than a word or phrase, listened to his patter in silence.

Eventually it wore him out. When he got back in the car and left, I watched the red taillights wink out behind the boundary wall before going back inside.

Was it Halloween? Were there ghosts in the air as I sat in the half-dark room, staring at the candle's flame?

I slipped back through the years, that phantom night, to the psychedelic days, when I'd calmed myself by staring at the Reshith between flame and wick, where the invisible source of life emerged from nothingness. There had been an exasperating dog then too, a girl who left it in my care and spent her nights elsewhere, an oily messenger who robbed me and left hallucinatory voices in his wake.

This was my karmic floor; I was sure of it. When I reached my particular intolerable limit of self-dissolution, this configuration would recur, in this lifetime and others.

It was late when Noreen finally walked in. She didn't look at me, perhaps didn't see me on the far side of the penumbral room partially illuminated by a candle. She went into the bedroom, light slashing out of the open door. After a moment I got up and went in myself. She was undressing.

I said, "We have to get rid of the dog. I spend all my time chasing him."

"He'll be all right," she replied, turning away as she pulled her nightgown on. "We'll find someone to train him."

Stupidly, for it wasn't the point, I said, "And who's going to pay for that?"

She shrugged as she turned, replied, "I will," and went into the bathroom.

I followed her, stood in the open doorway as she washed up, said, "It's more than that. You take advantage of my good nature, leave him here knowing I'll take care of him—"

"You don't have to take care of him if you don't want to," she replied neutrally, toweling her face.

"Then who else will?" I asked, raising my voice. "He runs away and there's no one here but me, so I'm the one who has to do it!"

"That's your choice," she said in the same even tone. "No one's telling you what to do." She brushed past me, reentered the bedroom, and I followed.

The light was on, but a dark cloud hovered at the low ceiling, a canopy of gloom. I felt petty, for arguing about a dog. And then thwarted, by an attitude that reduced my concerns to a moral weakness.

This was what Noreen did, I realized. This was what she'd become.

Suddenly infuriated, I shouted, "You *know* I'll take care of the dog if you don't! You count on it, don't you? And you throw it back at me as if it's a flaw!"

She was on the edge of the bed now, and I'd crossed to the other side. While waiting for her to come home, I'd taken out my contact lenses and put on my glasses. Now, as I perched on my side of the bed, giving vent to anger I'd curtailed for so long, she abruptly lashed out, slapping me hard across the face.

My glasses went flying, and with them a part of me seemed to fly away.

For several seconds I sat stunned, staring at her myopically ... then turned away and bent down to retrieve the glasses from the floor. Standing up, I linked one stem, then the other, behind each ear; deliberate movements that integrated my scattered fragments into a focused whole. That restored me.

I stared at her then, through the clarifying lenses, and realized I hadn't looked at her without justification for a long time; maybe forever.

Her shoulders were drawn up with tension as she looked at me with fearful eyes, afraid I might hit her back ... and then, realizing that I wouldn't, drawing upon the power I'd bequeathed her over the years—by not arguing, or disagreeing, or even expressing my own needs—her shoulders eased, lost their tension, and her thin lips crooked in a slight superior smile, as if it never occurred to her I could look at her and see what was there.

Which was when I left her for good.

Epilogue
Off Broadway

I heard footsteps behind me and knew it was her before I felt the tug on my arm.

"I didn't mean to frighten you," she said when I turned around.

Pale skin, flaxen hair, a high forehead and long chin; Noreen wasn't attractive. That never mattered to me, but seeing her now brought forth a deep, profound repulsion.

I'd seen her in the off-Broadway loft, and afterward, aware of her sitting up front, was unable to concentrate on the play. Associations chased each other, emotions roiling my gut. Too much had gone down between us for it to be any other way.

Why had I continued to sit there, trying to follow the garble of dialogue onstage? Knowing she was there had been more than enough reason to escape. Yet for some reason, perhaps to prove that I could, I stayed, forced myself to watch the play, ready to bolt as soon as it was over. Finally, it ended, and during the applause I quickly slipped out of the back row, crossed the empty loft expanse, hurried down the stairs, then across the street and up the block. Venturing a look behind me, seeing the expanse of empty street, I eased down to a walk.

Then the tug on my arm, turning me back to the past.

"You didn't frighten me," I replied, which was true; I was chagrined at being caught. "I was hoping to avoid you."

She recoiled as if I'd slapped her; slapped with the truth, I thought without regret.

"But why?" she asked after a moment, clutching my arm with both hands now, to keep me from bolting again.

It startled me, that she had to ask. How could she not know? How could her take on what happened be so different than mine?

"Because of the months when I was starving and couldn't afford to eat," I replied fiercely, words waiting for years to come out. "Because I had no money to buy food and had to drink soda to trick my stomach into feeling full. Because when you went on with your life, Noreen, I couldn't, because you took everything and left me nothing ..."

"But I tried to find out how you were. I called—"

"And said you wanted us to be 'friends.' And I told you then what I needed, and you wouldn't listen."

Jolted, she didn't answer for a moment, then said plaintively, "But that was so *long* ago. Who can even remember the details about what happened at the end?"

"*I* remember, Noreen ... I remember that what I had was always *ours*, not just mine. I remember that after paying the bills, I gave you whatever you said you needed, but in the end, when I was the one who needed something, you said no."

Abruptly, I fell silent. I hadn't meant to say anything; but that was before, when I thought I could get away.

In the sudden silence between us, the scenery flooded in: West Forty-second Street, a few blocks off Broadway, garishly illuminated with pink-hued anticrime lights; the empty street a stagy day-for-night setting. The theater district, my outburst an angry soliloquy. I'd never liked emotional scenes, and here I was, facing my ex-wife, whom I hadn't seen in ten years, after she'd run after me.

She was peering at me with tilted head. Was it a mime of puzzlement, or genuine?

Noreen was never an actor either, or maybe she was and I hadn't noticed as she'd developed a make-believe talent while I typecast her as the girl she once was.

She straightened, as if gathering her dignity, let go of my arm and said, "I'm sorry," without feeling. And then, more believably: "I didn't mean to hurt you."

I stared at her and said nothing.

"But it was hard for both of us," she went on. "For me too. For a while after I left, I cried all the time. I missed you and felt lost—"

"*I* was the one who left."

Startled, she took a step back. "What?"

I said, "*You* didn't leave—*I* did."

Again she reacted as if slapped, and with that conjured in me the girl, the adopted baby, left behind by her mother.

We'd visited the hospital where she was born, trying to locate the woman who gave birth to her; a schoolteacher who'd come to Spokane from a small town in Montana, presumably so no one would know she was pregnant. But the state had laws against divulging the identity of a mother who had given a child away. The hospital records had reverted to the doctor who delivered her, so we looked for him, and discovered that he'd died the week before.

"Well, whatever," Noreen said now, and flicked a hand, dismissing her history, which clearly still unsettled her. "What difference does it make who left who?" In a strained voice, perhaps angry that I'd stirred up that emotion, as if I said it to diminish her.

But I hadn't. I'd said it because I remembered our final scene, and because the truth always matters. If you hide from it, nothing else can come out right.

"But I *am* sorry if your life was difficult …"

She was not angry anymore. Her blue eyes were pale, nearly gray; pleading now. Not for forgiveness, but something else … What did she want from me? I battled the old inclination to comfort her, and once more gave in, heard myself saying, "Why don't we go get a cup of coffee somewhere."

Opening a second act in this overwrought drama I saw unfold as I stood there, stunned by my own words: the intractability, the frustration, the anger. What a fool I was!

If my point had been to offer forgiveness, to merge the past with the present and resolve them on a satisfying note, I might have understood my impulsive suggestion. But as we walked up toward Ninth Avenue, I had no intention of bestowing that gift.

At the corner it occurred to me to break away, to sprint across the street and up to Times Square, to leave her behind. Why not? I owed her nothing. Then the impulse passed and we were plodding up the avenue, spangles of neon light from occasional bars adding color without illumination to the gloomy street.

Noreen finally broke the silence, asking, "What did you think of Colin's play?"

Colin Shay, from Berkeley. He and I had our own reunion a few weeks before, at a poetry reading in Woodstock, where I lived now. It hadn't gone well. For one thing, I was ambivalent about Colin. For another, it didn't take long to see that my suspicions about him years ago had been accurate. He was a tricky sort, obdurate beneath a facade of agreeability.

"I didn't like it," I said about the play.

Noreen snickered. "It was terrible, wasn't it?"

"I didn't know he was planning to invite you too," I said as we paused at a corner.

"I think he thought he had to. He slept at our house a few times."

There it was, what Colin had told me: Noreen was married, with children, and lived in an affluent town in Rockland County, overlooking the Hudson.

"Maggie left him, you know."

"Yes, I heard."

Maggie O'Connell, with her fine features and porcelain complexion; mentally tough and emotionally vulnerable, especially when she drank. Colin told me about it, in a tone of betrayal, but not why she left, and I didn't ask. We were not that close anymore. He did say she was married now, living in Sonoma, had two children—this last the giveaway, the bitterness he tried to mask as he dismissed having children as if it were a character flaw.

Noreen and I were walking again.

"Tell me about your daughter," she said. "Colin mentioned her ..."

An alarm sounded in my head, at giving her anything that was now mine, at surrendering a part of myself she didn't know.

"How old is she?" she asked. "What's her name?"

Reluctantly, I answered, "Raphaela."

"That's a beautiful name."

Was I now supposed to ask about her children?

"Does she love you?" Noreen asked abruptly.

I stopped short and looked at her. "What kind of question is that? Of course she loves me. I'm her father."

She ducked her head, flustered. Had she thought to disarm me with talk of love? So I might then forget what lay between us?

I resumed walking, and she fell into step beside me. "Why did you do it, Noreen?" I asked. "Why did you treat me so badly?"

Her head lolled to the side, away from me.

I said: "I know your father must have spoken to you and told you to give me nothing." She shot a surprised look at me; I'd guessed right. "Maybe he didn't know I was legally entitled to half of the accident money"—a smash-up we'd had in Montreal, the summer we drove cross-country to visit, between school terms—"because the lawsuit was settled in California, and we were married at the time." Again she was surprised. "I could have sued you, Noreen, and I would have won."

"So why didn't you?" she asked.

I paused as we crossed another street. The question went to the heart of why I'd been such a pliable husband. Don't fight what life deals you, just accept it. "Maybe I should have," I finally replied, "but I wanted to believe that if we talked about what you needed and what I needed, you'd do the right thing."

She said nothing.

"I didn't begrudge you going to Europe," I went on, "setting out on your new life. But we were *both* beginning again, and I should have had something too, if only enough to be able to afford food and rent an apartment ..."

I stopped talking. A curtain had fallen over her. We walked along the sidewalk, Noreen shifting from side to side with that familiar, loping gait ...

Seeing her coming up the street one day in Manhattan after school, I was taken by the graceful way she moved, like the artist she was.

Now, she looked at me again, said, "You always talk about money," not angry, but put out. "It always comes down to that with you, doesn't it?"

"But I wasn't the one who took everything, Noreen—*you* did ... *You* were the one who put money first ... Why did you do that?"

She averted her eyes. "Maybe I thought I needed it more ..."

It was a convenient answer, but truer than she knew. I stopped, and she did too. "Okay," I said. "But why *all* of it? Why *everything*?"

She took a step back. These shifts and silences, surreptitious glances and hesitant responses ... she'd become so tricky, trying on answers to see how they fit. Again I wondered if she'd done that all along, or become strategic in the final months, to distance herself from me, to protect herself.

She was young when we met, and might have had more changes to go through than I did. Then the sixties were over and she moved on, while I was immersed in writing and thinking about that past. And one day it seemed she was no longer the same person; like when you wake up one morning and look in the mirror with shock at the face staring back at you. It might have happened gradually, but you discover it all at once.

Or was I ascribing qualities to Noreen that were my own? I had my own version of cleverness, in deduction. An ability to deduce truth from fact and then act on it. Now, considering the drawbacks of intuition, which characterized her, I gave her the benefit of doubt. Maybe she was more innocent than I assumed.

Then I thought about my daughter, who did not always grasp the consequences of her behavior. I didn't hold that against her. But Noreen was not a child. She'd had years to recognize her own limitations. To grow up.

We stopped for a light, standing side by side, the cup of coffee that began this trek forgotten, had there even been somewhere to get one. The stores up and down the avenue were shuttered, except for a corner bodega and a boozy-odored bar at mid block.

"Let's go back," I said, and without waiting for a response, turned and headed the other way.

Like a shadow, she fell into step beside me.

This couldn't have gone as she'd expected, or wanted. So why was she still with me? She didn't intend to apologize. I could see that much. Did she believe that between this block and the next I might see things her way? That she might come up with an answer to bring me around?

We walked without speaking, clattering across basement gratings, moving in and out of the light of hallways and neon signs. Abruptly, perhaps unnerved by the silence between us—always more characteristic of me than her—she began to offer disparate pieces of her life, as if I'd actually asked about her kids, her husband, her house on a hill. She told me names and ages, her husband's profession, what her brothers were doing now, her mother, her father …

"Dad's dying of cancer," she said quietly. "He's been in the hospital two years."

Her father, the corporate executive, supporter of reactionary causes. I'd tried to see him as merely human but couldn't get over his pride at making napalm jelly. Still, he was her father, and I heard myself saying, "My wife had cancer too, a few years ago."

"Oh, I'm sorry," Noreen said quickly.

"She's okay now," I said, just as quickly, regretting having made that commiserative offering. "She found the strength to deal with it."

We were at another corner, waiting for another light. "And you?" she said, looking at me with that sideways tilt of her head. "Have you found the strength to deal with things?"

All at once a black fury arose in me, uncoiling from the dark pit of the cottage where I'd spent so many nights alone.

"I've learned to endure," I replied coldly, my eyes boring into hers. "I had to."

She flinched and looked away.

Then, crossing the street, she said softly, "Maybe that's why I left you nothing."

I stopped in the gutter and stared at her. "You're saying you did it on purpose, for my own good?"

She smiled and nodded, once.

I was flabbergasted. The arrogance was hers, but the guise of a chess player, seeing moves in advance, was bizarre, impossible.

I crossed to the sidewalk, stopped on the corner, waited there for her and said, "If it's true, Noreen, don't expect me to thank you. It wasn't your place to decide what was best for me." I sounded so reasonable, I surprised myself. But what else was there to say?

Forty-second Street was an arc-lit contrast to Ninth Avenue. A concrete parking garage ran the length of one side of the block, facing run-down three- and four-story buildings across the way, in one of which we'd seen the play. No doubt Colin thought it amusing to invite both of us. A poet who yearned for recognition, who'd gotten a grant to write a play, and enlivened it with a personal drama his trickiness produced.

There was no one in sight, and only one car on the street, parked in the middle of the block. It appeared there, at the curb, as if out of the past, only this car was shiny and new, not a jalopy convertible painted with psychedelic splotches ...

Noreen had been in the backseat as I came up the block. I hardly noticed her, but she called my name, and as I approached, she smiled. When I stopped, she told me we'd met in the park a few days before. I didn't remember.

A few days later we met again, in the park, and not long after, she came to my pad, distraught, on acid. I sat her down, made tea, talked her through it.

Later that summer we hitchhiked to a farm in western Massachusetts, stayed in a commune in Boston, spent a night on the coast, in the house of her old high school friend. And then I left and she flew home to Michigan and I forgot about her.

When I began a new life—commuting to work, leading a solitary existence—she reappeared again, and again called upon me to rescue her. But she rescued me too, by moving in and ending my isolation. She was eighteen; I was twenty-three.

Now, I headed for the car gleaming in the arc lights and leaned against it, as I had on the jalopy long ago.

Following, then standing before me, she said: "Why do we have to talk about the bad times? I want to remember the good times. Why can't we talk about that?"

In fact, the money wasn't important anymore. By talking about it, after all those years, its significance evaporated. Not having money only limited what I could do. Though always a problem for me, the lack of it never affected my behavior.

"… the good times," she was saying. "The early years. The places we went, the things we did together … I can hardly remember what happened in the end. Why harp on that and forget the rest?"

The blizzard in the Midwest the day before we were married … camping in the Rockies … the panhandle of Idaho, the overgrown meadow in Mendocino … Europe … Friday nights at the Laskers' … the trip to L.A., to Ojai …

Suddenly I understood why she'd come to the play and run after me. She wanted to reclaim her past, to make it part of the life she led now.

"Please," she said. "Can't we talk about *that* instead?"

There was a quaver to her voice, and then a tear leaked out of each eye, sliding down her cheeks. With the assurance of an artist, she wiped them away with the back of her hand, a firm stroke on either side.

I pictured her in a gingerbread house overlooking the Hudson, a picket fence, a profusion of vines and flowers in front. The rooms inside were light and airy, as befit her, photographs and paintings on the walls. There was a little boy and a little girl, and a husband who came home from work in the evening. The stability she'd always wanted, and that I'd never given her. I didn't begrudge it to her now. On the contrary, as I leaned against the car and she regarded me hopefully, the house on the hill was a pleasant vision.

But then, it had nothing to do with me.

She had her life. That would have to be enough.

Breinigsville, PA USA
27 December 2010
252260BV00001B/141/P